IMAGES
of America

NEW GARDEN TOWNSHIP

On the Cover: In 1919, brothers Joseph (left) and Francis (right) Sheehan purchased the Landenberg supply store from W. W. Sullivan, who with S. John Pyle had begun selling coal before 1900. Nestled between Landenberg Road and the creamery, the business supplied farmers with livestock feeds, seeds, equipment, and household commodities. With the death of both brothers within a year in 1940, Wilson and Brosius bought the Sheehan property/business and began relocating to Toughkenamon as PennDel Supply Company. In the picture, employee Harry Griffin waits in his wagon while Joseph Sheehan's wife, Helen, looks on. (Courtesy New Garden Township Historic Commission. (NGTHC.)

IMAGES
of America

NEW GARDEN TOWNSHIP

Keith Craig

ARCADIA
PUBLISHING

ISBN 978-0-7385-7267-3

Published by Arcadia Publishing
Charleston SC, Chicago IL, Portsmouth NH, San Francisco CA

Printed in the United States of America

Library of Congress Control Number: 2009936495

For all general information contact Arcadia Publishing at:
Telephone 843-853-2070
Fax 843-853-0044
E-mail sales@arcadiapublishing.com
For customer service and orders:
Toll-Free 1-888-313-2665

Visit us on the Internet at www.arcadiapublishing.com

To Keigan, Elle, and Anya

Contents

ACKNOWLEDGMENTS

While we all are unwittingly part of local history, writing New Garden Township's narrative would have been impossible without the contributions of oral history subjects Jim Bertrando; David Carlin; Lewis Carter; G. Pownall Jones; Edward, Ruth, James, and Kathleen Lafferty; Rita Lafferty Brackin; Frank Manfredi; Jean and J. Roland Minshall; Louis and Norma Pia; Lewis Taylor; and Leon H. Wilkinson.

In addition, Alma and Earl Rigler have been crucial in providing photographs and stories. Peggy Empet shared photographs of the Wollaston Farm. Joan Bonnage Procino offered Quill Farm and Colonial Farms photographs, her local history tomes, and keen proofreading. Chris Robinson gave a firsthand account, guided tour, and photographs of Colonial Farms. Betsy Thompson Turner donated photographs of her father's greenhouses. Ruth Richards delivered family photographs of her grandfather-in-law's Toughkenamon house explosion. Carla Lucas gave carte blanche to use her contemporary photographs. Steve Hoffman let me peruse *Chester County Press* archives. Skippy Reynolds and his son, Mike, offered photographs and stories about running Bunny's Ice Cream. Philip Donahoe shared Mushroom Supply Company experiences. Lenny DiFilippo shared memories and mementos of life at his father's store. Vivian Miller unearthed some forgotten family photographs. Helen Piergiovanni supplied photos of Toughkenamon. At a moment's notice, Andrea Tauson put her keen eye behind a camera. And township supervisor Barclay Hoopes provided photographs and glimpses of dairy life from mid-20th century.

I'm grateful for the resources of the Chester County Historical Society and Anne Haggerty's *Once Upon A Time in New Garden Township*. Having the moral support of the New Garden Township Historical Committee (NGTHC) and free access to its files has been essential to the fruition of this project. Among many aids, David Hawk also identified errors of fact in the Landenberg manuscript.

For watching my children as I worked, I thank Alan and Jean Craig, my parents, Devon Steen, and Kelly Power.

I am grateful to have had the imprimatur of the 2009 New Garden Township Board of Supervisors (Steve Allaband, Barclay Hoopes, Jim Neal, Bob Norris, and Bob Perrotti) and township manager Carmen Raddi for this project.

And I, along with generations of township residents present and future, owe an eternal debt of gratitude to Dr. Margaret (Peggy) Jones for her stewardship and steadfast commitment to preserving the history of a vibrant and intriguing community. This book is an abridged collection of and a tribute to her expansive, ongoing, and thorough investigations.

Introduction

The story of New Garden Township began long ago, when the land was home to the Lenni Lenape Indians. Located in southern Chester County, Pennsylvania, New Garden was a land of deep woods, tumbling streams, and Native American trails until 1700 and the arrival of William Penn Jr.'s land agent. Within two decades, Quaker farmers from County Carlow, Ireland, settled the most arable land in the center of the township. Mary Rowland's 1708 patent for 700 acres east of Toughkenamon was the first. New Garden was the name these settlers gave to their log Meeting House, built in 1715. Here these Irish Quakers found religious freedom; they could follow their practice of silent worship without the threat of stoning, fines, loss of property, or imprisonment—the persecution that had been their lot in Ireland.

The Meeting House was the center of the settlers' lives; it was here they gathered to worship but also to learn news of the community, to provide support, and to care for each other. By the early 1800s, a village had begun to grow around the Meeting House. In his will of 1809, James Miller directed that his land be broken into small lots, some for family, some to be sold. Throughout the 19th century, there was a general store, a blacksmith, a cabinetmaker, a brick maker, a lawyer, a dressmaker, a doctor, and a post office—a village. By the mid-20th century, New Garden Village was reduced to a country crossroads, with a 19th-century house on each corner supporting the more-than-200-year-old Quaker Meeting House.

Almost 100 years elapsed between the coming of the Irish Quakers and the settlement of the southern part of the township, with its rough, hilly terrain drained by White Clay Creek. However, as soon as capital became available, White Clay Creek's potential to provide waterpower attracted a milling industry. A mill town had its beginning in the first decades of 1800, with a mill at Laurel and the Chandler gristmill downstream. In 1862, Martin Landenberger purchased the mills, promoted the building of a railroad, and gave the valley his name, Landenberg. From 1879 to 1917, when the last mill burned, Landenberg was owned by the Lund family. With the closing of the mill, workers drifted away and the once-booming mill town became a sleepy country village.

With the coming of steam power, factory owners had more flexibility about where to build. Strahorn's wheelworks was the first to leave Landenberg for the Toughkenamon valley. Strahorn's associate, Isaac Slack, the "Father of Toughkenamon," saw the possibility for a railroad town. He purchased 132 acres, where he built mills and houses for the workmen's families. To entice the railroad to make a regular stop in the village, Slack built a station, installed a water tank, and deeded the surrounding land to the railroad. Through the mid-1880s, Toughkenamon's economy depended on Slack's factories, but by 1900, the major employer was the Sharpless Creamery. In the 20th century, a mushroom cannery, basket factory, and mushroom supply houses provided employment.

The coming of railroads also marked the impetus for the kaolin industry. As early as 1802, kaolin, clay used for making porcelain and firebricks, was known to lie beneath the soil south of the Gap-Newport Pike near the Delaware line. By 1863, when clay could be shipped by rail to major cities, the industry exploded; New Garden's kaolin industry hit its zenith in the mid-1880s. With as many as 175 men digging in open-pit mines, a train car a day, loaded with white firebricks, was being shipped to Chester iron foundries. Fortunes were made, a mansion was built, and the kaolin pits provided employment for a generation. However, when richer deposits of clay were discovered in Georgia, the local mines could not meet the competition. In 1940, when the Gap-Newport Pike was relocated, most vestiges of the village of Kaolin disappeared; only the water-filled pits now called "lakes" remained.

The 19th century saw the growth of industrial villages in the township, but farming remained the norm for most New Garden families. New Garden was essentially a rural township; typical farm size was between 70 and 100 acres, as much as a farmer and two or three hands could cultivate. It was subsistence farming, with a portion remaining to trade at the country store or drive/cart to market in Wilmington. The railroads opened new markets and spurred the growth of a dairy industry. The term "milk train" became part of the language.

In the 1880s, creameries to process milk into butter and cottage cheese opened in both Landenberg and Toughkenamon. They processed milk from about 100 small dairy farms; 50 years later, the dairy farms had declined by 90 percent. Several factors contributed to this decrease: the low price of milk during the Great Depression, a scarcity of farm labor during World War II, and increased regulations for quality control of milk. Although the number of dairy herds decreased, the amount of milk produced by the few remaining herds actually increased. With pressure from residential development, however, the early 21st century saw the end of the dairy industry in New Garden Township.

By 1900, New Garden Township was known as the "Township of Glass Houses." More greenhouses were reputed to be in New Garden Township than in any other township in Chester County. Beginning about 1870, Charles Starr began to grow carnations and tuber roses for the Philadelphia market. Soon he was followed by others—Edward Marshall, Joseph Chambers, Lawrence Thompson, and Frank Pratt. Samuel Thompson started a greenhouse business that remained in his family for 120 years.

It was sons of greenhouse men who experimented with mushroom culture. They were trying to find a use for the wasted dark space under greenhouse benches. Soon dairy farmers began to experiment with growing mushrooms in their barns and chicken houses. Because mushrooms were grown only during the winter months, farmers saw this crop as a way to supplement their incomes. Gradually the number of mushroom growers increased. Until the 1950s, however, if a crop were successful, it was good luck; if it failed, bad luck. The turning point was the development of scientific cultural practices and the use of air handlers to control temperature and air quality. Today, with an average of 4.5 crops a year and a yield of about 200 million pounds of mushrooms, the industry dominates the township's agricultural economy. More mushrooms are grown in New Garden Township than in any other municipality in the United States.

Another change came to the township in the 1950s. At the same time the mushroom industry was expanding, the first residential housing development was built. In 1955, Pineleigh was begun, with 20 houses on 20 acres of the Dutton farm on New Garden Road. Landenberg Manor on Laurel Heights Road was next, and the building boom began. The population of the township grew from 3,027 in 1950 to 9,083 in the year 2000. New Garden Township's rural character, with its farmhouses, barns, mushroom houses, and open fields, began to be eclipsed by the houses and manicured lawns of suburbia.

—Margaret B. Jones, Ph.D.
New Garden Historical Commission

One

New Garden Village

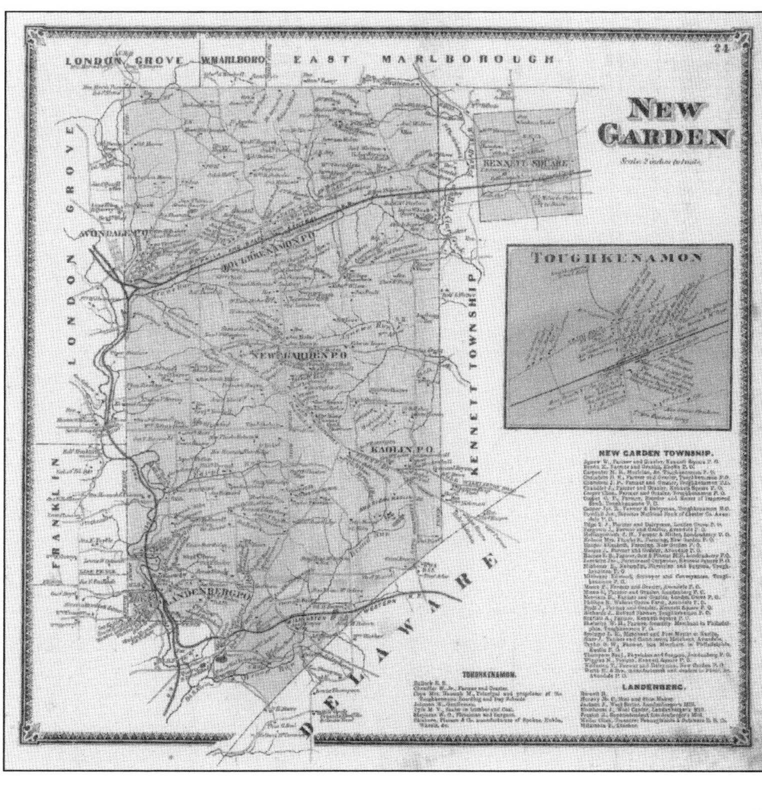

This 1873 Witmer Map identified streams and buildings and showed the names of property owners of New Garden Township. New Garden Village is dead center, at the convergence of numerous roads. For most of the 20th century, New Garden Crossroads at the intersection of Newark and New Garden Roads consisted of a few residences dominated by the Quaker Meeting House. These remaining vestiges only hint at the once-busy village life of the 19th century. (Courtesy NGTHC.)

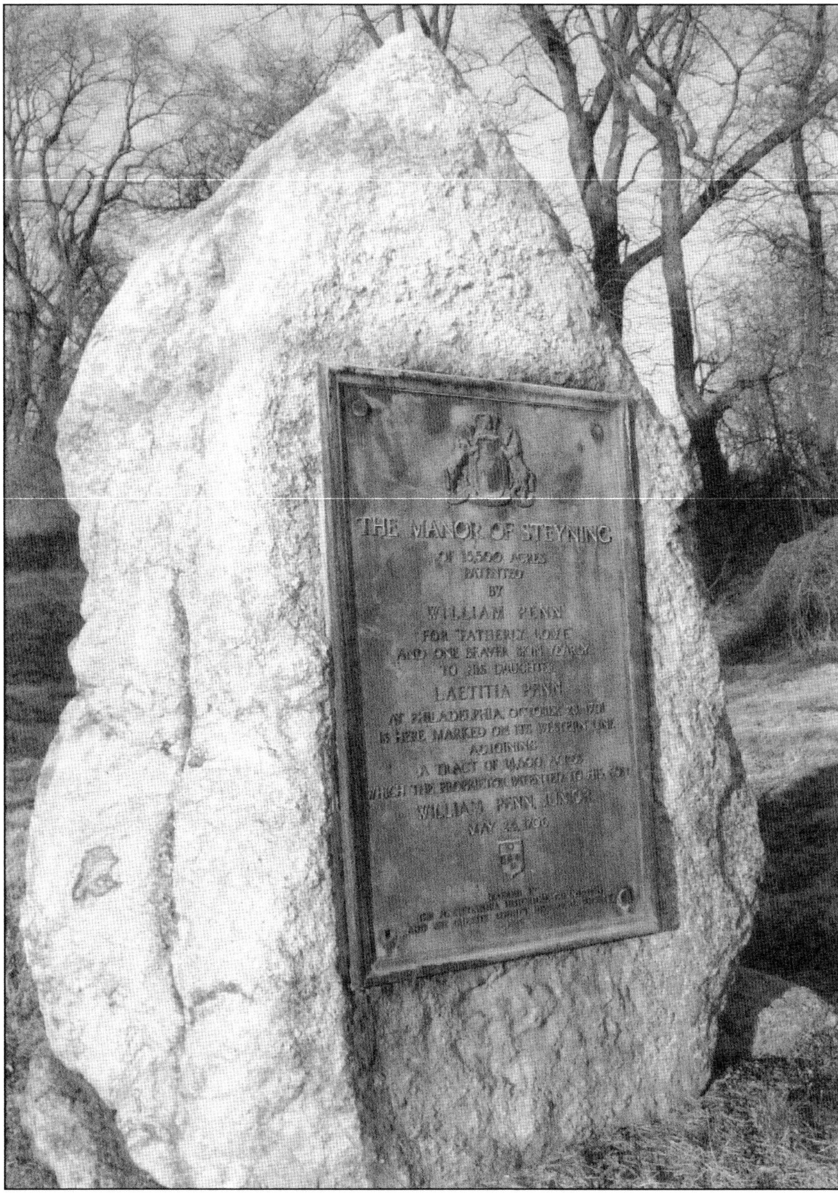

William Penn's colony of Pennsylvania was conceived as a haven for Penn's fellow Quakers. From the mid-1600s, these Quakers, followers of George Fox, had been persecuted because they refused to worship in the established Church of England. Quakers believed each person could commune directly with God without the need for a priest, and this, in 17th-century England, was heresy. Pennsylvania was to be a place of religious freedom where Quakers would be free to hold their meetings for worship, the silence broken only by spontaneous vocal ministry. Pennsylvania, however, was to be an inheritance for Penn's children. A 1700 survey divided 35,000 acres between the grants of William Penn Jr. and Laetitia Penn; this plaque on Baltimore Pike marks the dividing line and the gift "for fatherly love and one beaver skin yearly." William Penn Jr.'s Stenning Manor on the west became the home for 23 Quaker families from County Carlow, Ireland. Their settlement, named for their Quaker meeting in Ireland, was formally designated New Garden Township in 1714. (Author's collection.)

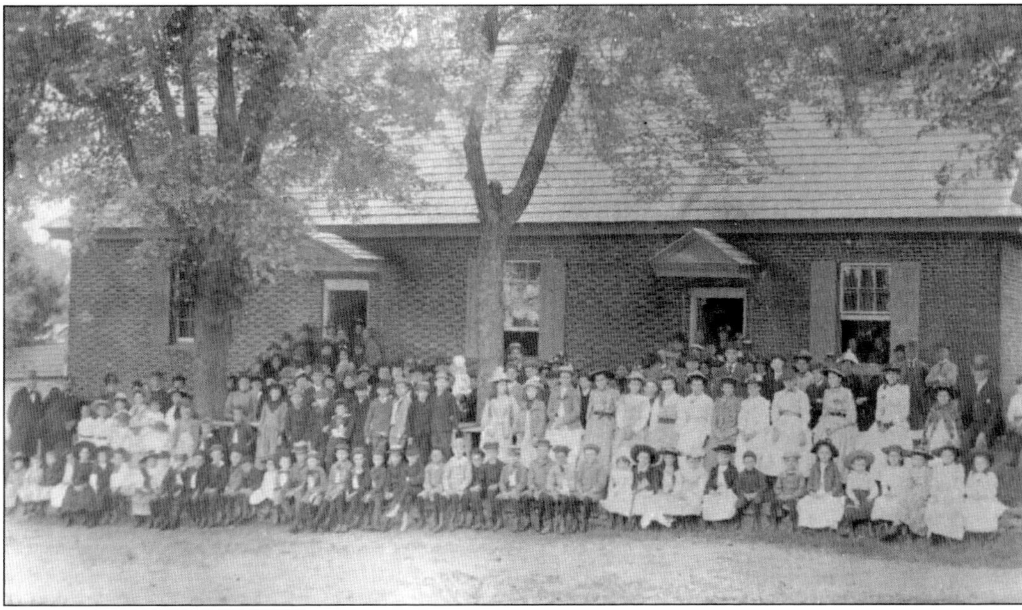

In 1712, Quakers gathered for worship in the home of John Miller, whose 1,013-acre land grant skirted modern Baltimore Pike to the south. However, seven years after their arrival, with all the demands of settling a new country, these Quakers built a log meeting house on the southern corner of Miller's land. By 1743, the membership had grown, and the log building was replaced by a brick meeting house. (Courtesy NGTHC.)

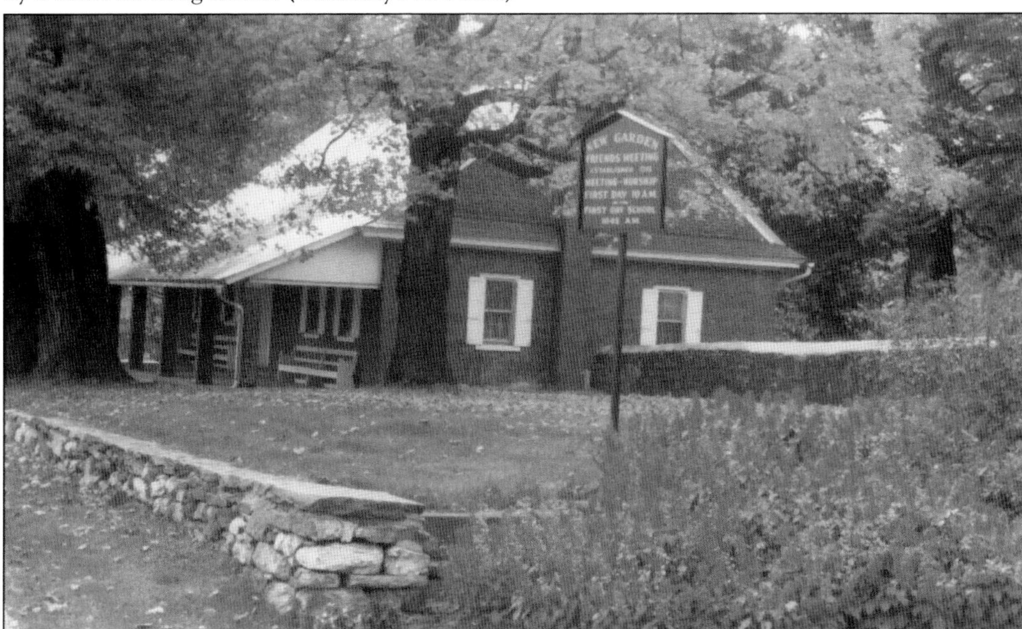

In 1790, New Garden Meeting House was enlarged with a brick addition to the north. The final changes to the exterior of the building occurred in 1905, when the long porch and porte cochere were added. Throughout the history of the Meeting House, social issues of the day have been discussed within its walls. Members have been concerned with the abolition of slavery, Native American affairs, temperance, women's rights, war, and peace. (Courtesy Margaret Jones.)

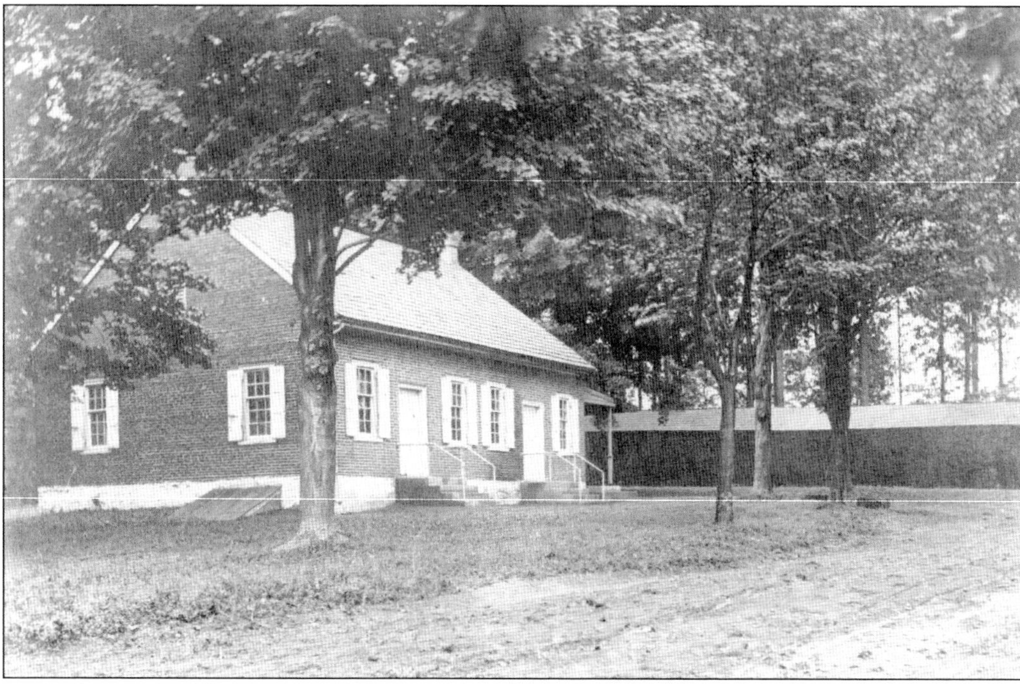

In the late 1820s, there was a schism among Quakers; the more liberal Hicksite were interested in causes of social justice such as temperance, slavery, and the plight of the Native Americans, while the conservative Orthodox were more concerned with issues of theology. At New Garden, the Orthodox Friends left and built a meeting house at the intersection of the Gap-Newport Pike and Newark Road. This "Lower New Garden Meeting House" was used from about 1831 until 1938, when the membership became too small to continue. In 1949, the building was sold to Mario Testa, who remodeled it for a dwelling. (Above courtesy Chester County Historical Society [CCHS]; below courtesy NGTHC.)

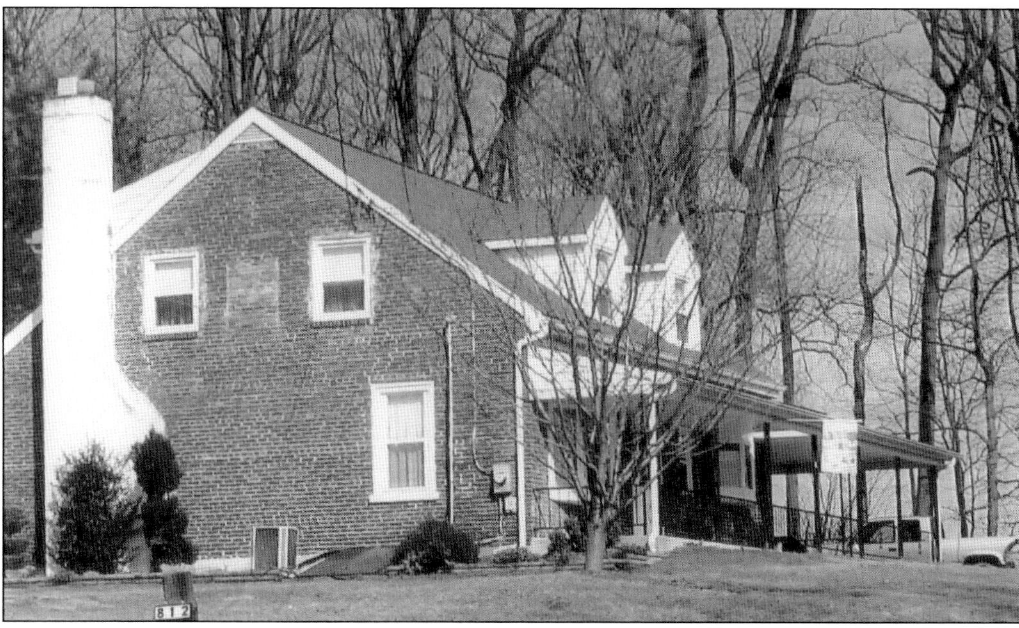

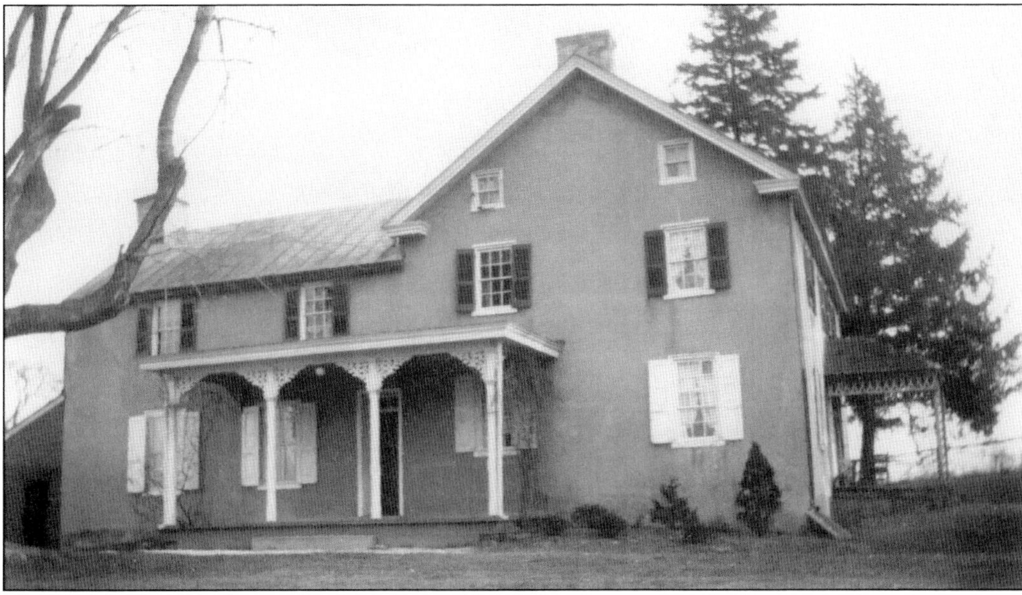

James Miller's stone house on West New Garden Road is the oldest documented house in New Garden Township. Built in 1730, the front two rooms of the present house were James and Ann Miller's original house. In the 1940s, Heatherly Dutton planted the trees and shrubs that surround the old house. (Courtesy NGTHC.)

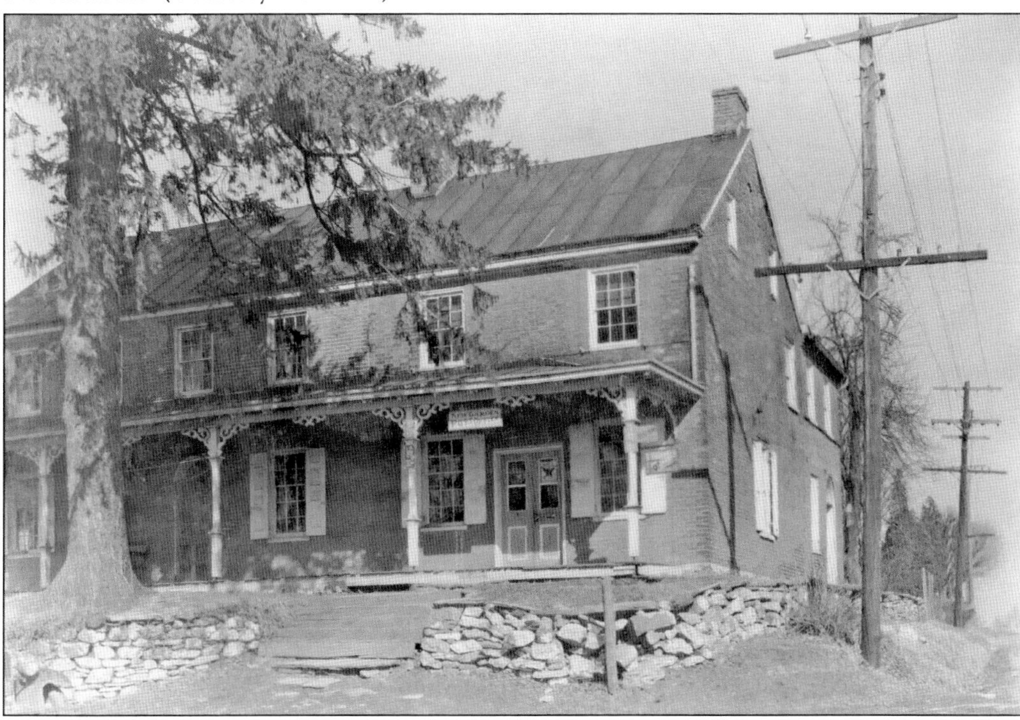

Gradually a village grew around the meeting house; log buildings were replaced by more substantial houses. In 1829, James Hughes built the brick store that would also eventually house the post office. Houses and shops extended west on New Garden Road to James Miller's house and north along Newark Road to Hillendale Road. (Courtesy CCHS.)

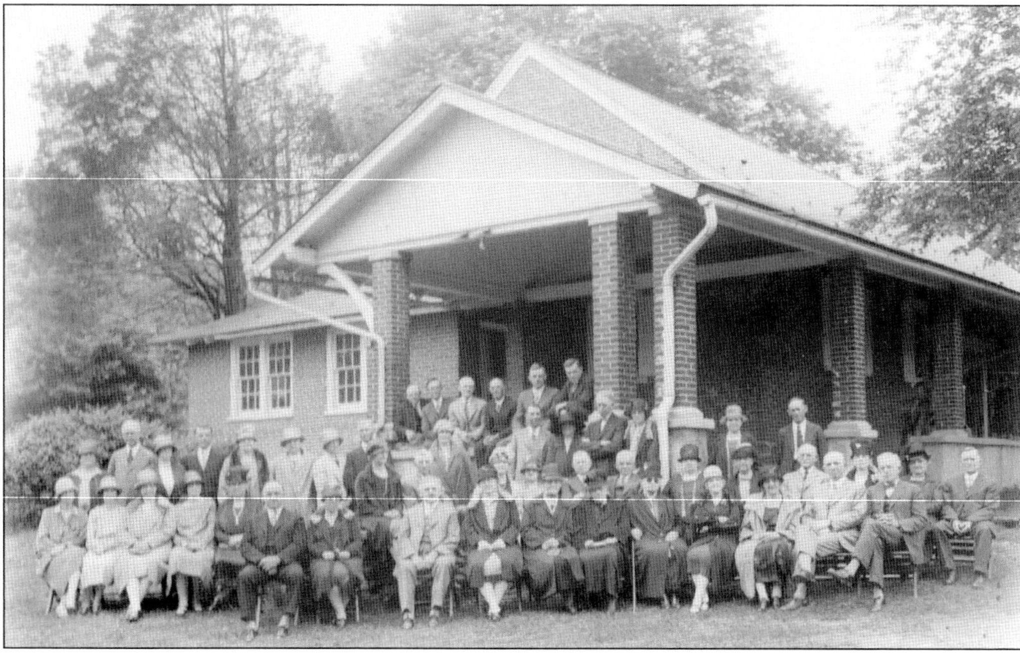

Members of New Garden Meeting pose about 1925 for this picture. By this time, New Garden Village had been reduced to a country crossroads anchored by the Meeting House. The store and post office remained open until the mid-1940s, but all other commercial enterprises were gone. (Courtesy NGTHC.)

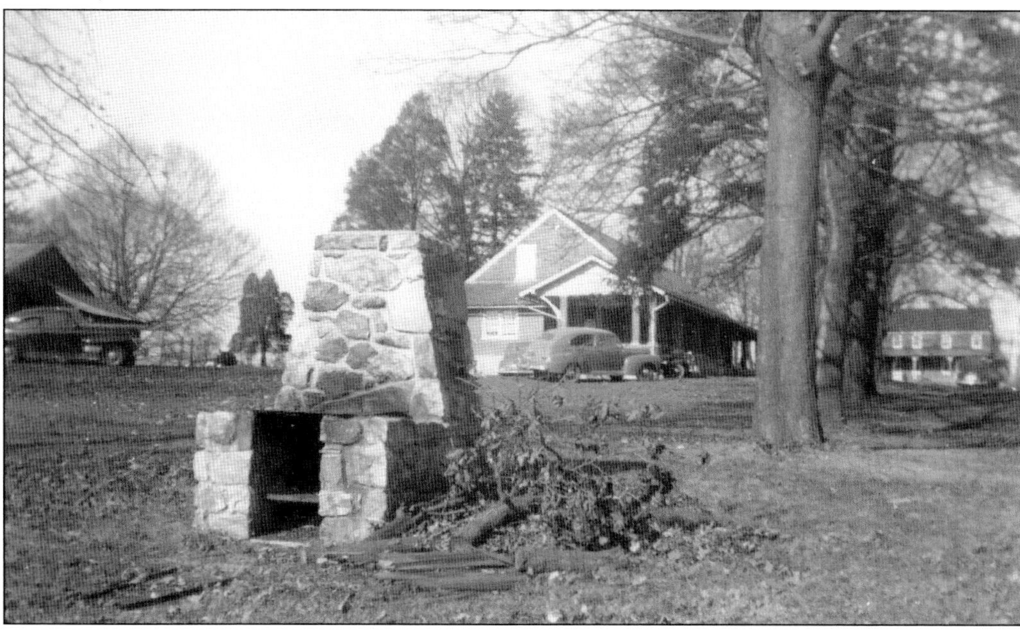

By the mid-20th century, only the meeting house remained on the Meeting property. The row of carriage sheds to the southwest had been removed, as had the Friends school. The school, a log structure with a stone fireplace forming an entire wall, stood where the present outdoor fireplace is located. Built in 1777, it was a "subscription school" (where parents paid tuition) until the Public School Act was passed in 1837. The building was demolished in 1872. (Courtesy NGTHC.)

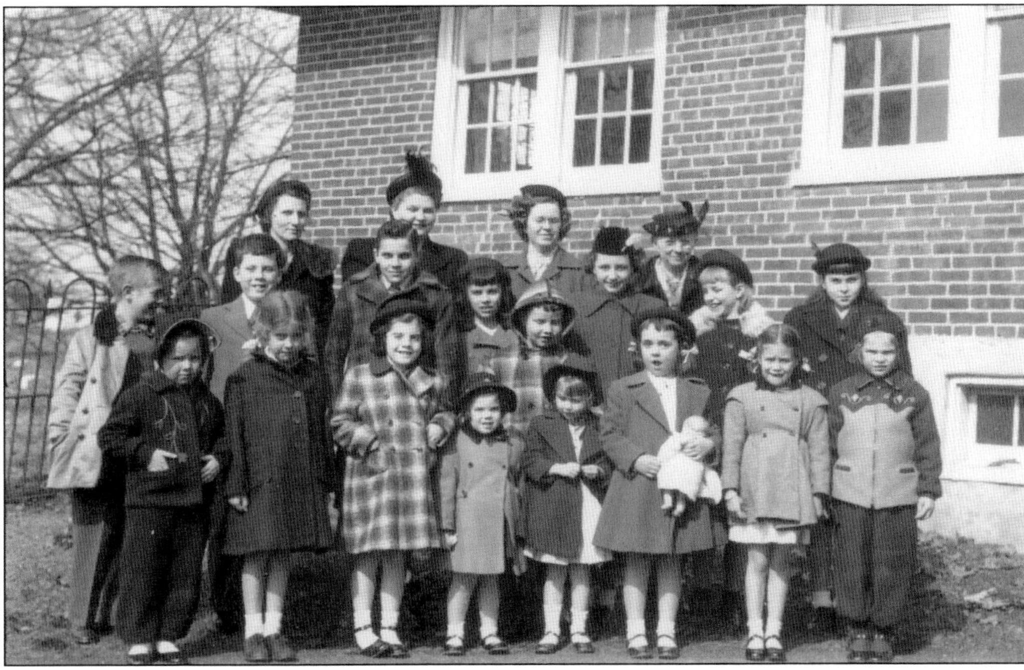

New Garden Meeting's First-day School children pose with their teachers in the 1940s. Teachers are, from left to right, Margaret Thomas, Katherine Parrish, Eleanor Wollaston, and Ellen Wollaston. The children are, from left to right, (first row) Kathy Wollaston, Marty Wollaston, Karen Darlington, Tina Darlington, Gail Wood, Patty Wood, and two unidentified; (second row) Tommy Maddox, Morton Darlington, David Parrish, Karen Maddox, unidentified, Barbara Davidson, and Mary Jane Parrish. (Courtesy NGTHC.)

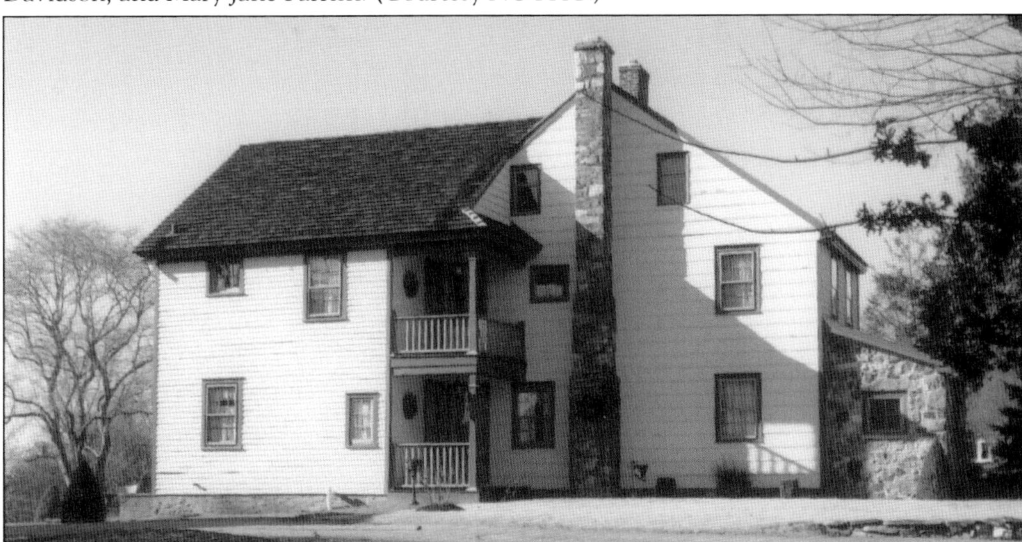

In 1829, John W. Thomas built his frame house and carriage shed north of the Meeting House. From 1835 to the 1860s, he maintained his law office in a room in his carriage house; his name appears on many deeds, wills, and other legal documents from the period. Prior to opening his law office, Thomas kept store in a log building on the northwest corner of the New Garden intersection. (Author's collection.)

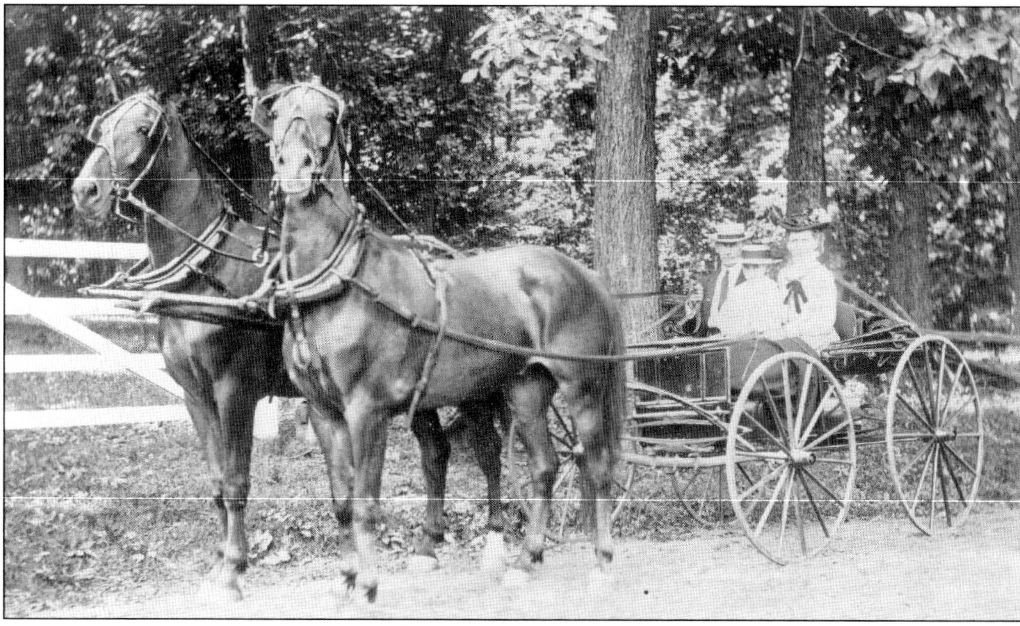

Frank and Ella Pratt and their son, Howard, were a Quaker family whose farm was on Hillendale Road. In 1900, when this picture was taken, they would have traveled about 2 miles by horse and buggy to attend New Garden Meeting. (Courtesy NGTHC.)

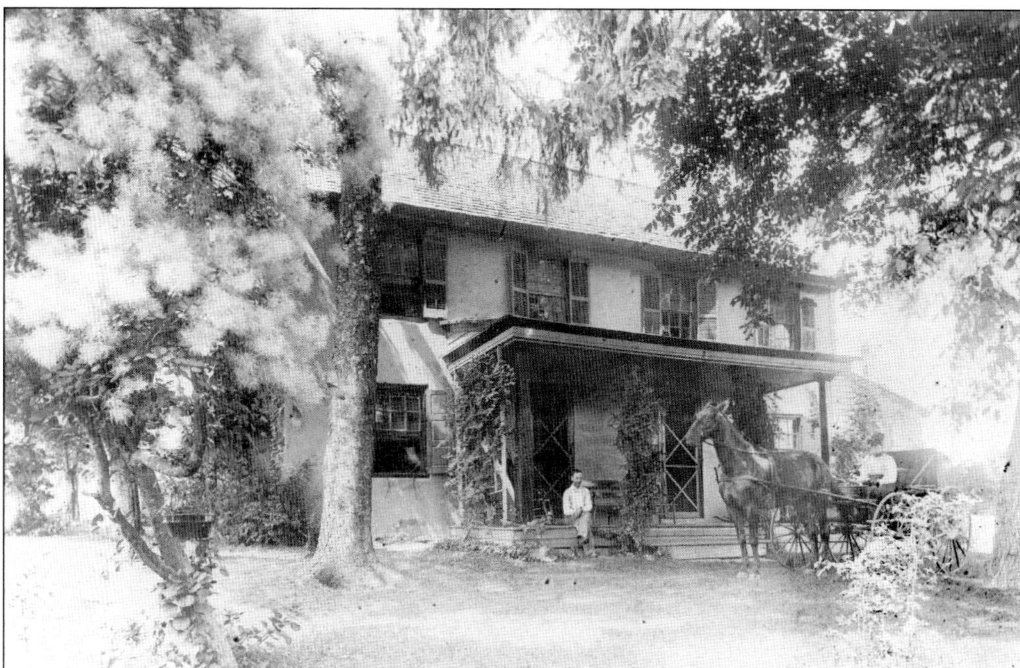

The Pratt's 121-acre farm had been purchased by Frank's father, John E. Pratt, in the 1870s. The John Pratt family had come from Delaware County to this farm, described in a sale notice as having a good stone house with 13 rooms, fine shade, and a young apple orchard. There was unfailing water, a large frame and stone barn built in 1881, a carriage house, and a corn house. (Courtesy NGTHC.)

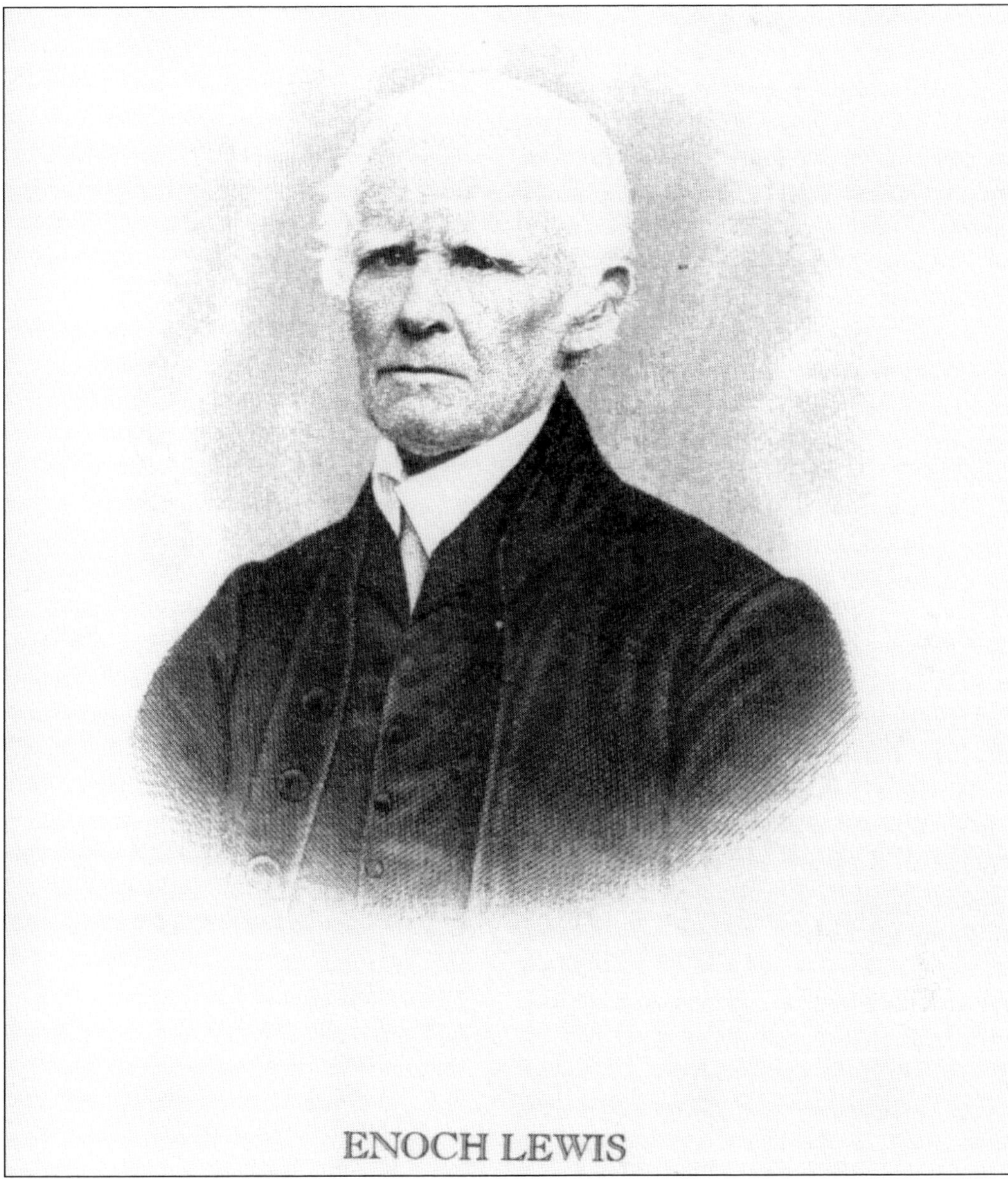

Enoch Lewis (1776–1856) was a prominent Friend and member of the New Garden community. Largely a self-taught scholar, Lewis was a teacher, writer, editor, and reformer. He spent 14 years at Westtown School, although not consecutively, where he taught mathematics and astronomy. In 1808, he opened a boys' boarding school on his New Garden farm. At the death of his wife in 1814, however, Lewis closed this school and devoted his life to the anti-slavery movement; his proposal that the U.S. government purchase and free all slaves placed him in the gradualist camp of abolitionists. Beginning in 1828, Lewis began to write about the economics of slave labor, lobbied legislators in Washington, D.C., and traveled on behalf of the Free Produce Movement, encouraging people to purchase goods not produced by slaves. Lewis was not only an active member of New Garden Meeting but was also much involved with the work of Philadelphia Friends. In his later years, Lewis began work on a multivolume history of the United States using social issues rather than wars as benchmarks. (Courtesy NGTHC.)

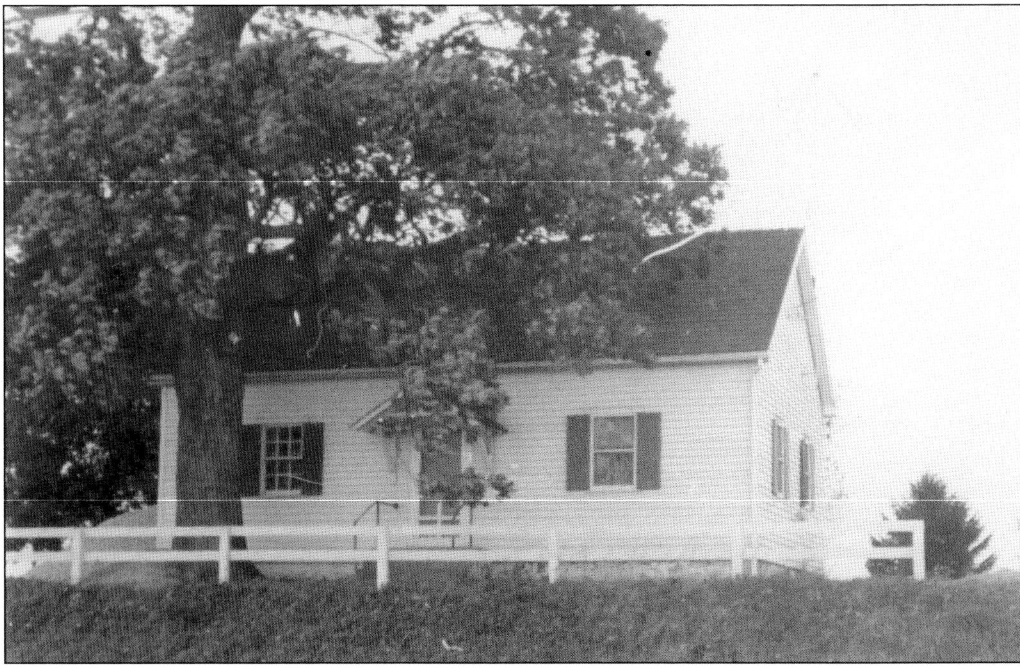

In 1852, Enoch Lewis sold a quarter of an acre to the New Garden Lyceum House Company, which built a frame building, 25 feet by 35 feet, at the intersection of East New Garden Road and the Gap-Newport Pike. Here temperance debates, abolitionist meetings, lectures, and other entertainments were held. The township purchased the Lyceum House in 1884, using it as a school; it was a meeting and polling place until 1966. (Courtesy NGTHC.)

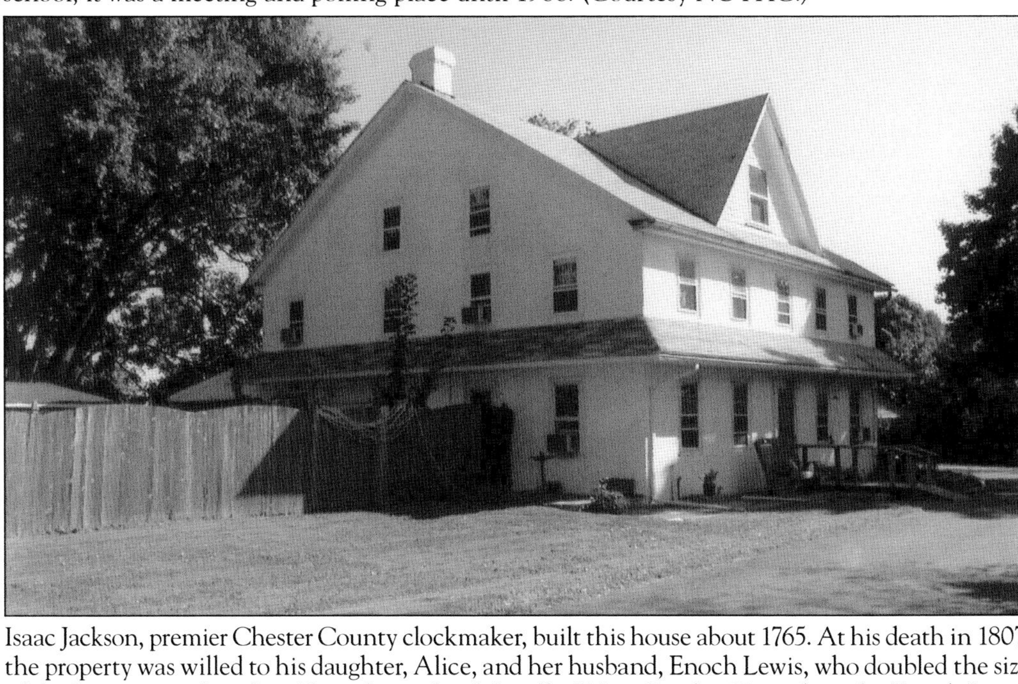

Isaac Jackson, premier Chester County clockmaker, built this house about 1765. At his death in 1807, the property was willed to his daughter, Alice, and her husband, Enoch Lewis, who doubled the size of the house to make a boys' boarding school. In all of New Garden Township, the Enoch Lewis house is the only documented station on the Underground Railroad. (Courtesy NGTHC.)

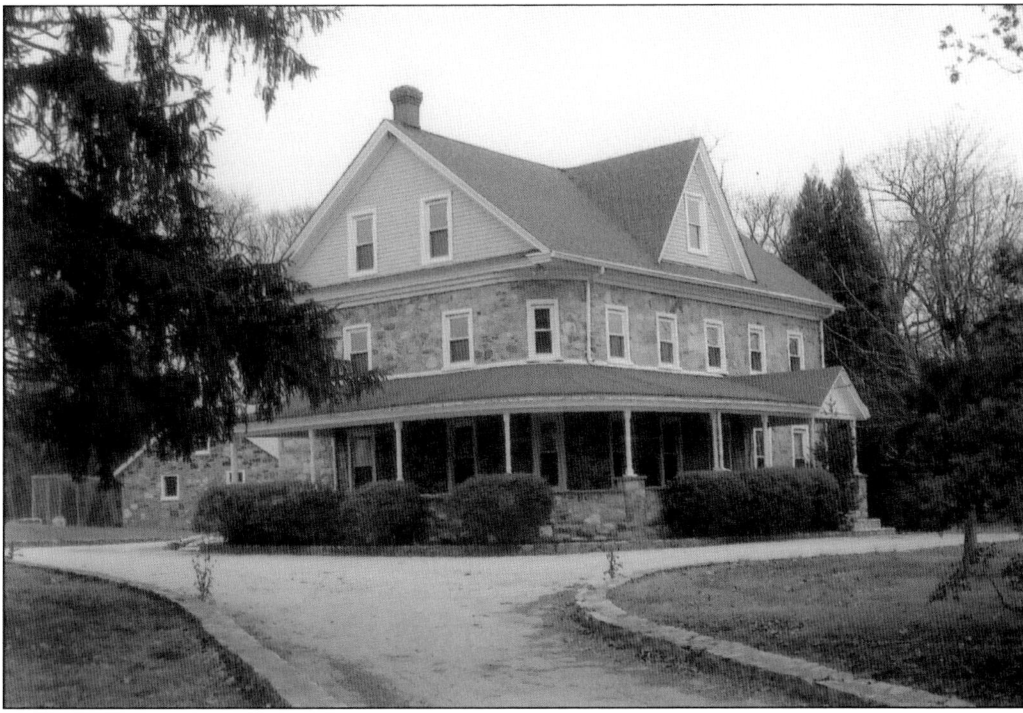

George W. Taylor (1803–1891) was a student of Enoch Lewis and much influenced by Lewis's anti-slavery views. Taylor thought that refusing to buy slave-produced goods could end slavery without war. He opened a "Free Produce" store in Philadelphia, leased a cotton mill at Doe Run, and traveled to the West Indies to secure sugar and molasses to supply his store. Despite financial losses, he never regretted his effort to abolish slavery. Taylor built his stone house on the north side of Sheehan Road and spent his last years as a dairy farmer, keeping his herd of Alderney cows in this stone barn. The barn, with stone to the peak of its roof, predates 1830 and may have been built by George's father, Jacob. (Both author's collection.)

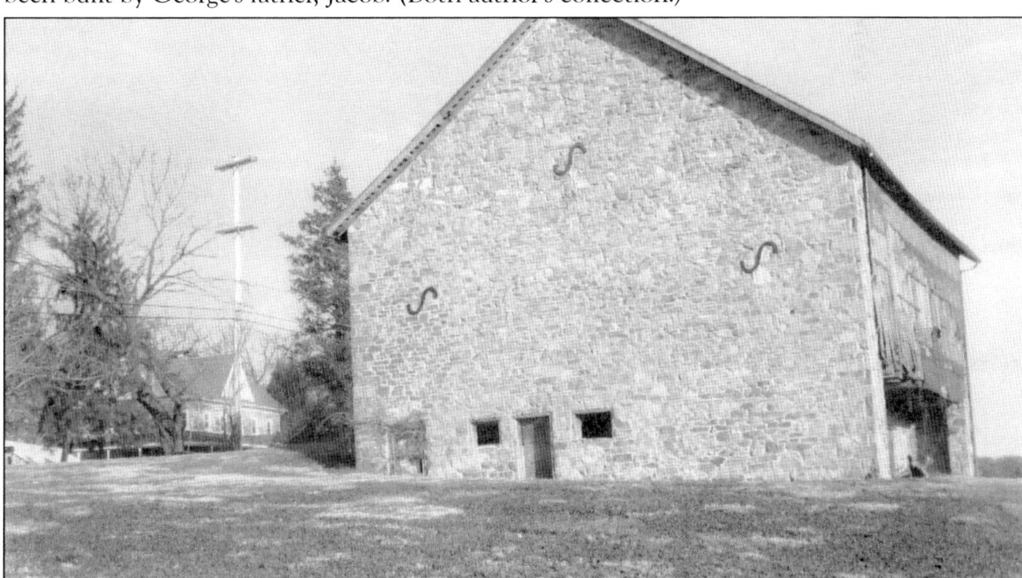

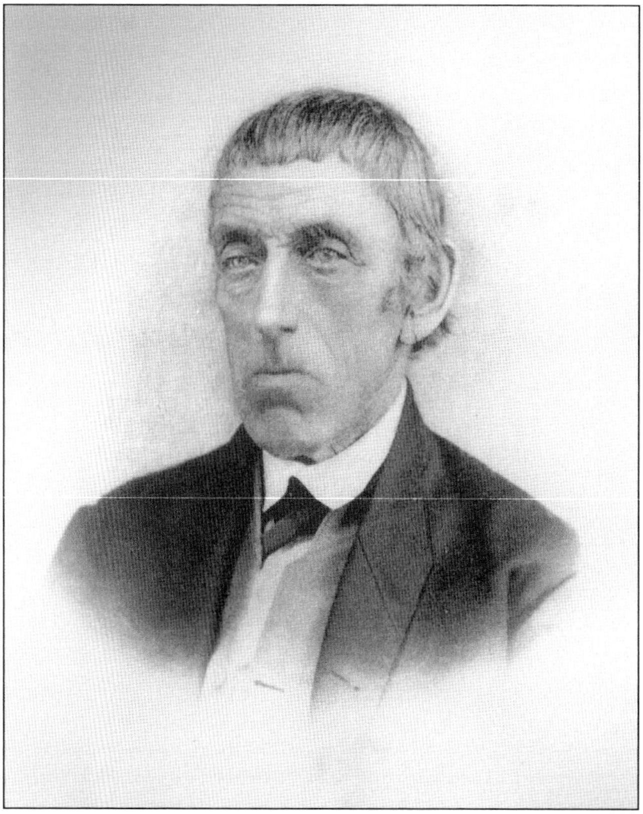

Dr. Ezra Michener (1794–1887), scientist, writer, temperance advocate, and prominent member of the Society of Friends, established his medical practice in New Garden in 1829. In addition to serving residents of the community for over 60 years, Dr. Michener also organized the first temperance society in the county and helped establish the Chester County Medical Society. Dr. Michener found time to study the natural sciences; he wrote 15 books on birds, plants, and shells. His writing extended to an autobiography and to a history called *A Retrospect of Early Quakerism*. In 1855, Dr. Michener built his brick house on Newark Road. Calling his home Sylvania, he surrounded the house with an arboretum of trees collected from around the world. (Left courtesy Margaret Jones; below author's collection.)

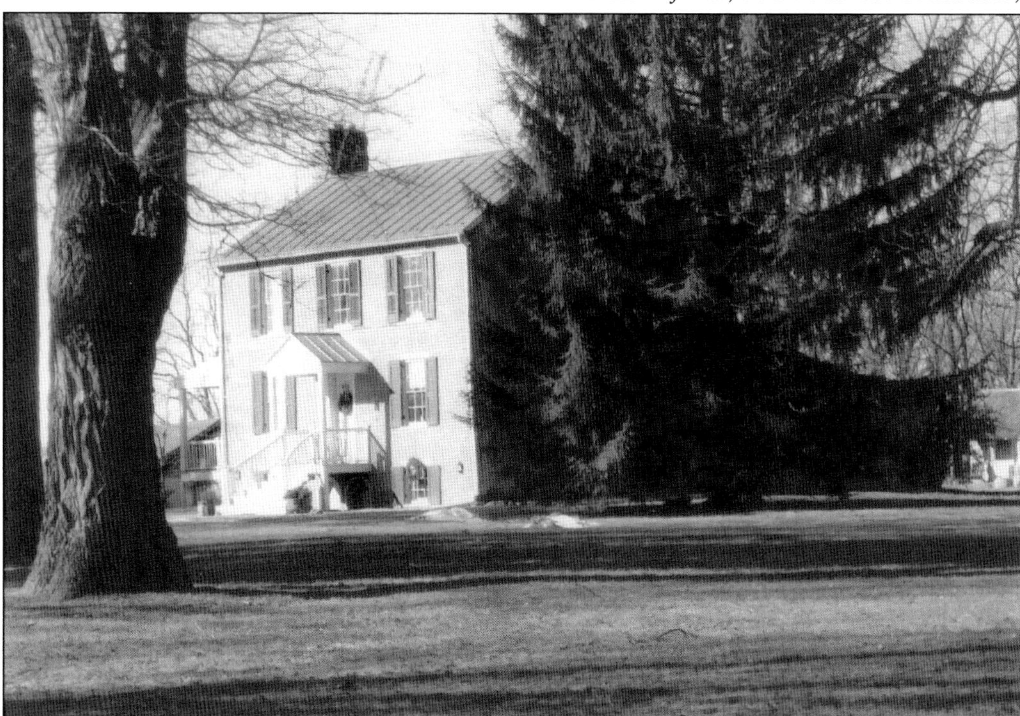

Two

LANDENBERG

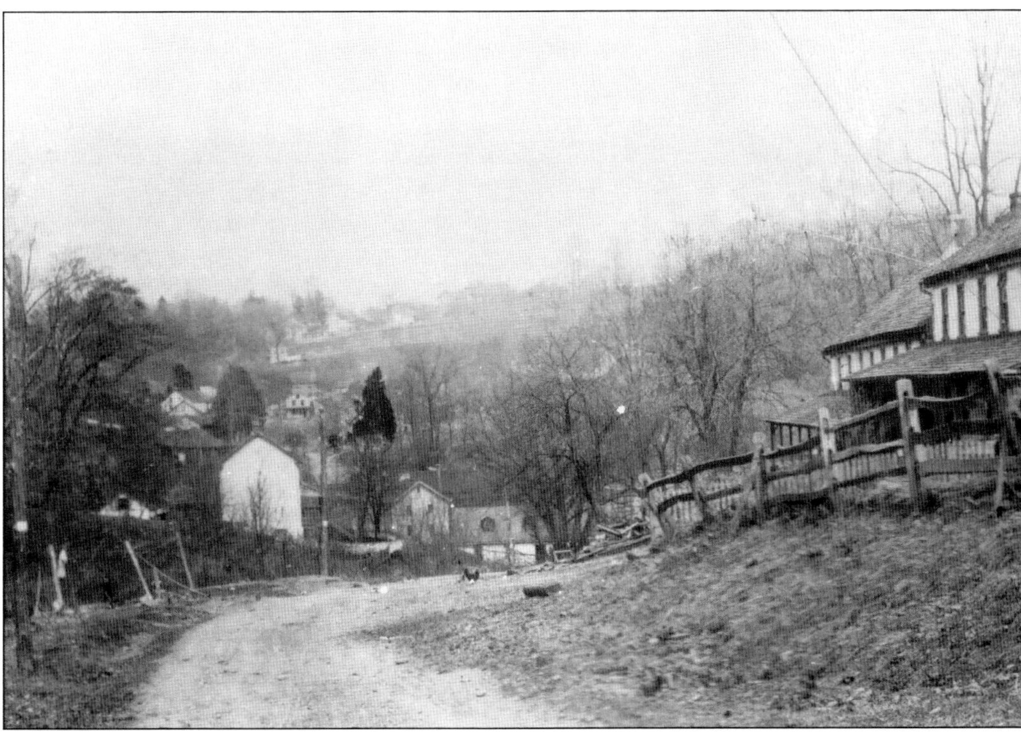

Throughout the 19th century, Landenberg evolved on parts of two tracts: a 1,000-acre land purchase by John Evans Jr. from William Penn Jr., and 1,000 acres known as the Wastelands, originally purchased by William Miller in the early 1700s. This scene is taken from Mercer's Mill Road approaching Landenberg from the west. (Courtesy NGTHC.)

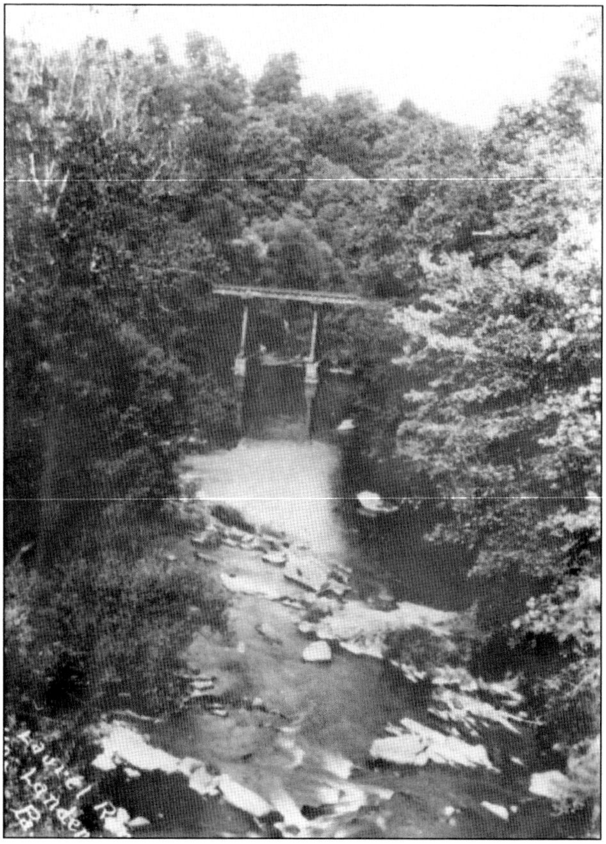

Recognizing the financial potential associated with waterpower, Philadelphian Cadwallader Evans purchased 371 acres of Miller's Wastelands in 1809. Within two years, Evans had erected a sawmill and 20-foot dam just upstream of today's Laurel Bridge, pictured. This was the first of three Laurel mills. (Courtesy Alma Rigler.)

In 1814, Evans sold his mill and dam to Joseph Johnson, who added two cotton factories and four tenant houses. Eventually, three mills and 14 two-story tenant houses comprised Laurel Mills, operated by Aaron Osmond in the 1840s. However, the cost of transporting cotton from the South doomed commercial prospects. Bankruptcy and fire took their toll on the mills, as seen in this picture. (Courtesy NGTHC.)

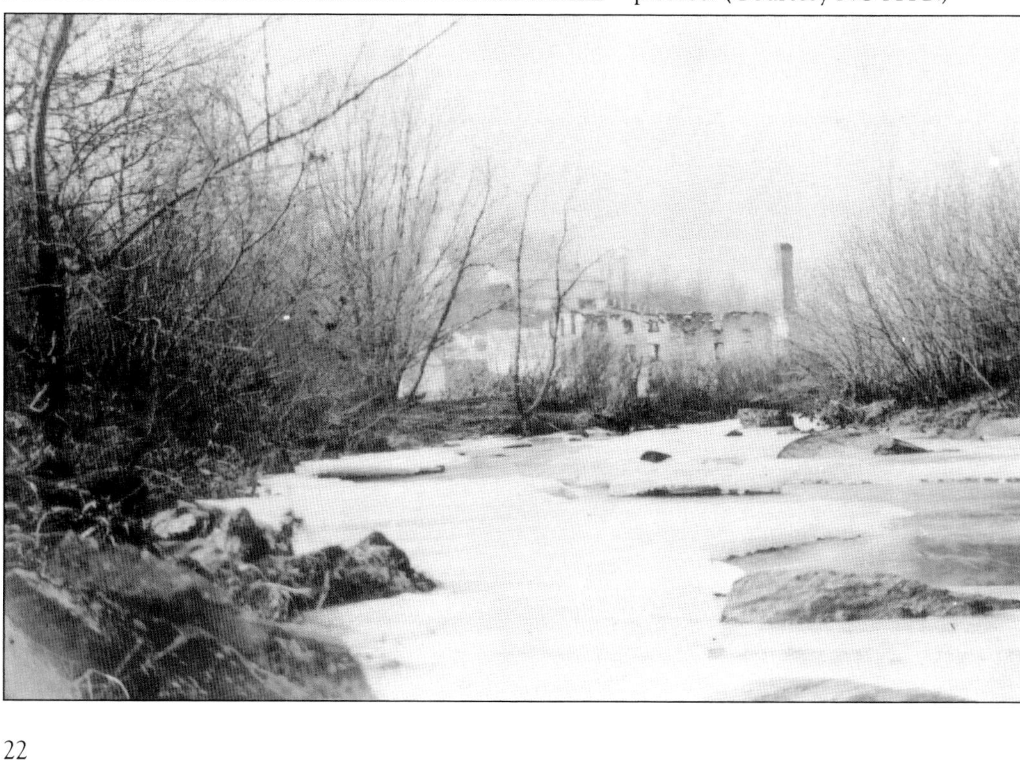

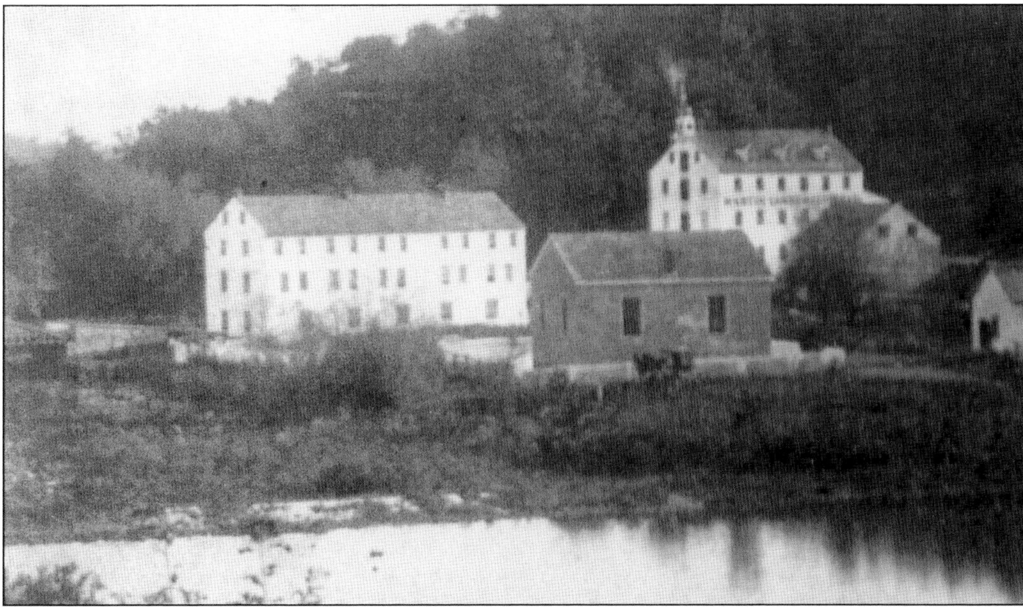

In 1817, Enoch Chandler, New Garden Inn owner, saw an opportunity to invest his profits. Over time, he built a sawmill, gristmill, fulling (felting) mill, and in 1825, a large cotton factory, establishing Chandlerville. Although Chandler died in the early 1830s, his mills remained in operation through 1841, when Joseph Ripka, a Prussian immigrant and Philadelphia industrialist who developed Manayunk, purchased the cotton mill. Financial panic in 1857 wiped out Ripka. (Courtesy NGTHC.)

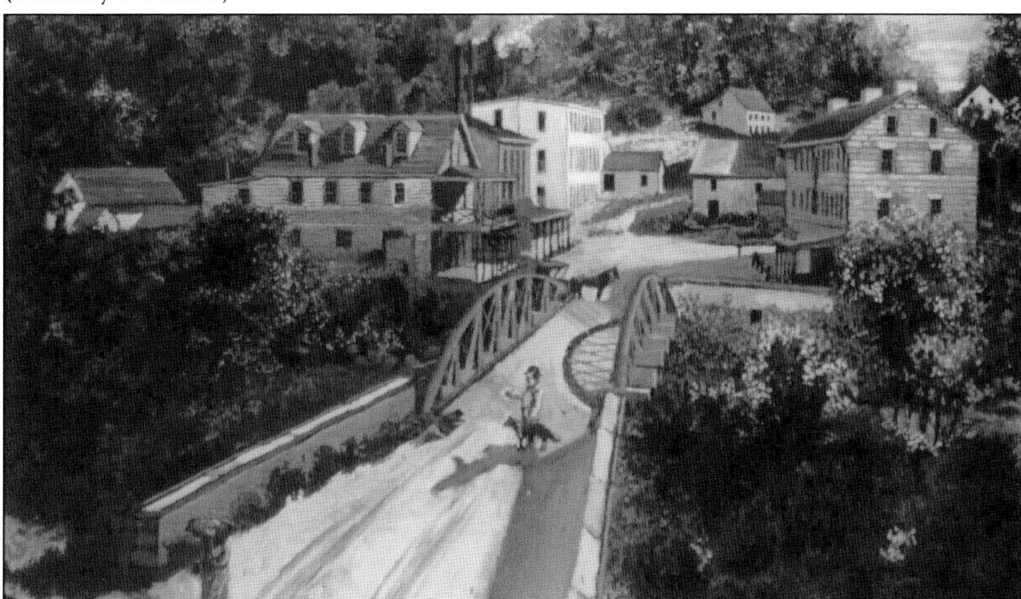

By mid-century, four dams and six mills had harnessed the power of the creek as it dropped nearly 60 feet over the course of a meandering mile. At the time, a *Daily Local News* advertisement described the Chandler property: "cotton factory, 64 by 24 feet in size, a saw mill, a new stone dwelling house, a stone barn, and two small stone and frame houses . . . machinery . . . including 588 spindles and two wool carding engines—a Billy and a Jenny." (Courtesy NGTHC.)

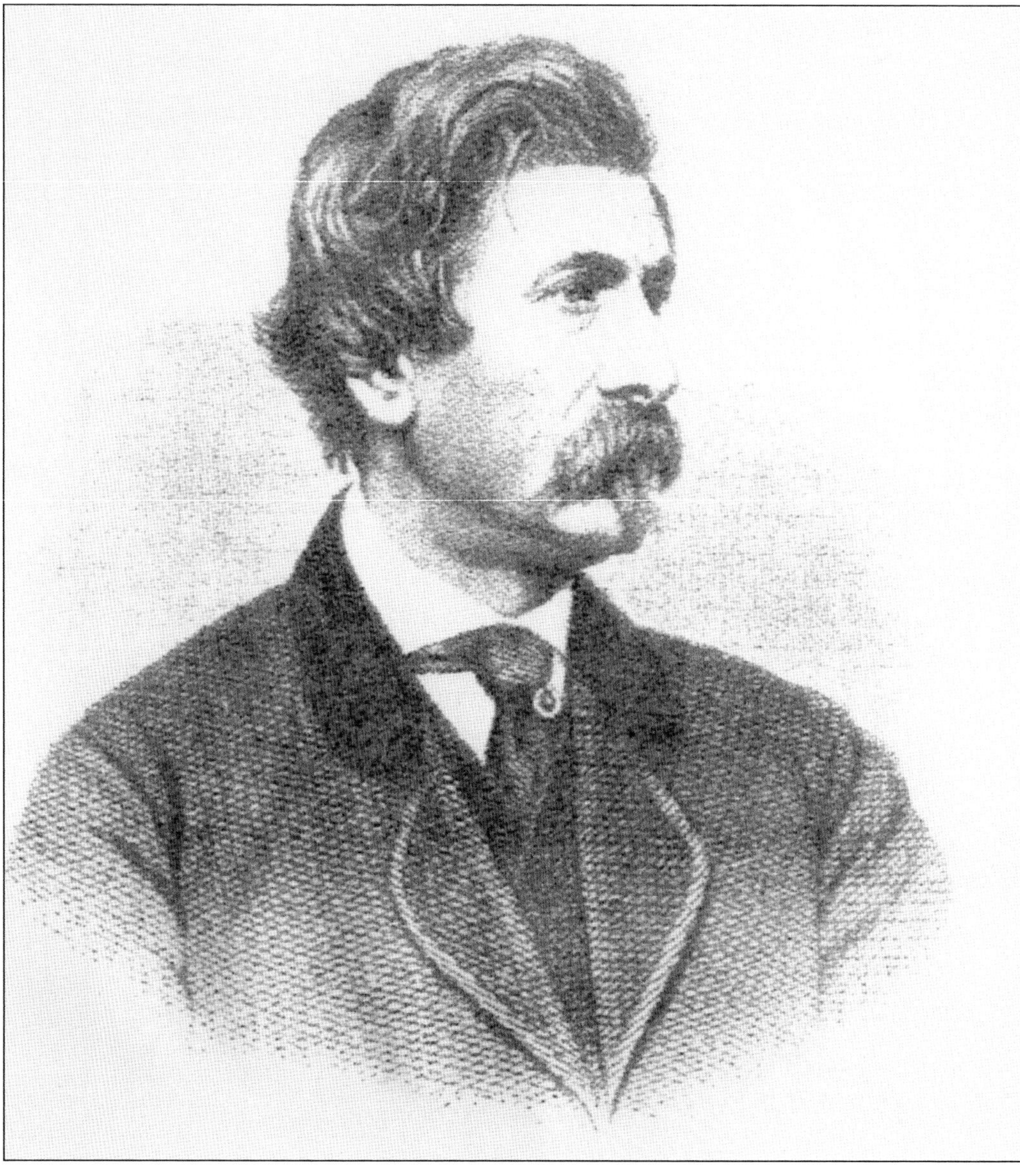

In 1832 Martin Landenberger immigrated to Philadelphia from Ebingen, Germany, a stocking manufacturing town. An enterprising hosiery weaver, Landenberger eventually owned a factory in Germantown that wove paisley shawls, popular in early Victorian America. In 1864, because of the available waterpower, he purchased the Laurel and Chandlerville mills and their villages. This consolidation of the two mill sites allowed him to produce needed wool yarn to supply his hosiery factory in Germantown. Between his large hosiery mill in Germantown and his yarn manufacture in Landenberg, he employed about 1,000 people and produced about $1 million of merchandise. Landenberg saw the advantage a railroad would bring to Landenburgh and invested heavily in the Pennsylvania and Delaware Railroad, which reached Landenburgh in 1872. A financial crash in 1873 threw Landenberger and other industrialists into bankruptcy; in 1879, the railroad too declared bankruptcy. About this time, a series of fires devastated the Laurel Mills; they were never rebuilt. Martin Landenberger died penniless in 1884 on a small farm in Millville, New Jersey. (Courtesy NGTHC.)

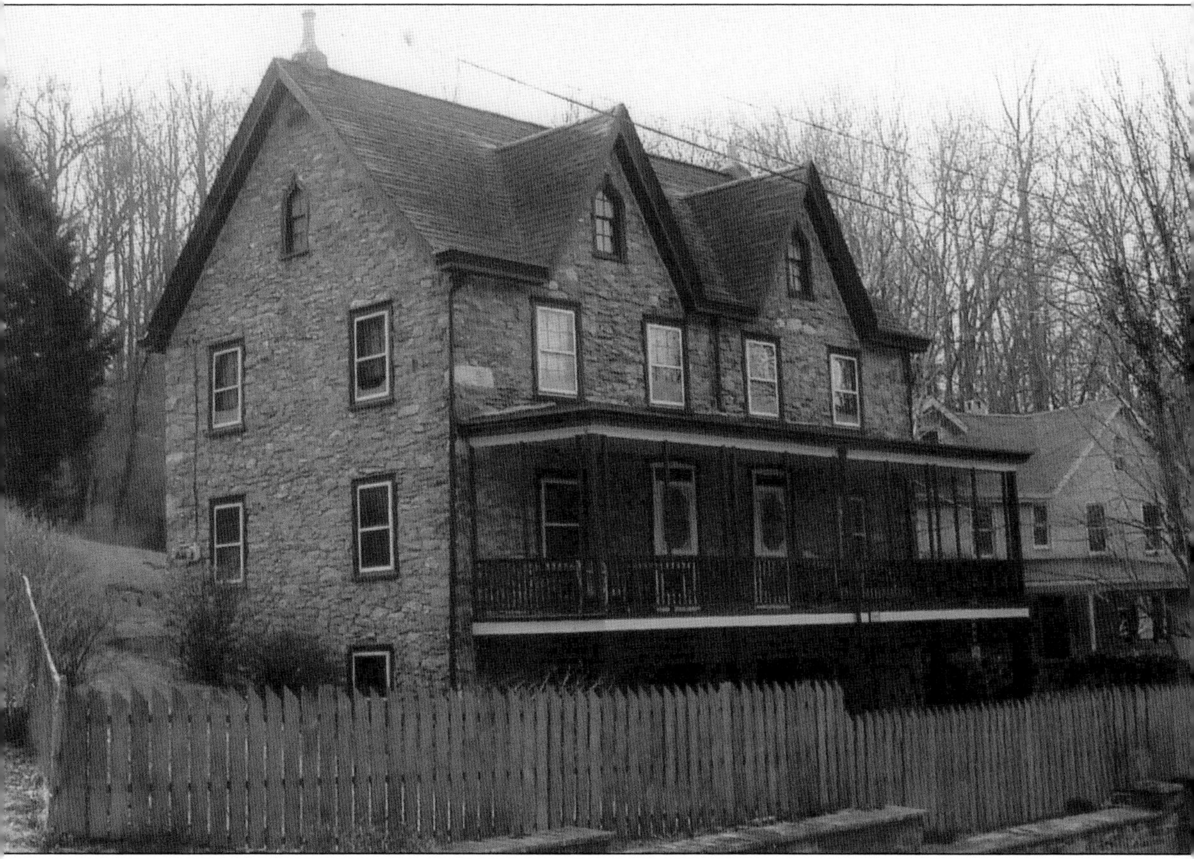

At the height of business, Landenberger hired several hundred local hands to operate the village mill's machines. Those employees needed lodgings and transportation. Landenberger built tenements and boardinghouses, like that above, and became a principal force (along with his son-in-law Charles Weiler, supervisor of the town's mills) behind bringing the railroad through Landenburgh, or Landenberg, as it has been spelled from 1904. (Courtesy Chris Robinson.)

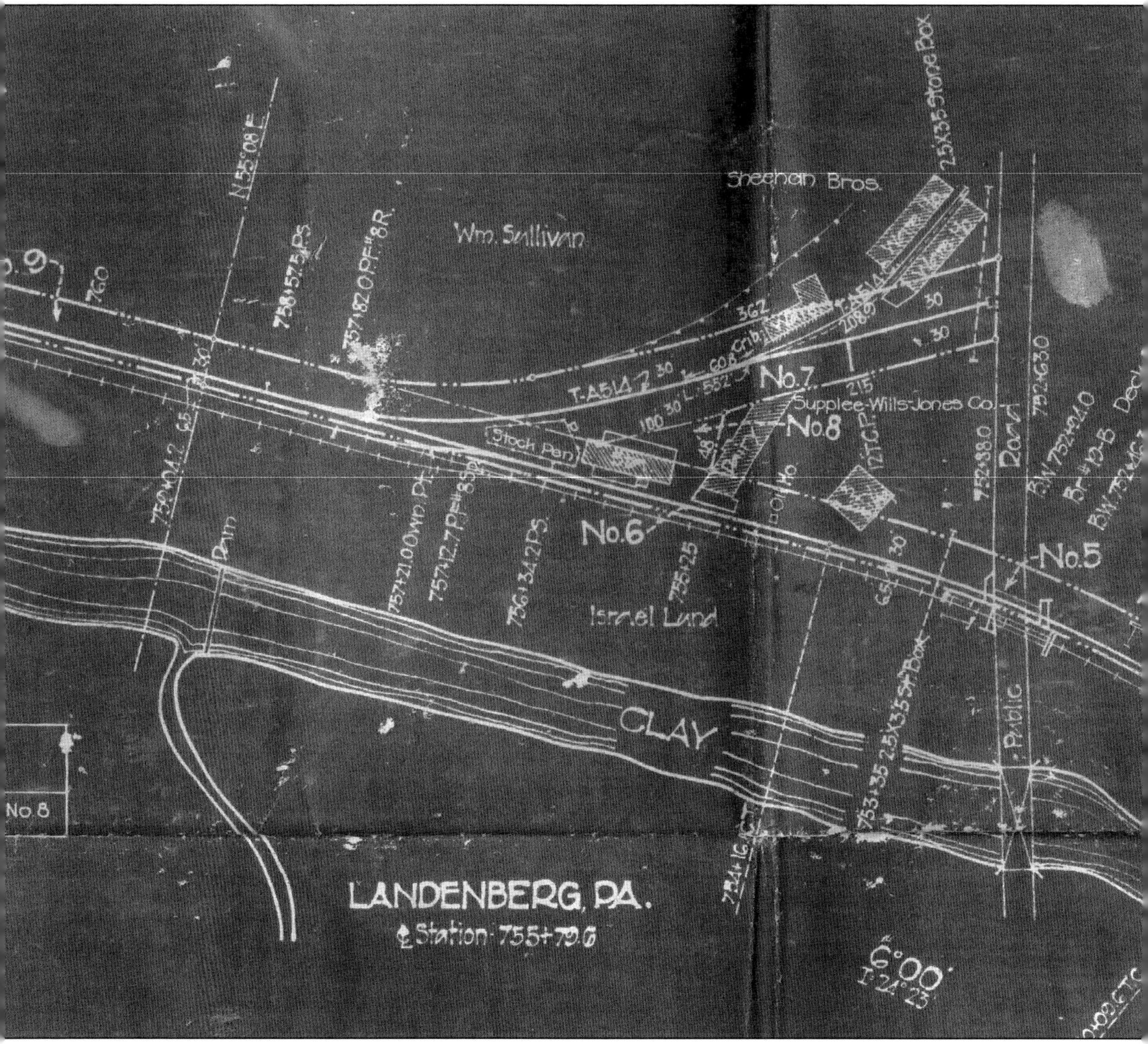

Bustling mills along the creek justified building a railroad through Landenburgh. The mills needed raw material and a way to distribute finished products. A railroad was also transportation for mill workers. At one time, there were hundreds employed. Eventually the railroad hauled kaolin clay, and, by the 1890s, the dairy industry used the railroad to ship milk, butter, and cheese. This surveyor's blueprint is from the early 1900s. (Courtesy Bob Norris.)

The The Pomeroy-Newark Railroad's route had necessitated leveling land, blowing cuts through the granite hills, and erecting trestles in order to follow the creek and minimize sloped grades. By autumn 1872, construction of the railroad was six months behind schedule because of these engineering challenges. (Courtesy NGTHC.)

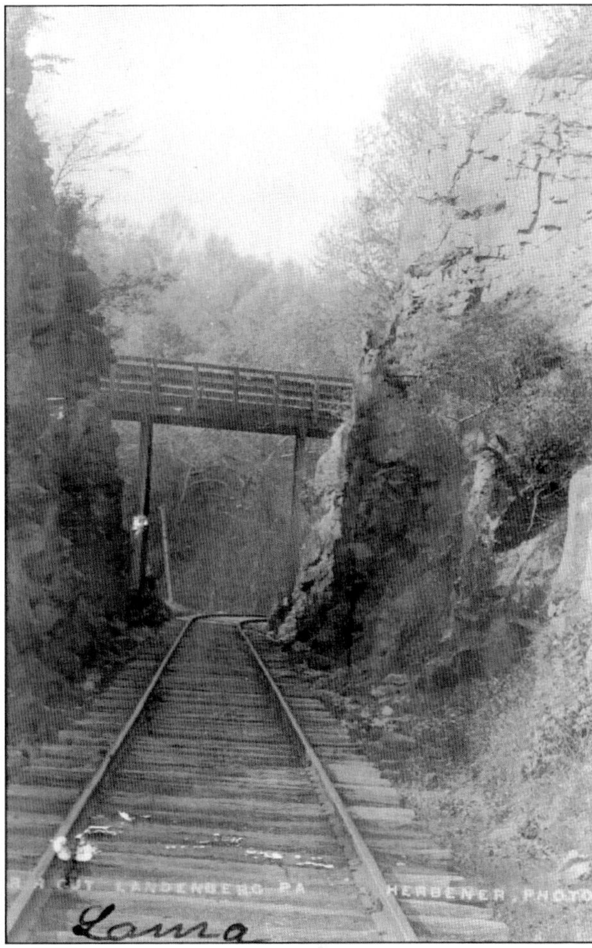

By 1871, the Wilmington and Western Railroad had broken ground. Its path would take it from Wilmington's riverfront to Landenburgh, with Pittsburgh as its proposed western terminus. But like planned spurs to Kennett Square and Oxford, the line to Pittsburgh never materialized. (Courtesy NGTHC.)

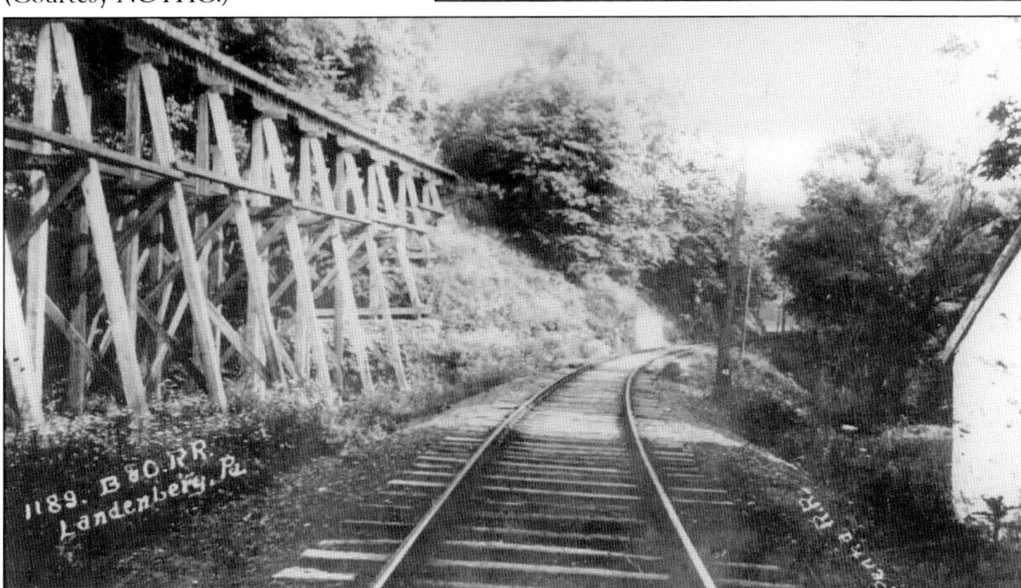

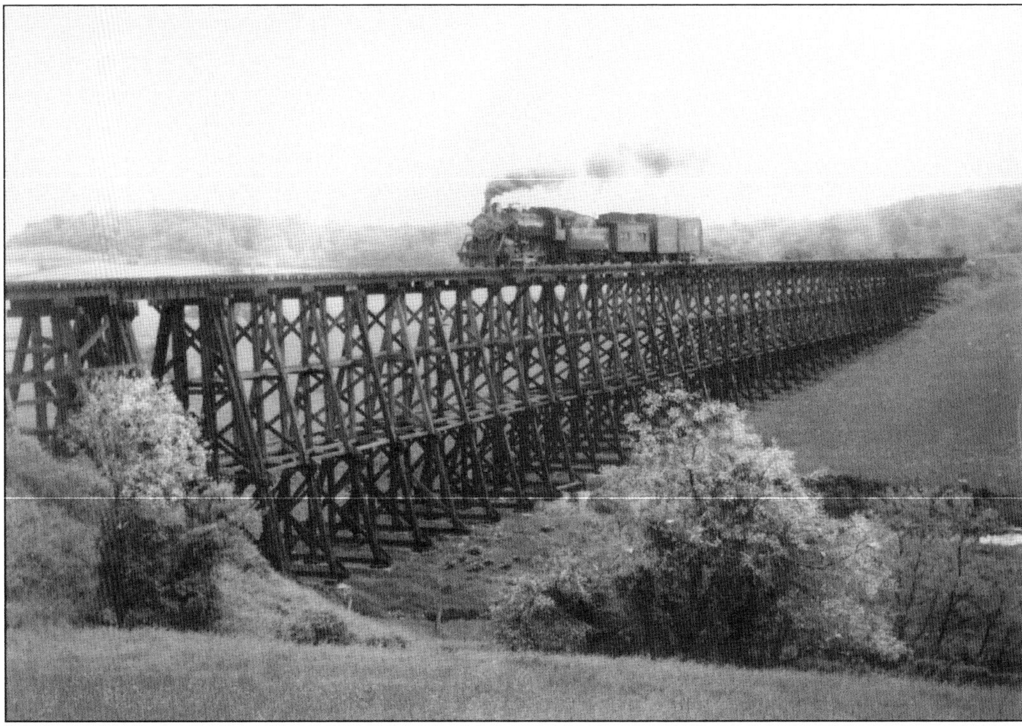

"On Saturday evening about 4 o'clock the track layers . . . spiked down and secured the track across the Broad Run Trestle, and then indulged in hearty cheers over the completion of the job. . . . All parties expressed their pleasure upon noting . . . how solidly the structure stood without a jar or tremble," reported the Wilmington *Every Evening* on October 19, 1872. A trestle-spanning series of barrels collected rainwater should sparks ignite a fire. (Courtesy NGTHC.)

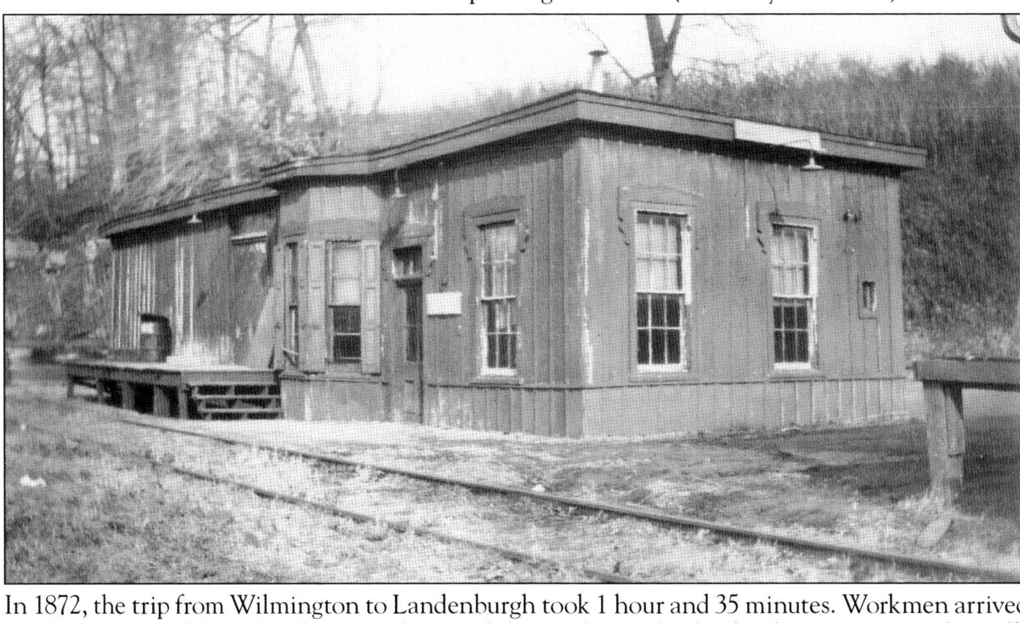

In 1872, the trip from Wilmington to Landenburgh took 1 hour and 35 minutes. Workmen arrived on the train, sped from this depot, and crossed the creek on a footbridge, hastening into the mills before the starting whistle. (Courtesy NGTHC.)

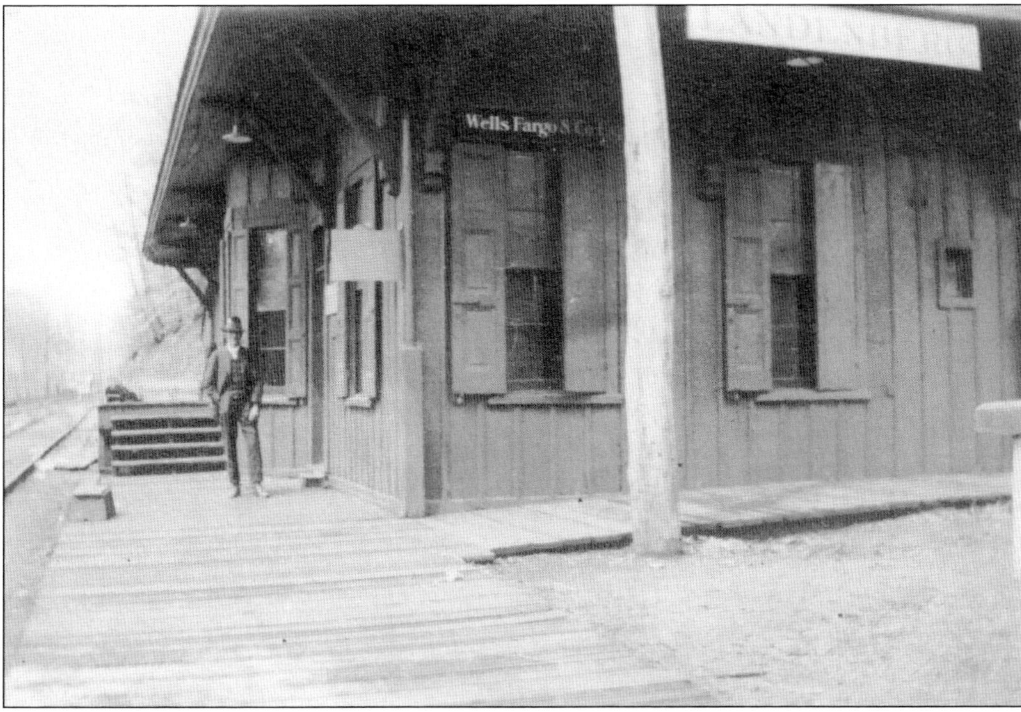

Fashioned with gender-segregated waiting parlors, an agent's room, ticket office, and a freight wharf, this modern railroad station replaced the old shed in 1875. (Courtesy Alma Rigler.)

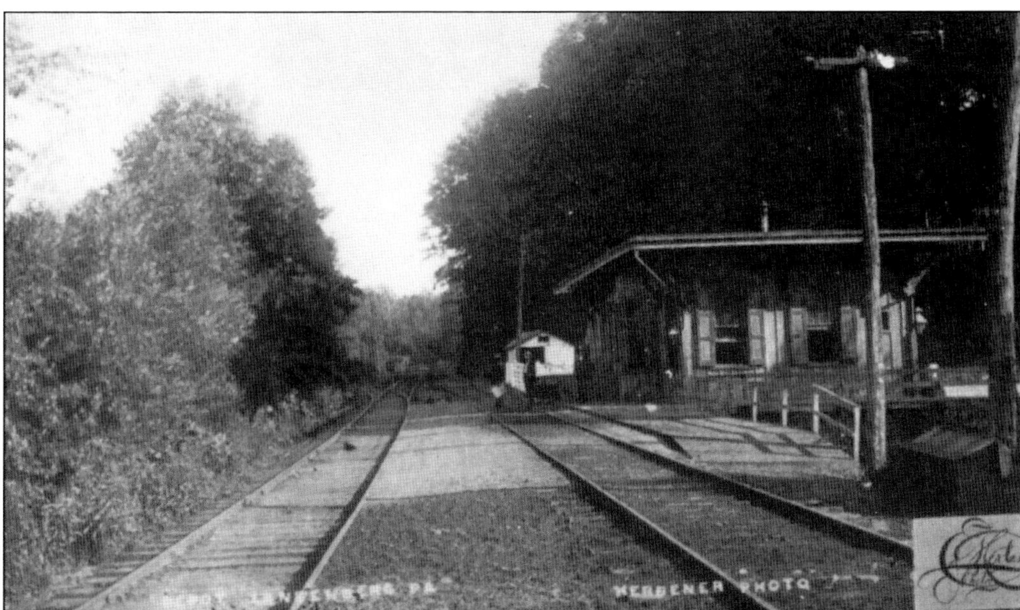

The Pennsylvania and Delaware Railway officially opened in 1873. It was built to carry coal from the Pennsylvania coalfields to the ice-free port of Delaware City; passenger service soon followed. This railroad shared the station with the Wilmington and Western Railroad, which reached Landenburgh in 1872. (Courtesy NGTHC.)

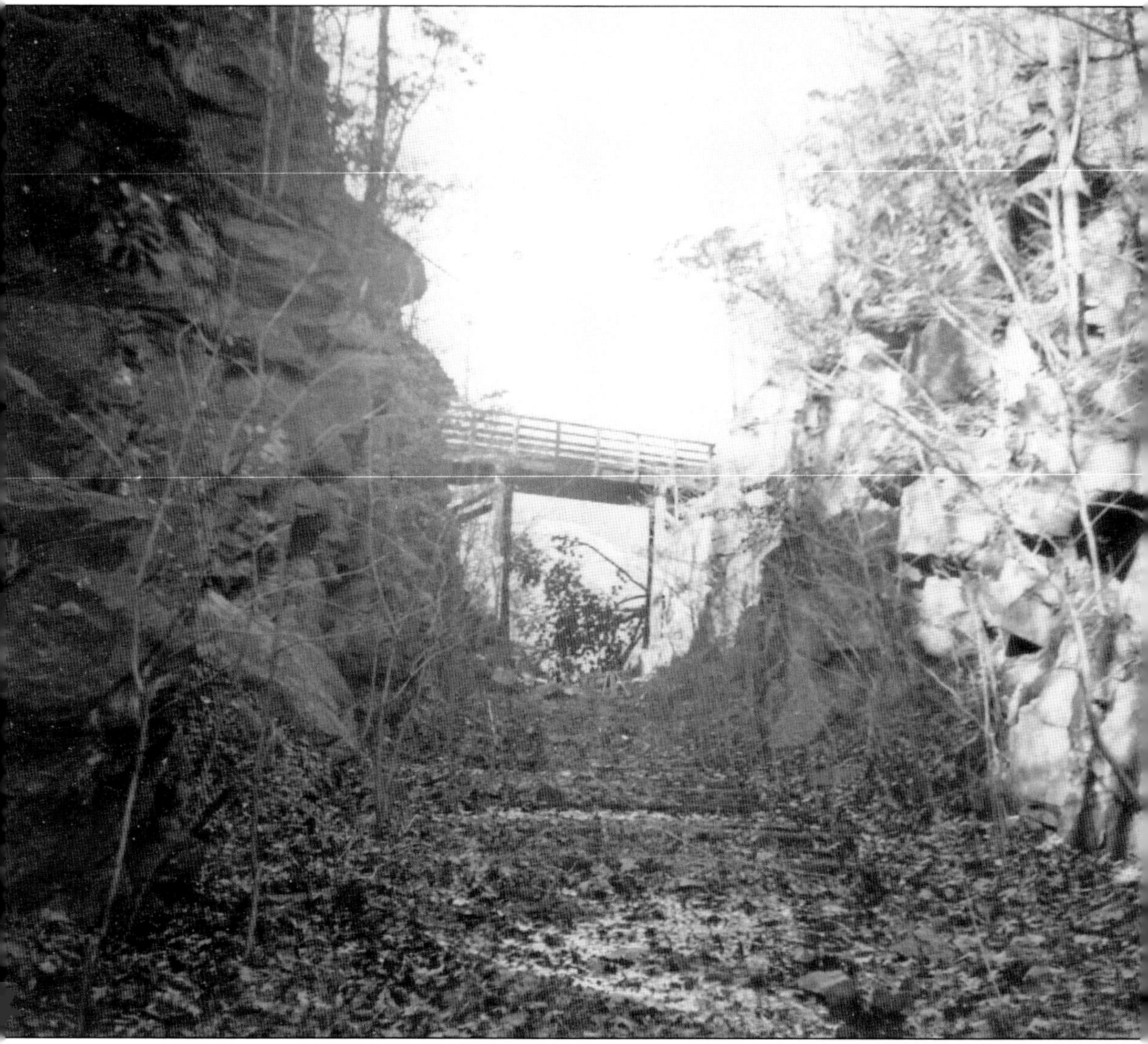

This cut is an example of the challenges the railroad faced making its way through the rough terrain along the White Clay. In addition to dynamiting through granite, engineers constructed five trestles over the White Clay between Auburn Road and Landenburgh to make the right-of-way not exceed a grade of two percent. (Courtesy NGTHC.)

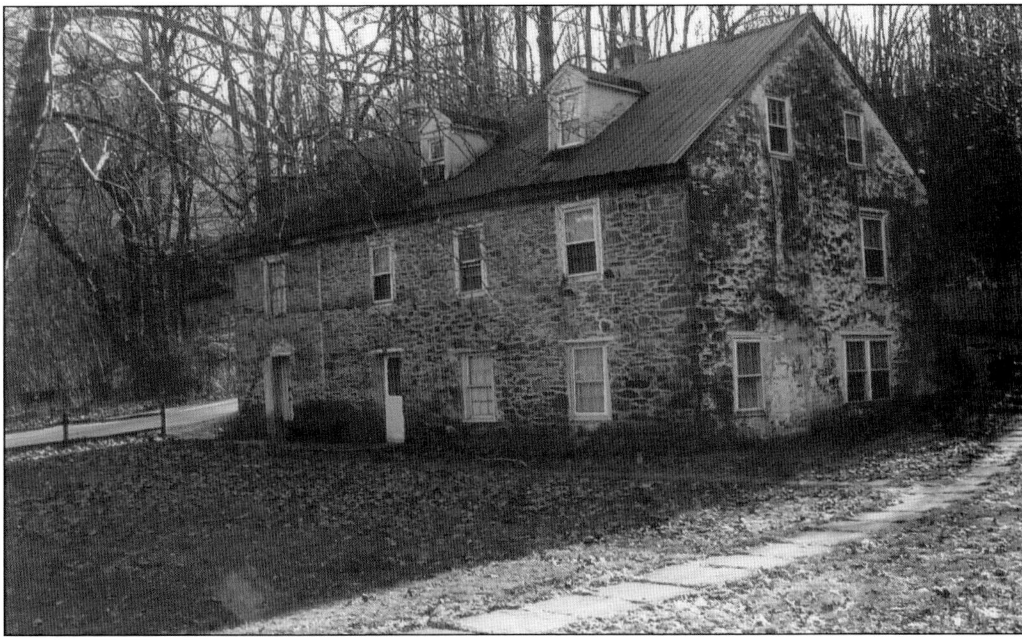

The wool house still standing on the southwest corner of Penn Green and Mercer Mill Road is the only remaining building from the era of the woolen mills. It had various uses during mill years, from storing raw wool to holding mill offices to later becoming a dormitory. (Courtesy Chris Robinson.)

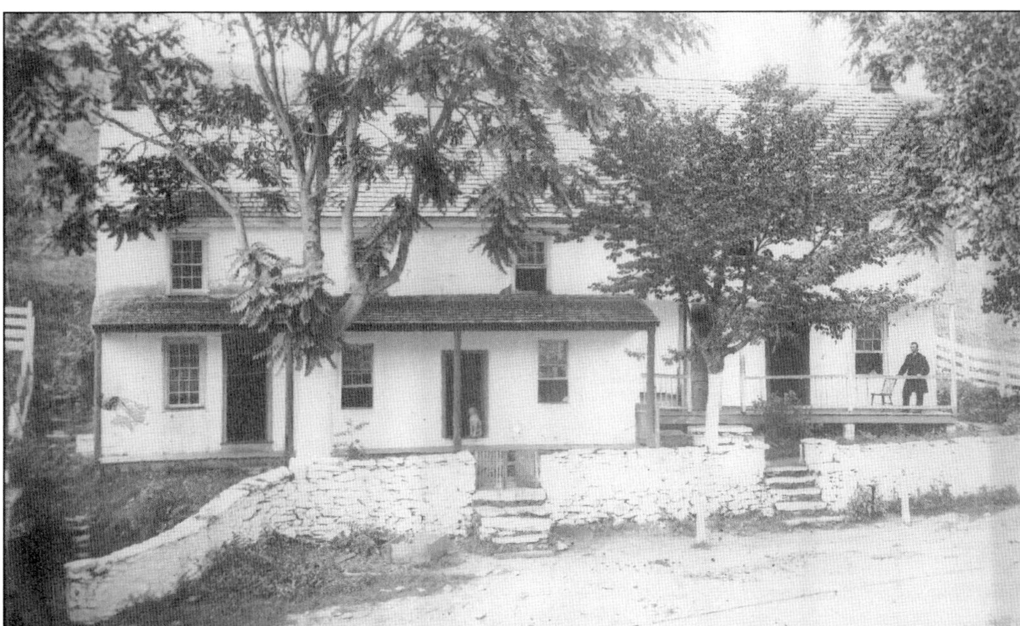

Although Landenberger encountered financial difficulties during the economic depression of 1873, and his businesses closed, his town persisted. Numerous houses appeared. Storekeeper and postmaster Washington Ewing built upwards of six houses including this hotel, which was always known as Wash Ewing's Hotel. (Courtesy NGTHC.)

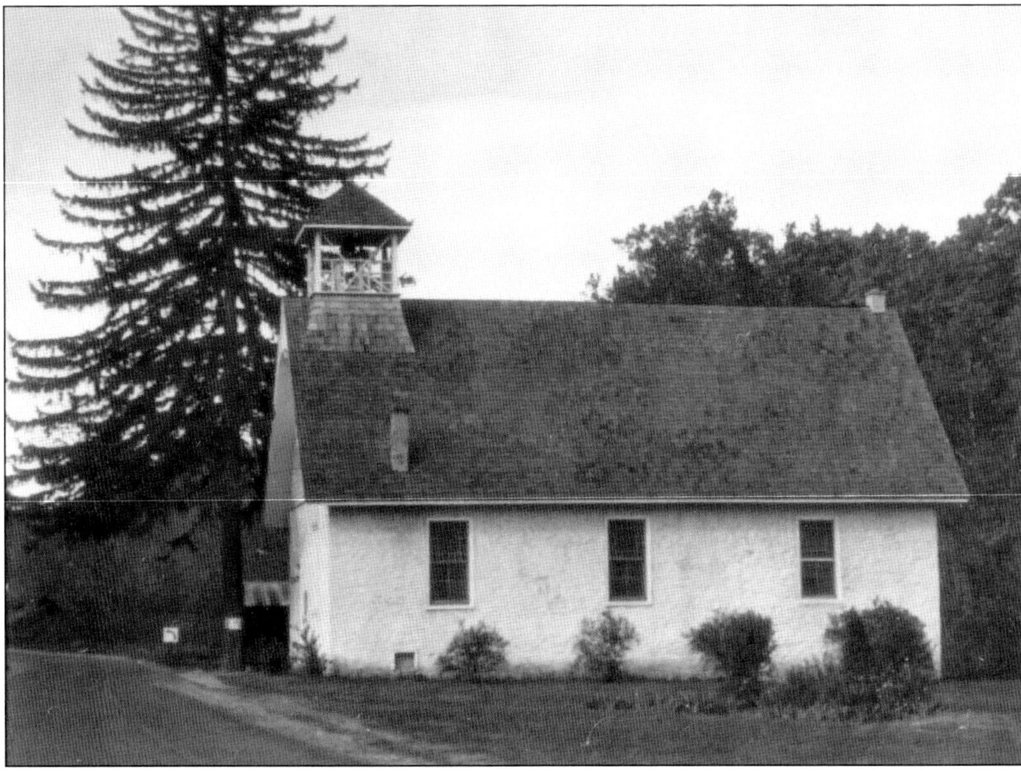

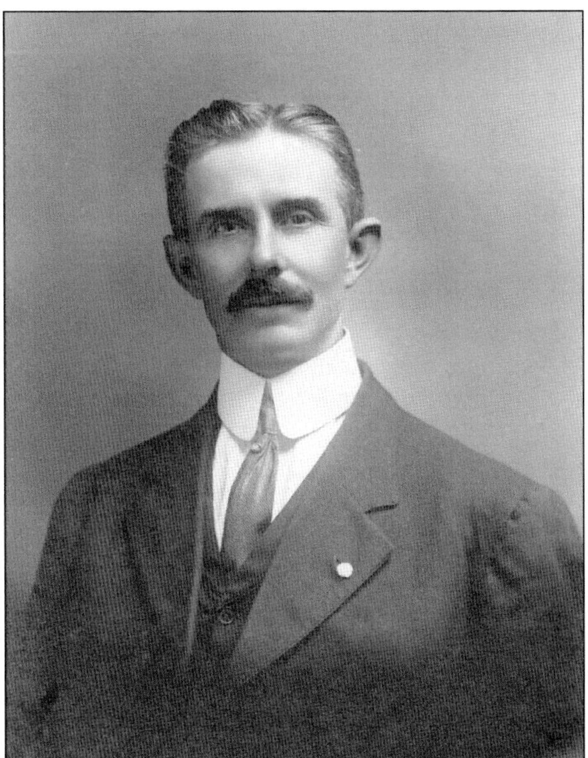

As early as 1846, a group of Chandlerville citizens pursued the notion of erecting a Methodist Episcopal church. The first church (above) was built in 1848 between Penn Green Road and White Clay Creek. A Sunday school was established in 1871, and in 1888, the original structure was renovated. The building was enlarged and a steeple with church bell erected. (Courtesy NGTHC.)

John Lefevre, the first engineer for the Baltimore and Ohio (B&O) Railroad's Baltimore-to-Wilmington route, spent 30 years delivering passengers and freight to Landenberg. His daughter, Jean Minshall, recalled that she and her sister frequently joined him for lunch in the caboose of the midday train. (Courtesy Jean Minshall.)

After the 1888 renovation of the Methodist Church (pictured), a parsonage was built in 1902. Subsequent renovations commenced in 1915, providing more facilities for service organizations like Ladies Aid, Junior Epworth League, Queen Esther Circle, Boy Scouts, and the Women's Society of Christian Service. Just before Christmas in 1953, fire destroyed the sanctuary amid a third renovation. The new Sunday school wing survived, but the worship hall incurred $25,000 worth of damage that took another year to fix. (Courtesy Alma Rigler.)

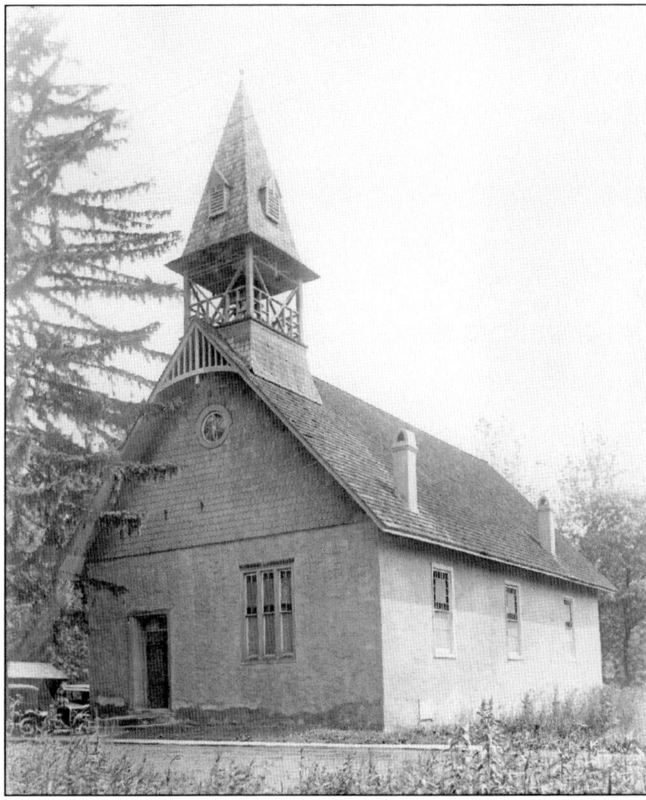

To raise funds to renovate the church manse in 1915, the Landenberg Methodist Church issued and congregants purchased stock certificates for $1 to be redeemed in 1999. (Courtesy Alma Rigler.)

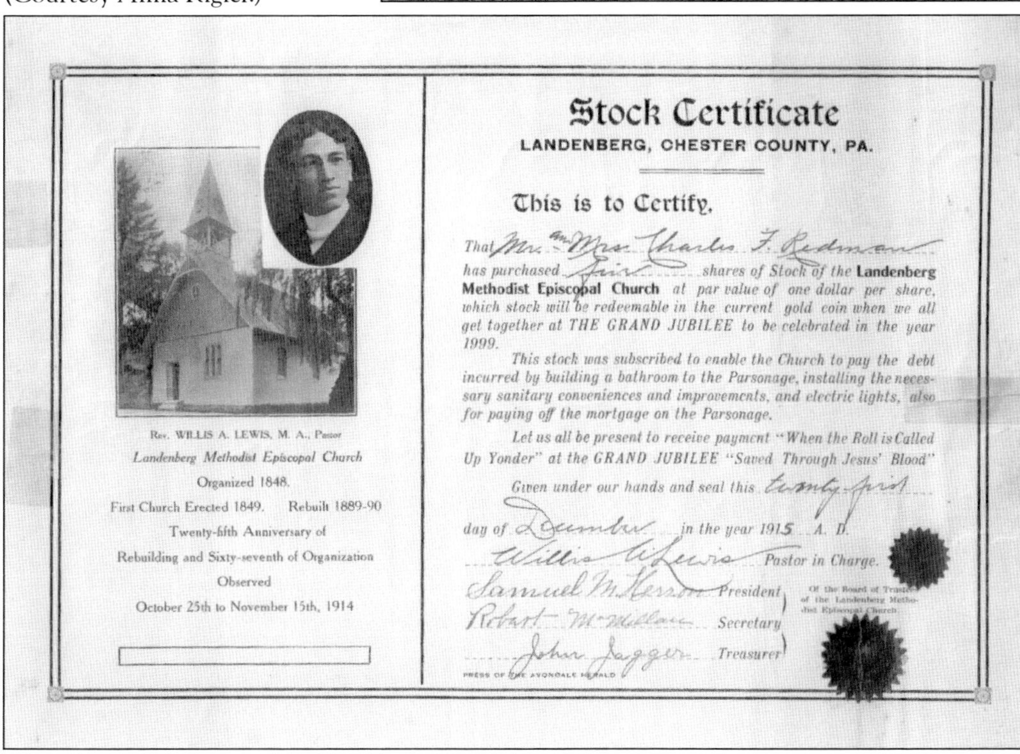

Rev. WILLIS A. LEWIS, M. A., Pastor

Landenberg Methodist Episcopal Church

Organized 1848.

First Church Erected 1849. Rebuilt 1889-90

Twenty-fifth Anniversary of Rebuilding and Sixty-seventh of Organization Observed

October 25th to November 15th, 1914

Stock Certificate

LANDENBERG, CHESTER COUNTY, PA.

This is to Certify,

That Mr. and Mrs. Charles F. Redman *has purchased* Five *shares of Stock of the* **Landenberg Methodist Episcopal Church** *at par value of one dollar per share, which stock will be redeemable in the current gold coin when we all get together at THE GRAND JUBILEE to be celebrated in the year 1999.*

This stock was subscribed to enable the Church to pay the debt incurred by building a bathroom to the Parsonage, installing the necessary sanitary conveniences and improvements, and electric lights, also for paying off the mortgage on the Parsonage.

Let us all be present to receive payment "When the Roll is Called Up Yonder" at the GRAND JUBILEE "Saved Through Jesus' Blood"

Given under our hands and seal this twenty-first *day of* December *in the year 1915 A. D.*

Willis A. Lewis *Pastor in Charge.*

Samuel M. Herron *President*
Robert McMillan *Secretary*
John Jagger *Treasurer*

Of the Board of Trustees of the Landenberg Methodist Episcopal Church

PRESS OF THE AVONDALE HERALD

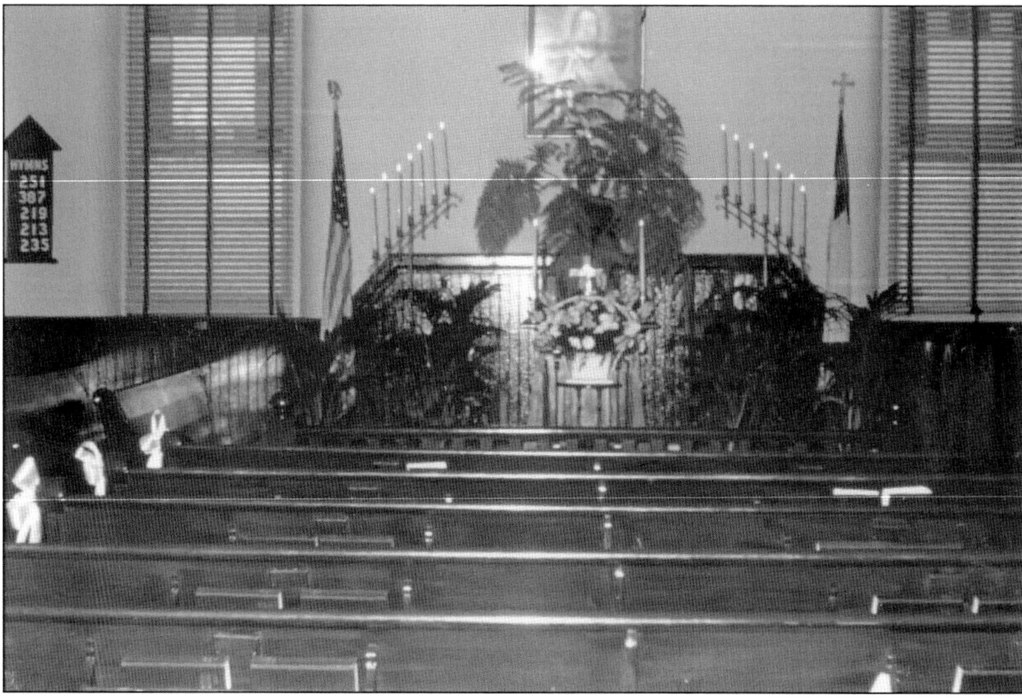

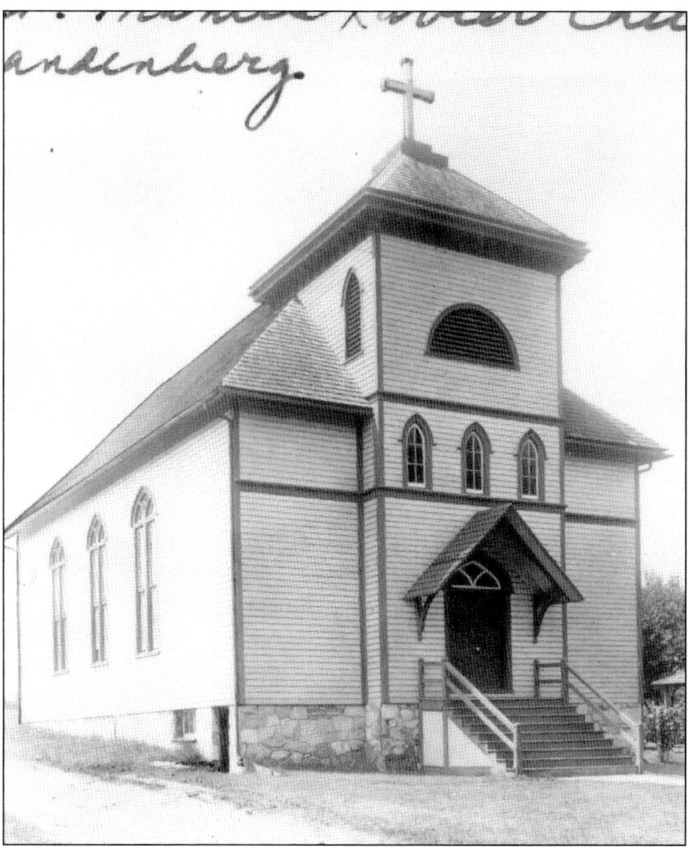

The Landenberg Methodist Church sanctuary has welcomed parishioners for over 130 years and is little changed from this photograph taken before the wedding of Alma Hendrickson and Earl Rigler in 1950. (Courtesy Alma Rigler.)

Mary McMahon donated a parcel of land on the corner of Saw Mill and Landenberg Roads to St. Patrick's parish of Kennett Square. Rising atop Landenberg Hill, St. Francis Xavier Church was begun in April 1893 and completed and dedicated in less than six months. It held nearly 250 congregants, closed in 1966, and is today a private residence. (Courtesy NGTHC.)

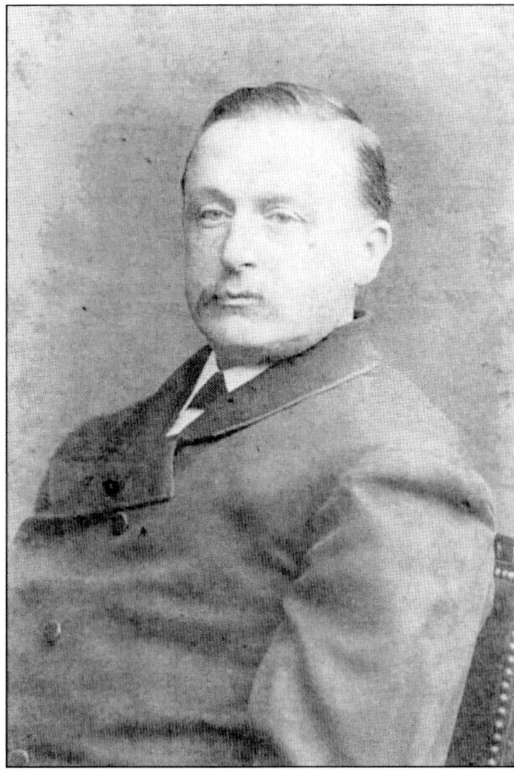

James Lund, a weaver from Yorkshire, England, arrived in Landenburgh in 1878 to work in the Landenburgh mills. In 1880, after Landenberger's default, Lund purchased much of the town's property. Equipping the factories with steam power, Lund's enterprise met with success despite a fire that consumed the mill soon after his purchase. Within nine months, Lund rebuilt the mill to twice its size and incorporated two steam engines yielding a combined 80 horsepower. Business operated intermittently until May 1888, when the *Daily Local News* reported "the Sheriff closed him out as the Sheriff had done to Chandler, Ripka and Landenberger." The mill business was risky because it was subject to the swings of the national economy. Newspaper articles of the time note that "the mills are operating full time" or "the mills have been closed for two months, but are expected to open soon." (Both courtesy NGTHC.)

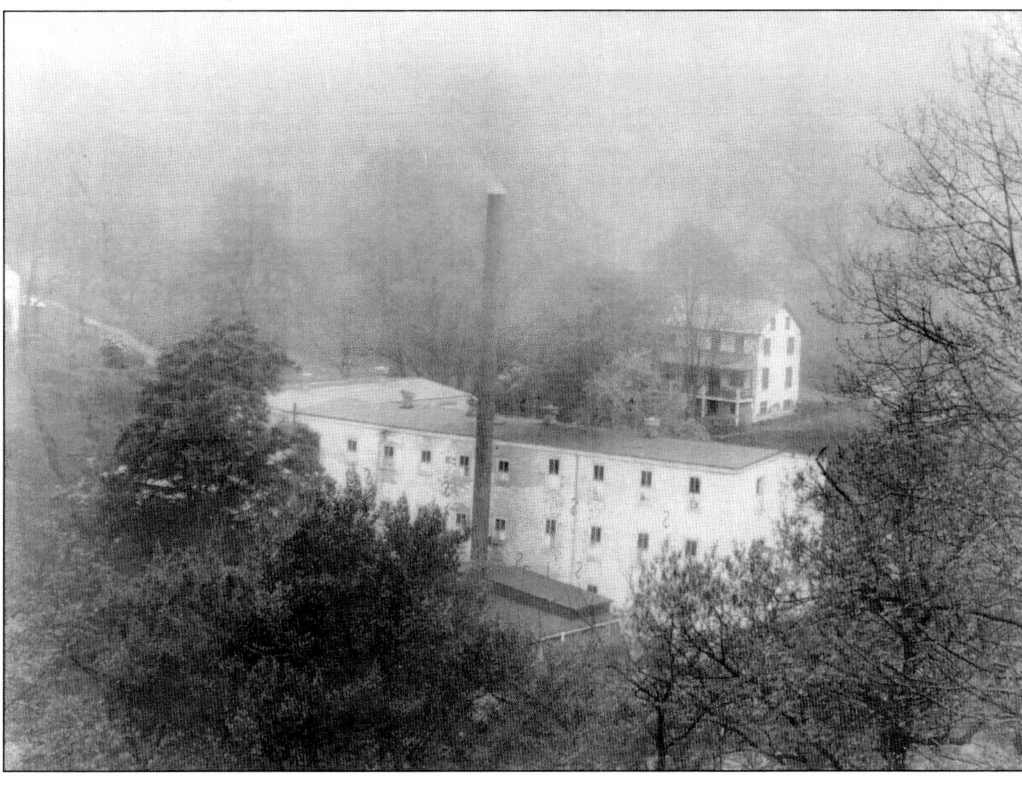

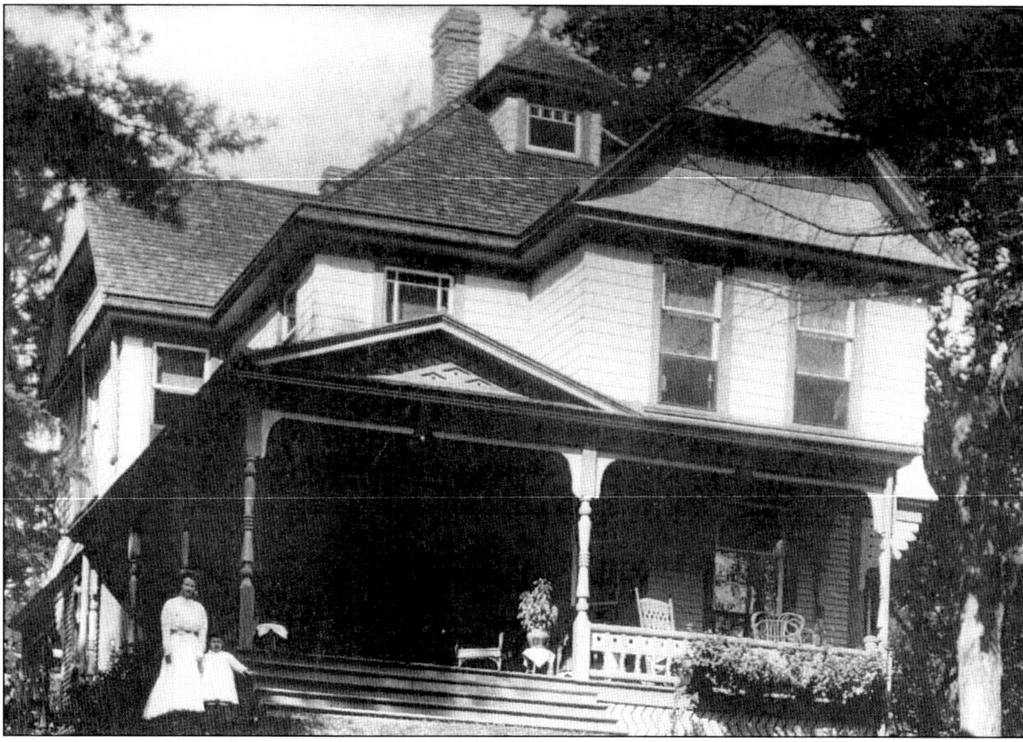

Lund's brothers, Thomas and Alfred, and his son, Ezra, purchased the mill and other properties in 1890 and met with success. Ezra supervised the mill operation, paid his workers weekly, and ran the hotel and general store. The town prospered for more than a decade as Ezra, his wife Lizzie, and their four children assumed societal prominence. James Lund built this house high on the hill for Ezra's family. (Courtesy NGTHC.)

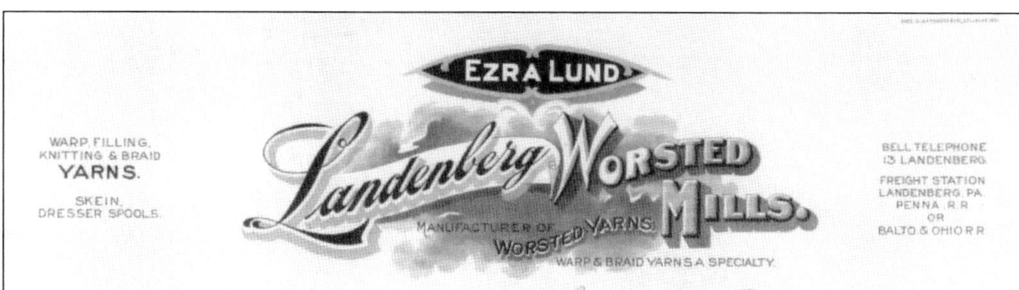

The Lunds were the last of a long string of mill owners in Landenberg. Although Ezra Lund had been managing the large woolen mill for a number of years, he purchased it in 1904. Always at the mercy of countrywide economic conditions, Lund was forced by slack demand to shut down the mill in 1912. It never reopened; on the night of September 9, 1917, the unoccupied mill burned. (Courtesy NGTHC.)

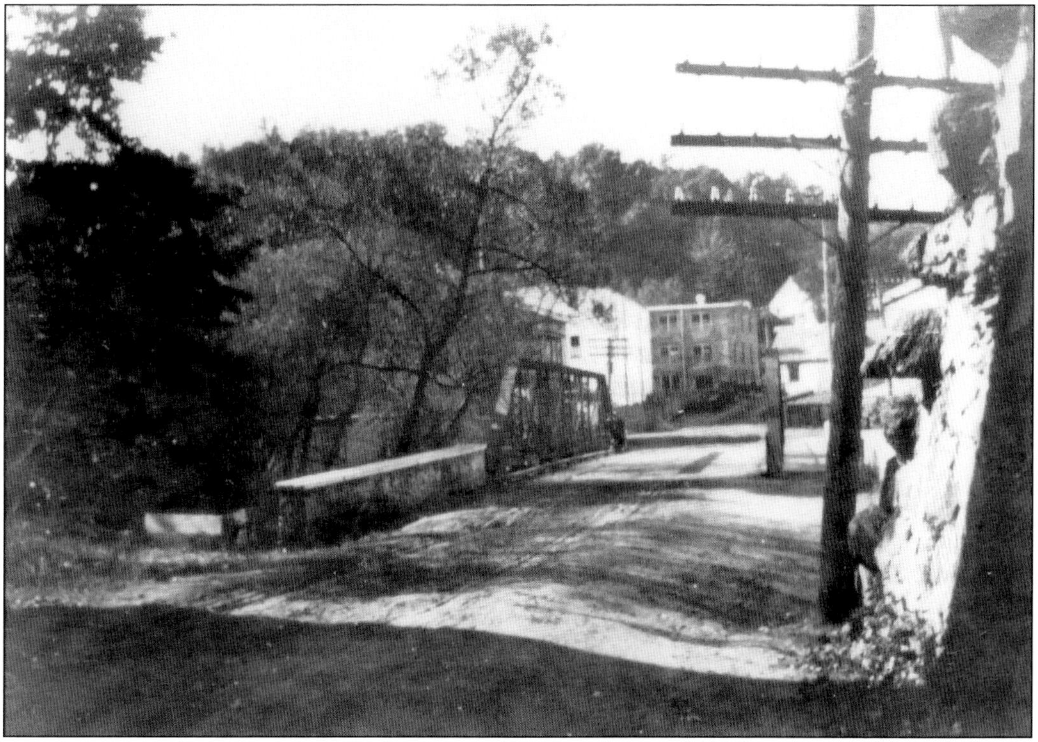

In 1871, an arched iron bridge replaced an 1856 covered bridge over the White Clay Creek and provided a wider right-of-way. The year 1898 saw a Pratt Pony Truss bridge, manufactured in Phoenixville by the Phoenix Iron Works, supplant the arched bridge. This latest bridge sported a cantilevered walkway built atop the northern truss and separated from the roadway by a lattice railing. The bridge offered an 18-foot right-of-way for teams and the newfangled automobile. The bridge overpass seen in the lower picture was the track of the Pomeroy Newark Railroad. (Both courtesy NGTHC.)

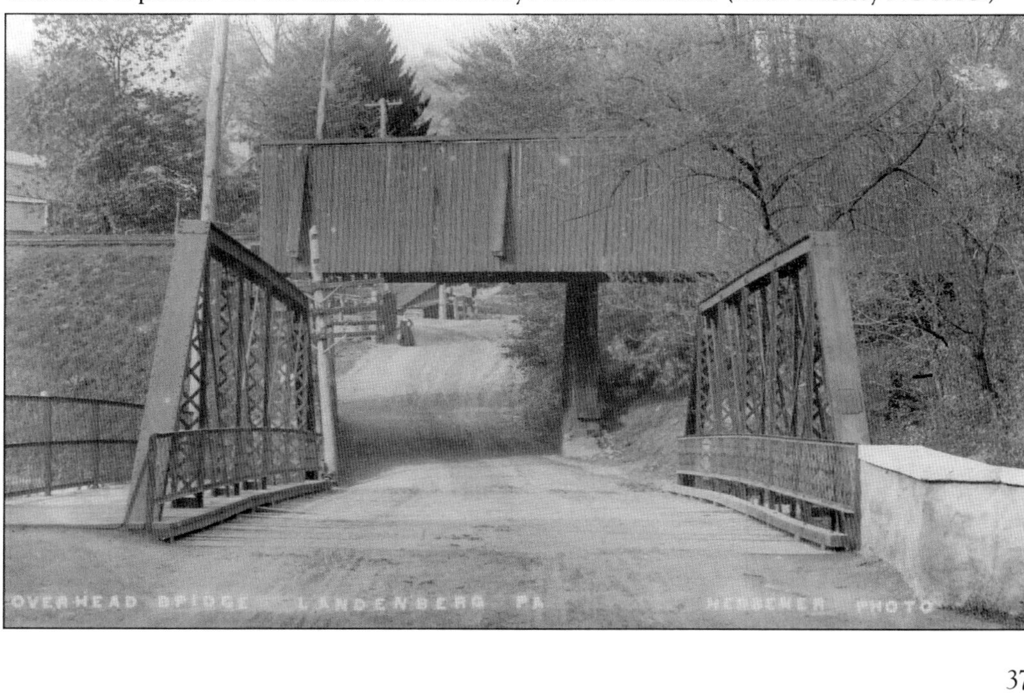

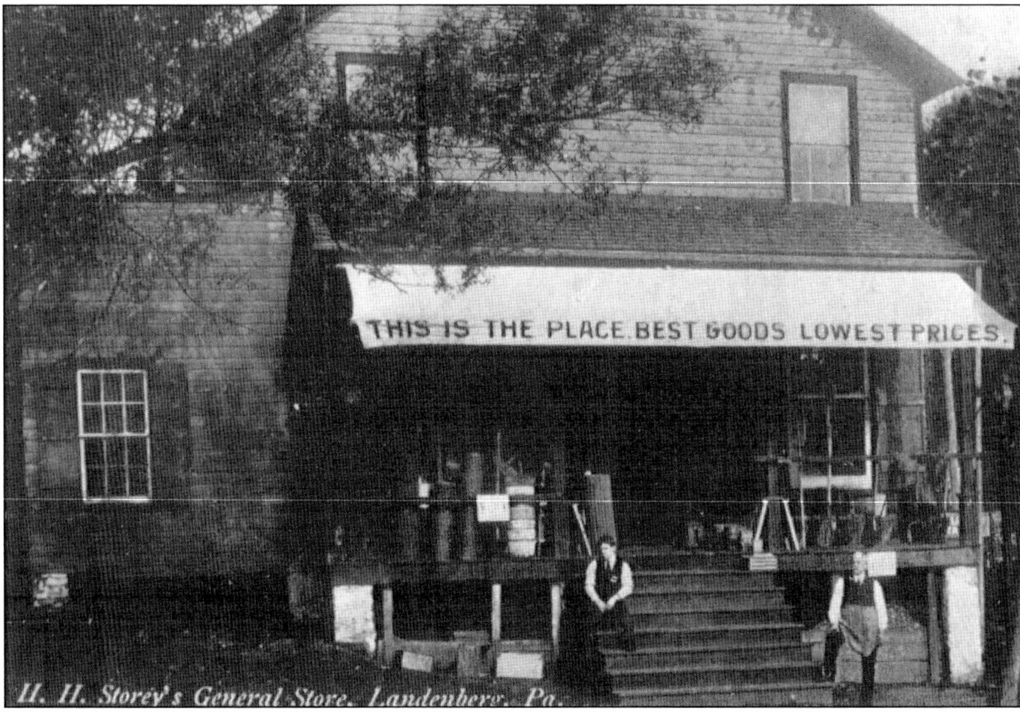

Hiram Storey established his dry goods store and harness shop in 1880 at the junction of Chesterville and Penn Green Roads. For 32 years, locals patronized Storey. Before he died in 1912, Storey had built a community hall atop his business that served numerous local groups—especially the Methodist church's Willing Workers—for dances, dinners, festivals, plays, lectures, and even spelling bees. (Courtesy NGTHC.)

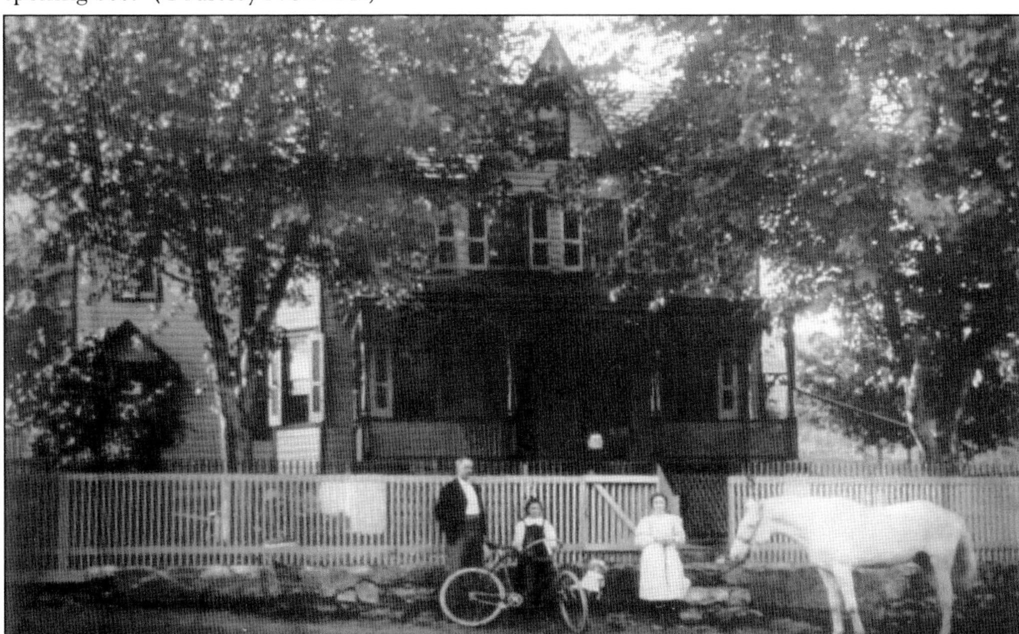

Storey built his house on Chesterville Road in 1886. (Courtesy David Hawk.)

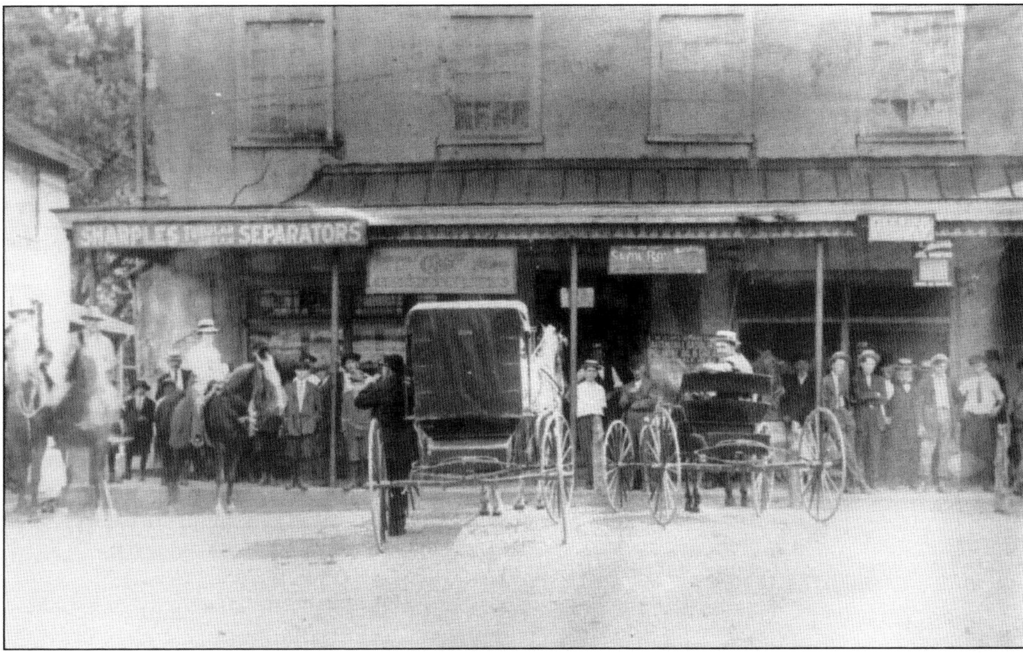

Landenburgh's burgeoning late-Victorian population supported ample commerce. Boyd's Business Directory reported a population of 414 in 1882, 600 in 1888, 900 in 1893, and 1,000 in 1900. Besides general store purveyors Hiram Storey, William Watson, and Ezra Lund; cobblers W. H. Alexander and Joseph Ross; builders Greenwalt, Hoopes, and Strickland; itinerant meat merchant Irvin Guest; collier W. W. Sullivan; and barber Harry Rigler transacted business. (Courtesy NGTHC.)

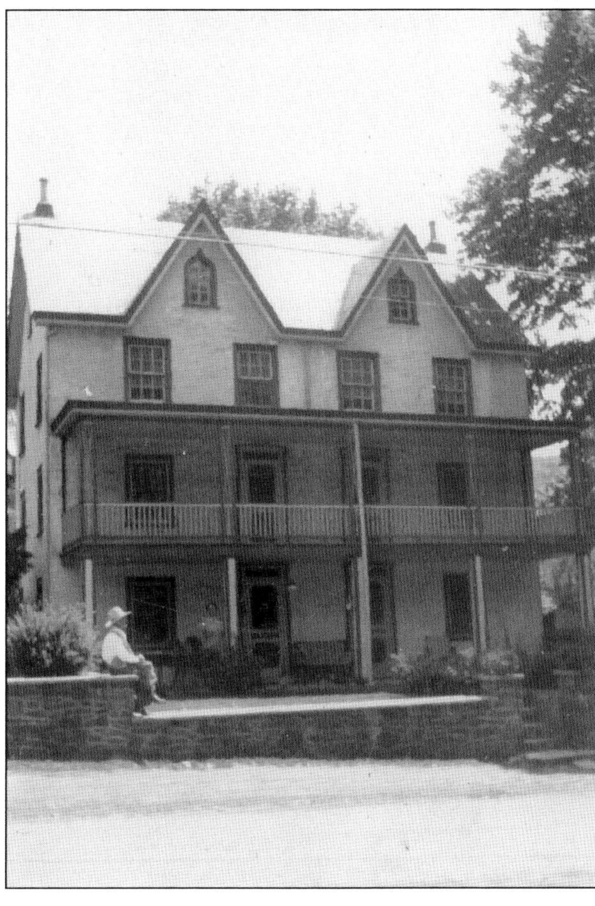

Throughout the 1890s, the Lunds, Washington Ewing, and others erected larger and more opulent homes along the incline of the hill. At town's center, mill workers lived in tenement houses and dormitories. According to author Anne Haggerty, "The Hill People had a status far above that of the Mill People. The 'Mill Dolly' or 'Wool Dolly' was looked upon scornfully by women who pursued more 'ladylike' activities." (Courtesy NGTHC.)

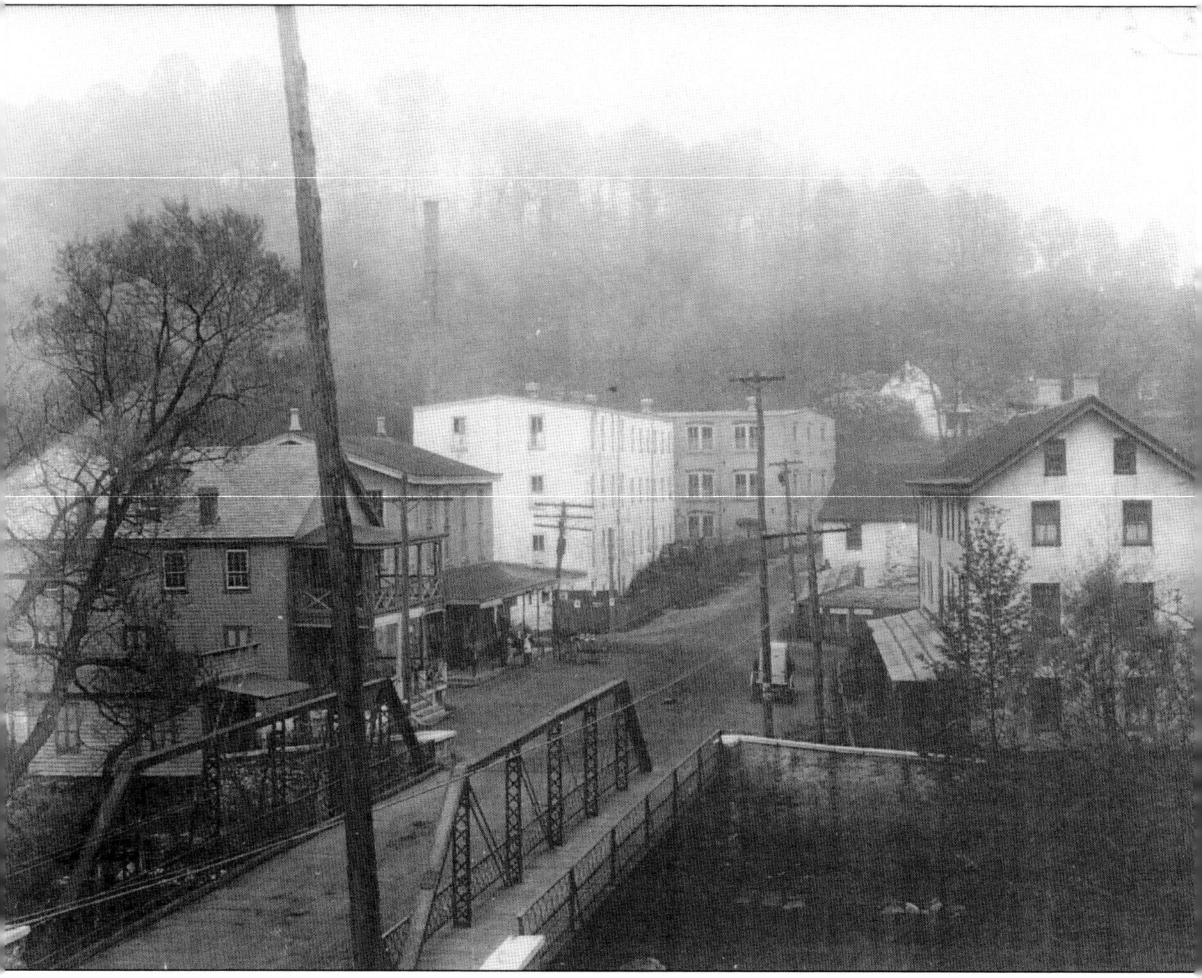

This view of Landenberg, taken from the east side of the bridge, dates from sometime between 1899 and 1917. The Pratt Pony Truss Bridge in the foreground was built in 1898. The Lund Woolen Mill in the background was destroyed by fire in 1917. Landenberg's bridge was always an important link between industrial Landenberg and the homes of the managerial class on the hill. At the bottom of steep hillsides along the narrow valley of the White Clay Creek, smoke, steam, dust, and noise prevailed. This was where the mill workers lived and toiled. In the foreground to the left of the bridge was the hotel, which often served as a boarding house, and the store with its second-story community hall. To the right of the bridge was a large frame boarding house, and beyond the roof of the blacksmith shop was the wool house, used both for storage and as an office. (Courtesy NGTHC.)

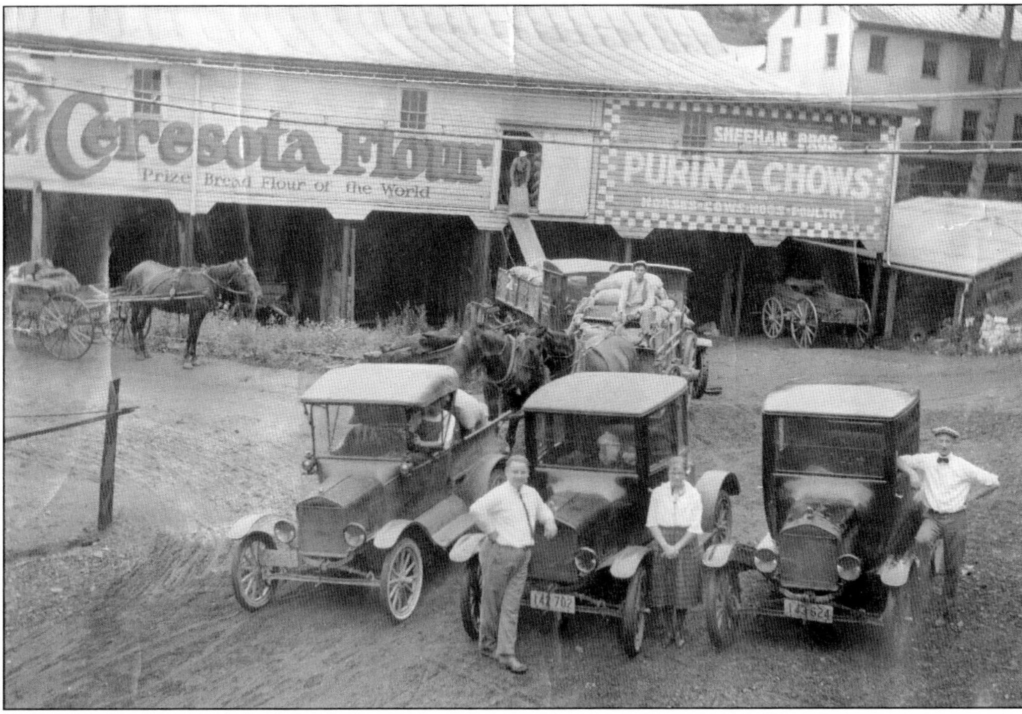

Joseph and Francis Sheehan purchased their coal and lumberyard in 1919 and received their inventory by rail, either from the Pomeroy Newark or the Wilmington and Western Railroad. By 1942, truck traffic had eclipsed rail service; that year, Sheehan's received only 17 carloads on the Pomeroy Newark. Their lumberyard had been the only remaining Landenberg customer. Despite protests, both railroads abandoned their tracks, citing a dearth of traffic. (Both courtesy NGTHC.)

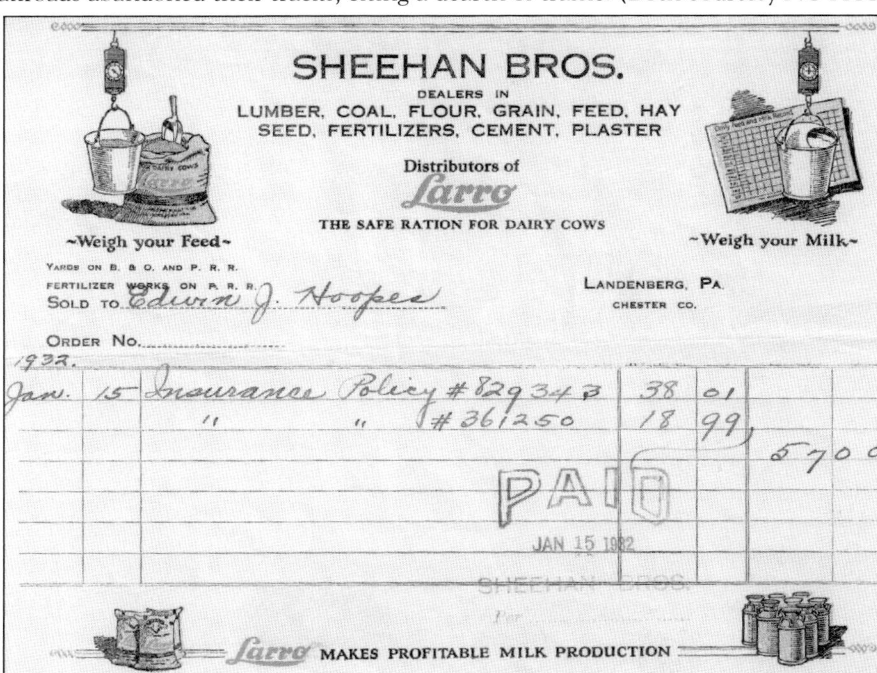

SHEEHAN BROS.
DEALERS IN
LUMBER, COAL, FLOUR, GRAIN, FEED, HAY
SEED, FERTILIZERS, CEMENT, PLASTER

Distributors of
Larro
THE SAFE RATION FOR DAIRY COWS

~Weigh your Feed~ ~Weigh your Milk~

YARDS ON B. & O. AND P. R. R.
FERTILIZER WORKS ON P. R. R.
SOLD TO Edwin J. Hoopes

LANDENBERG, PA.
CHESTER CO.

ORDER NO.

1932.				
Jan.	15	Insurance Policy #829343	38 01	
		" " #361250	18 99	57 00

PAID
JAN 15 1932
SHEEHAN BROS.

Larro MAKES PROFITABLE MILK PRODUCTION

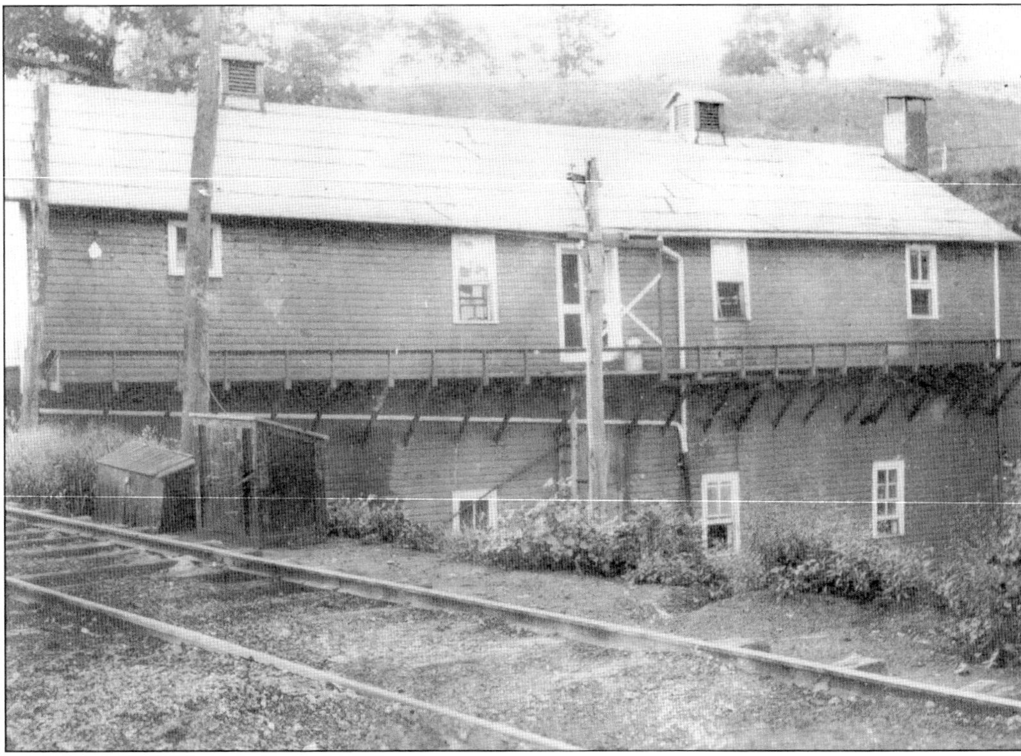

For decades, beginning in the 1880s, dairy farmers brought raw milk to Sharpless's Valley View Creamery. Each morning, wagons and later trucks would queue from the dairy, out to Landenberg Road, across the bridge, and down into the town proper. (Courtesy NGTHC.)

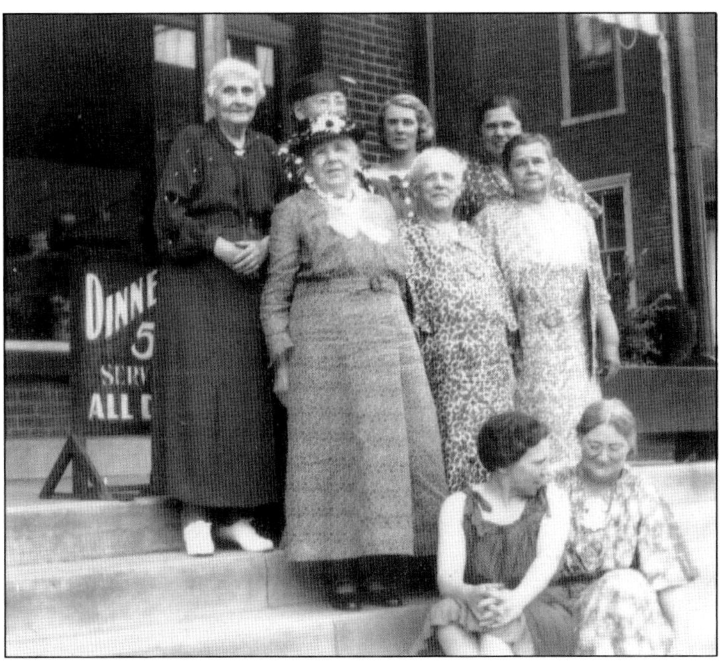

The Willing Workers, a Methodist women's group, organized in 1917 to commit what Jean Minshall describes as "deeds of kindness." Using a November turkey dinner fund-raiser, the group maintained Storey's Landenberg Hall, sent soldiers care packages during World War I, and purchased a tenement opposite the store, razed it, and donated the land to the church. On the steps of John Kennedy's Store in the 1930s, Willing Workers, so-called "Crossan widows," pose. (Courtesy Jean Minshall.)

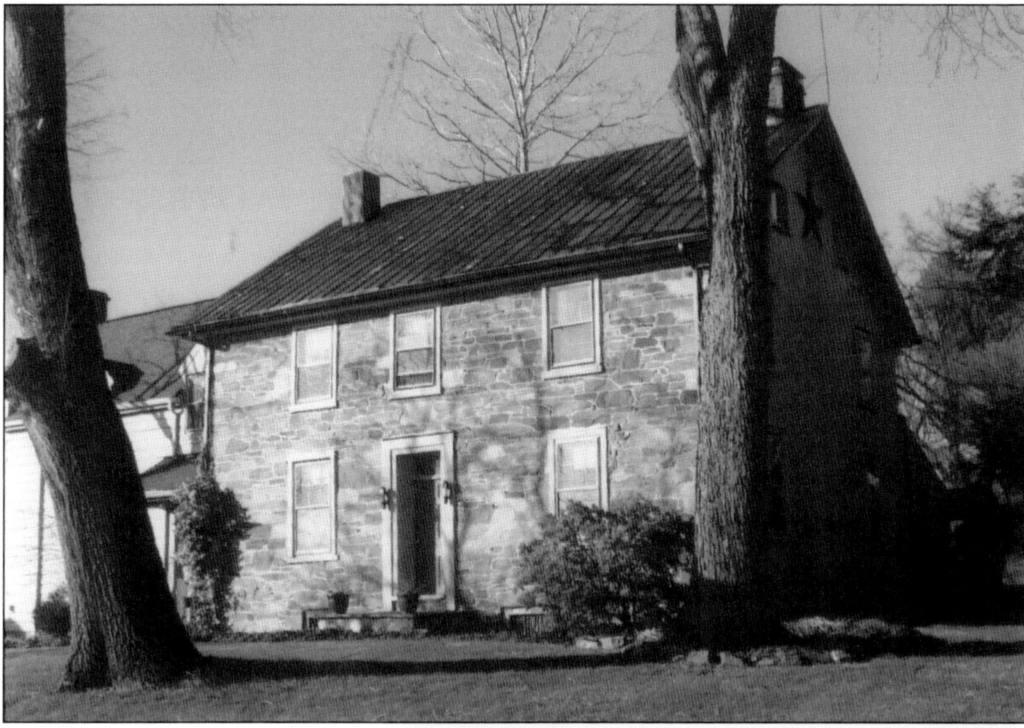

In 1764, Samuel Miller Jr. inherited 233 acres from his uncle, also named Samuel Miller. By 1774, Samuel Miller Jr. had built a brick house and a sawmill on the White Clay at the intersection of Penn Green and Egypt Run Roads. When the farm was sold in 1801, the mill was described as a large three-storied stone, brick, and frame gristmill with an attached clover and sawmill. (Author's collection.)

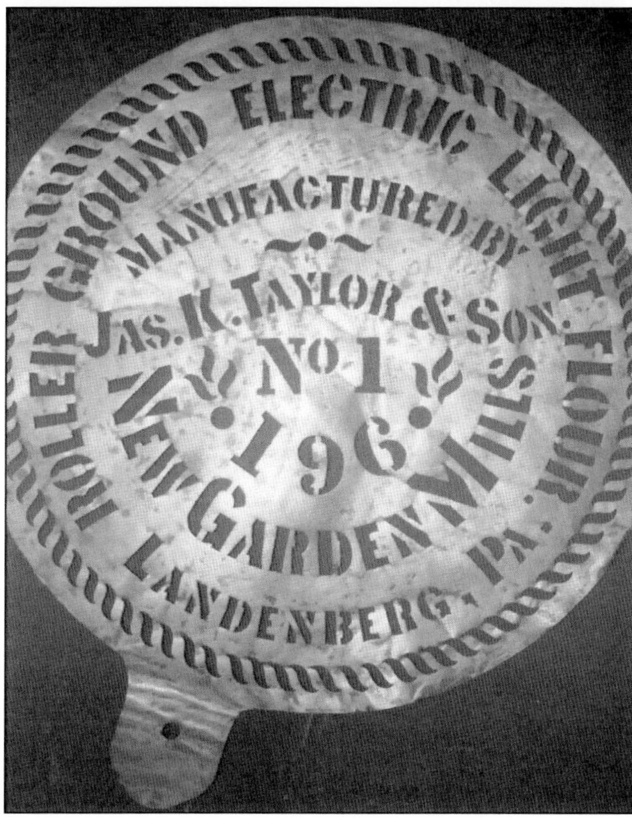

James K. Taylor, who used this brass stencil to stamp his barrels of flour, operated Miller's mill until 1901. Described as having waterpower that never failed, the mill had the capacity to process 50 barrels of flour a day. Harry Crossan, who purchased the mill, operated it until it burned in 1910. It was one of the last flour mills in New Garden Township to operate on the White Clay. (Courtesy David Hawk.)

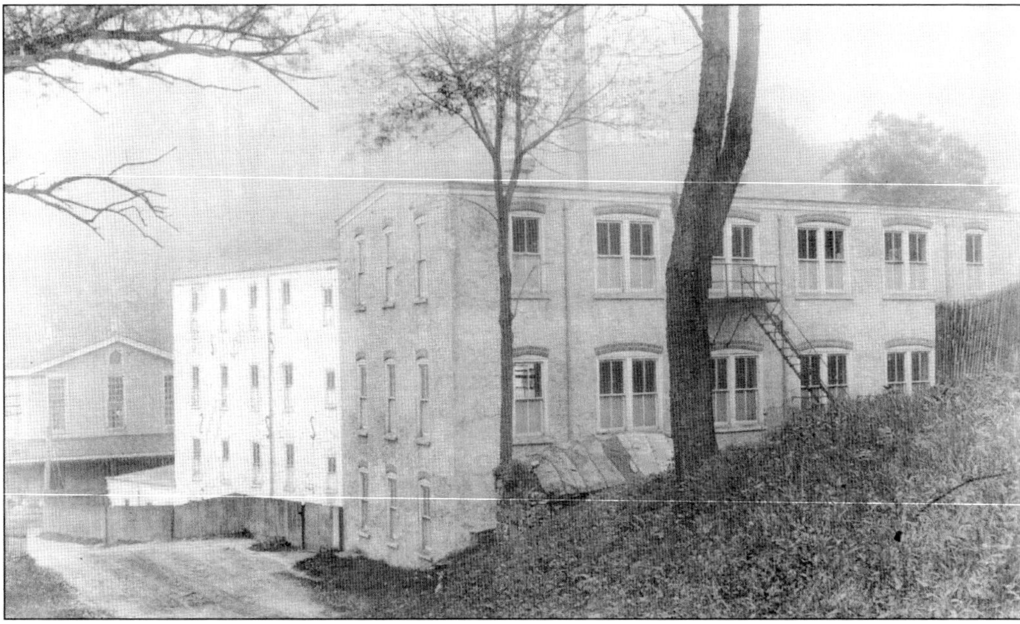

In 1904, Landenburgh officially became Landenberg, and the entire town was put up for sale. The *Daily Local News* reported: "The Lund Woolen Mills . . . forty miles from Philadelphia with ample railroad facilities and well equipped for manufacture of worsted yarns. About 200 acres of land with all necessary buildings, houses for employees, etc. 280-horse power engine, 3 boilers, 2300 spindles, employs 85 to 90 hands. Good water power." A month later, another advertisement listed "woolen mill, 14 houses, 40 acres, Storey's Store, 2 upper water powers, 91 acres, farm of 34 acres, coal and lumber yard and warehouse and lot, 7 acres, 3 dwelling houses." After 1905, Landenberg's population sharply decreased. Except for a brief period of business around 1910, the mill era, and thus the industrial era of Landenberg, ended by 1913. Closed that year, the abandoned woolen mill burned to the ground in 1917. In 1933, its ruins were used to build Landenberg's roads. (Both courtesy NGTHC.)

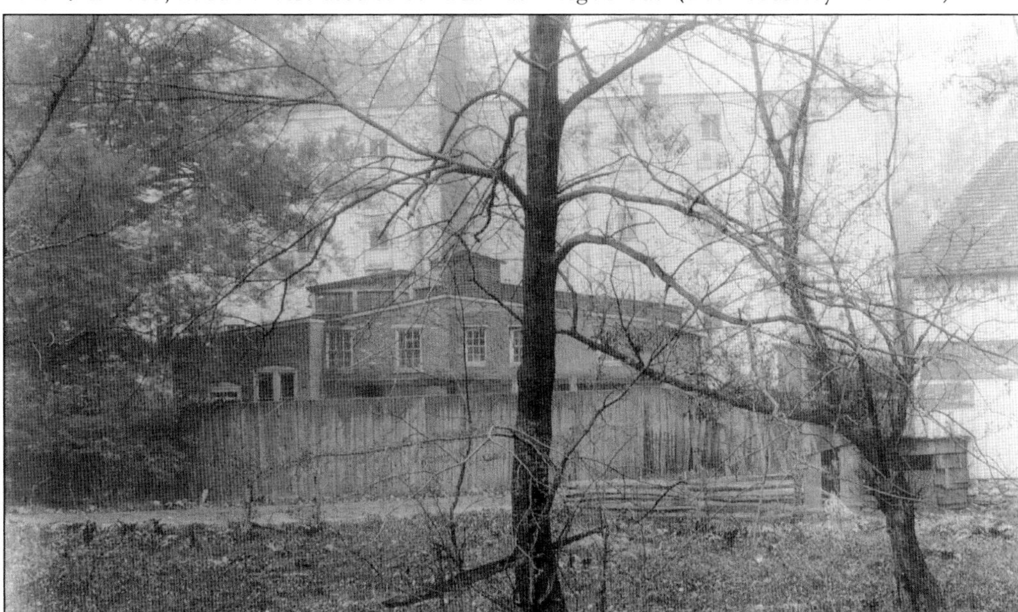

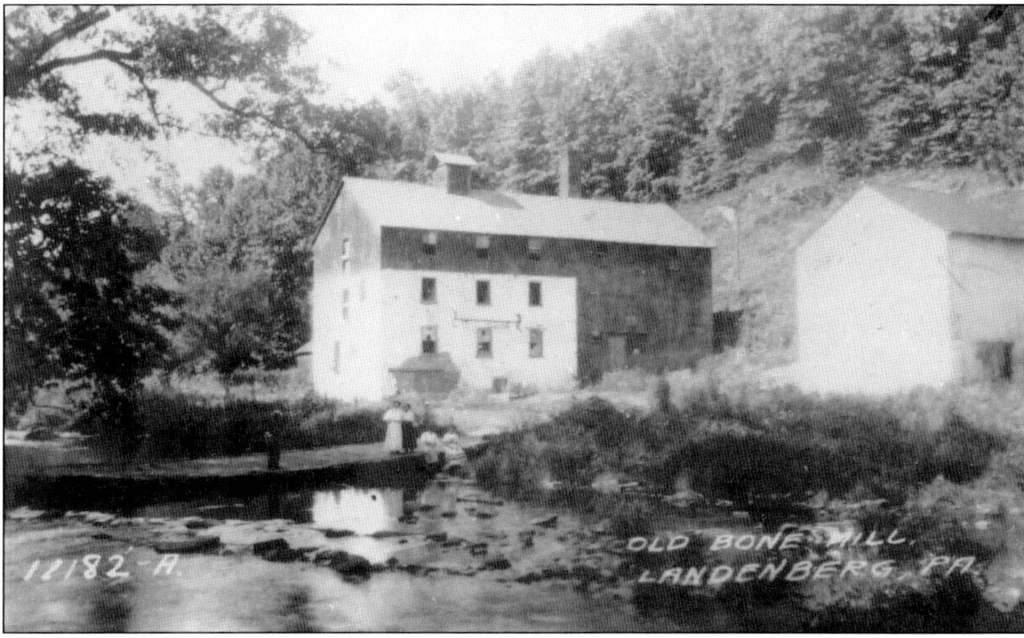

Waterpower was harnessed from White Clay Creek by the construction of dams. However, dams were always at risk of washing out in high water. This dam, known as the Bone Mill Dam, originally built by Enoch Chandler, washed out in 1904. The Keystone Super-Phosphate Mills made fertilizer from ground buffalo bones that were shipped from the western plains. It was rebuilt by the owner of the Bone Mill, William W. Sullivan, who etched his initials and the date into the dam's concrete. (Above courtesy CCHS; below author's collection.)

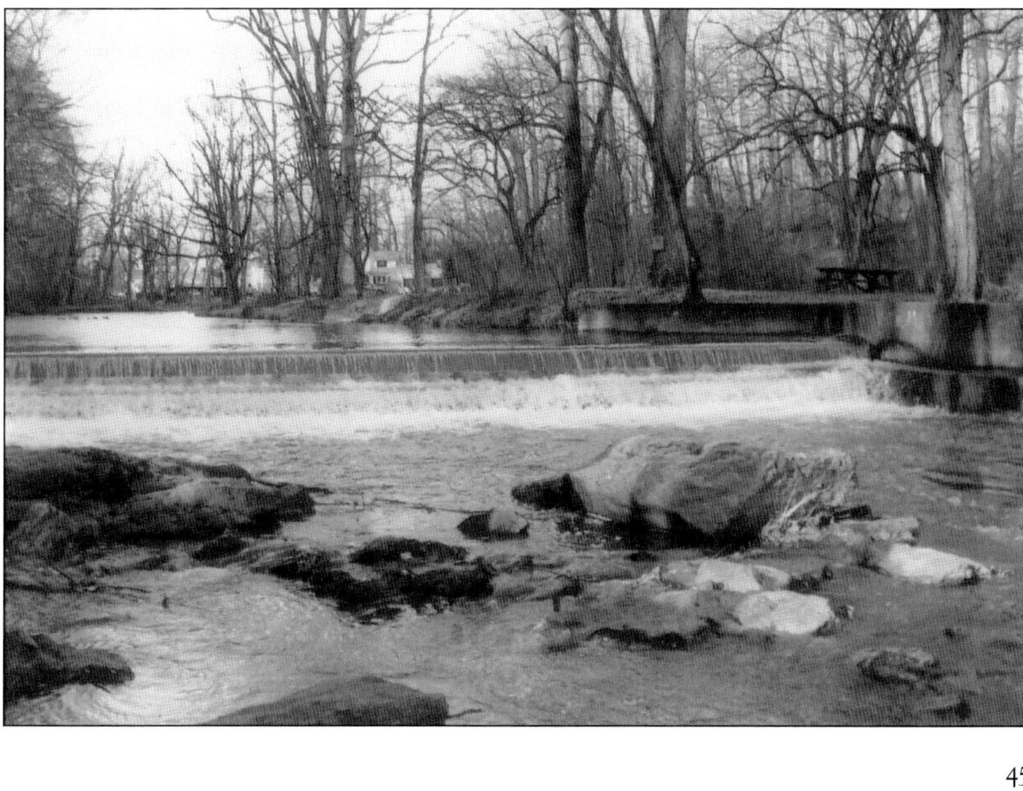

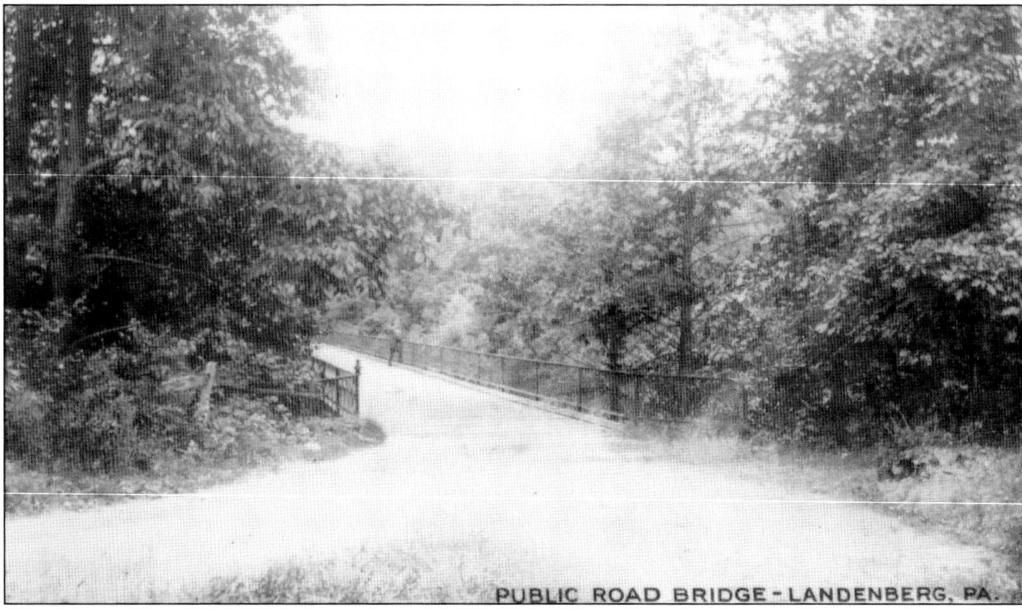

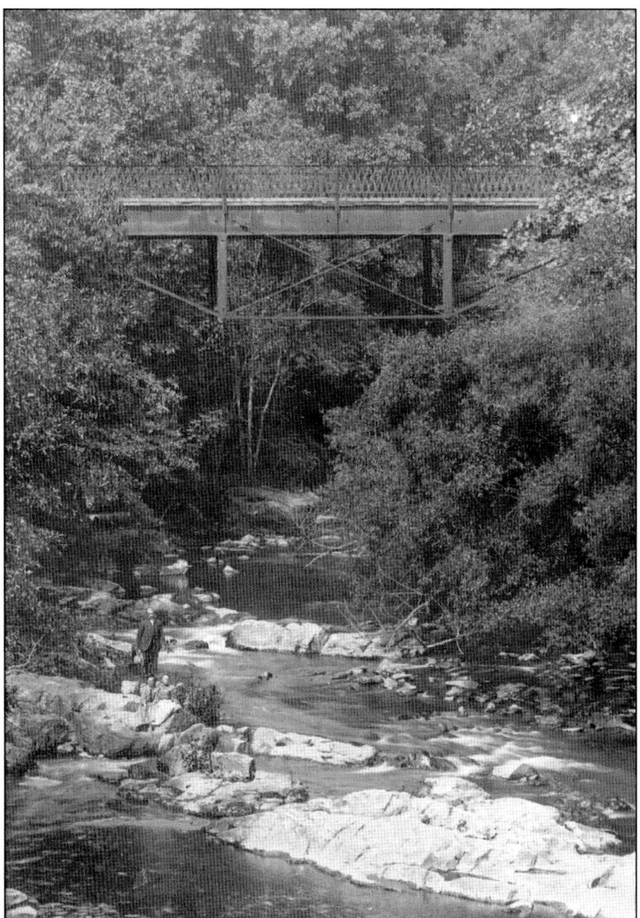

In 1863, when Martin Landenberger purchased both villages, Laurel and Chandlerville were combined. To travel between the two villages was difficult, with the only route following Sawmill Road, which continued west, dropping down the hill to Laurel; no direct route existed until the building of Penn Green Road about 1840. This Laurel Bridge, built on Penn Green Road in the 1870s, served the community for 100 years. (Both courtesy NGTHC.)

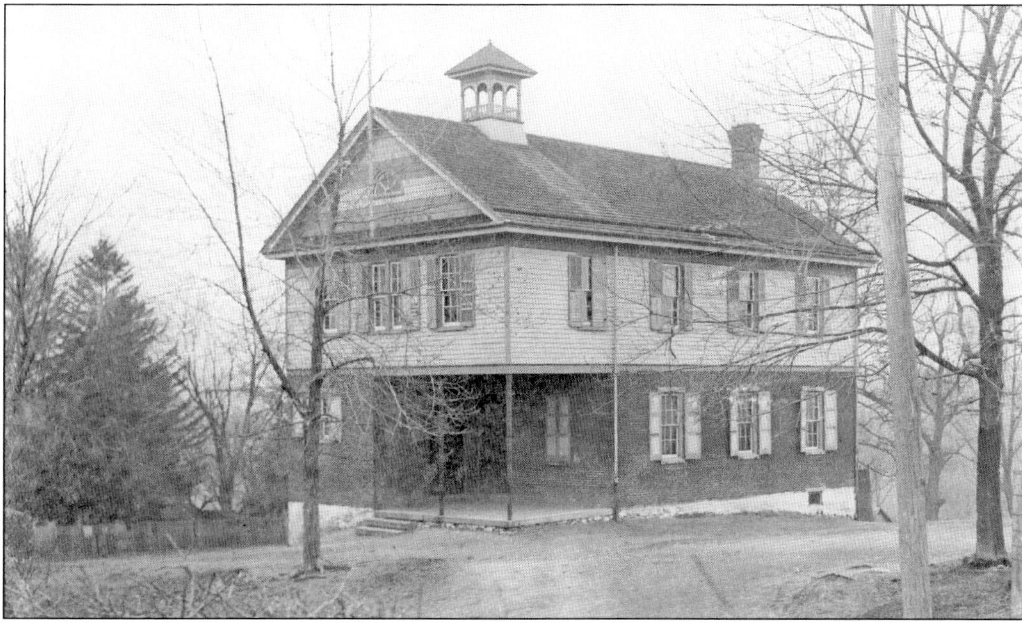

Many Landenberg children worked in the mills. As late as 1906, mill owner Ezra Lund was advertising for child laborers. One account told of how he and his 100 girls and boys were converting wool into vast quantities of the finest yarns. With the passage of the 1930 Child Labor Law, all of Landenberg's children began to go to school. This school, built on the hill in 1875, served the community until 1932. (Courtesy NGTHC.)

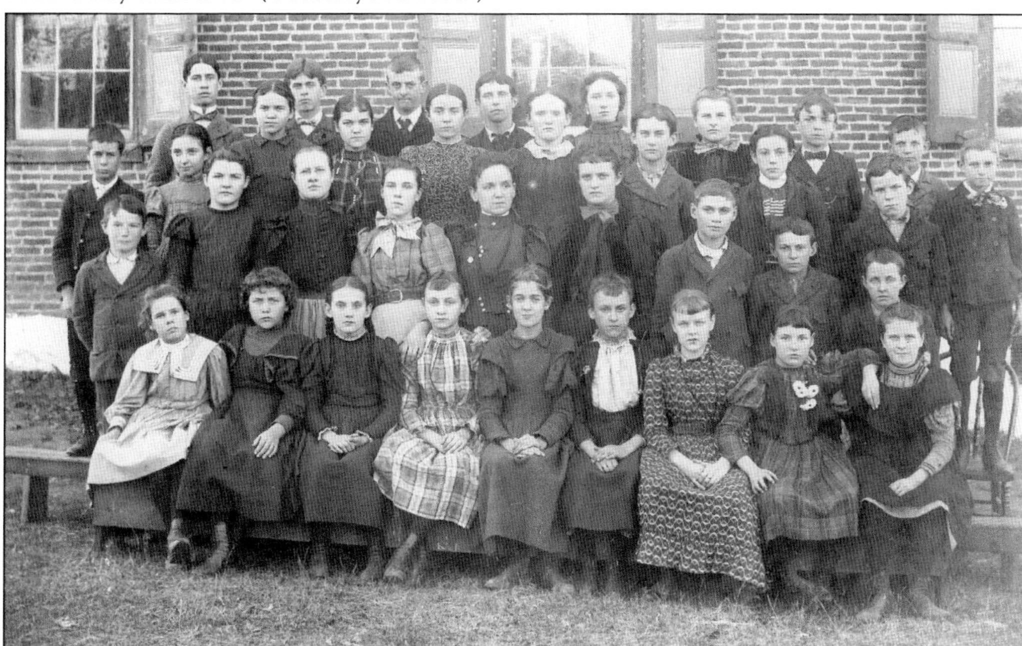

In this 1898 picture, Landenberg's schoolchildren pose on the lawn beside the school. Landenberg was a safe place in which to grow up. Children swam in the creek, sledded down Landenberg and Mercer's Mill hills, played on ball teams and in marbles competitions, ice-skated, and danced. (Courtesy CCHS.)

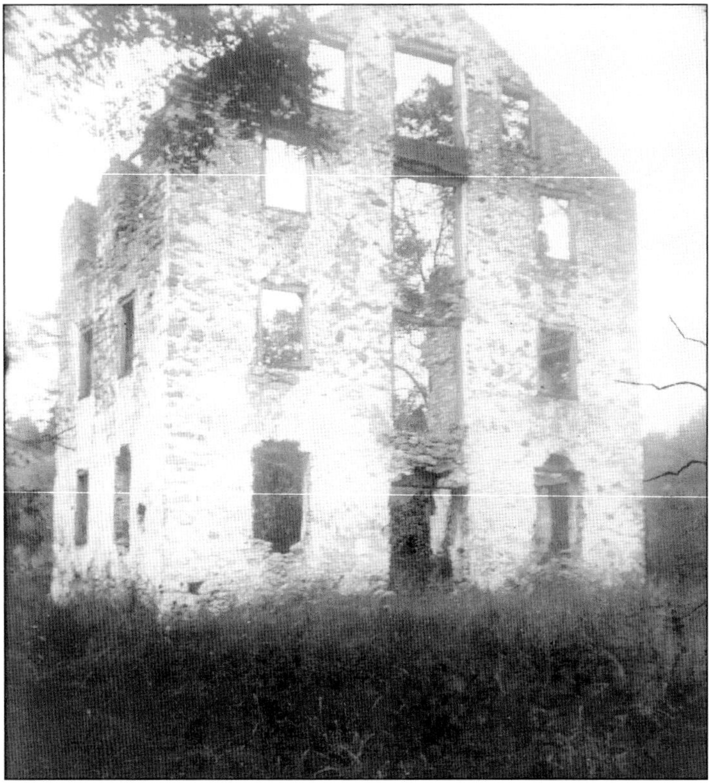

Fire was a constant threat in the mills. Although built of stone, most of the Chandlerville and Laurel mills suffered fires and were rebuilt. This Laurel mill burned in 1876, and 75 of Landenberger's employees lost their jobs. However, because of Landenberger's financial difficulties compounded by the economic depression of 1873, the yarn factory was never rebuilt, and the waste of good water power was widely lamented. (Courtesy CCHS.)

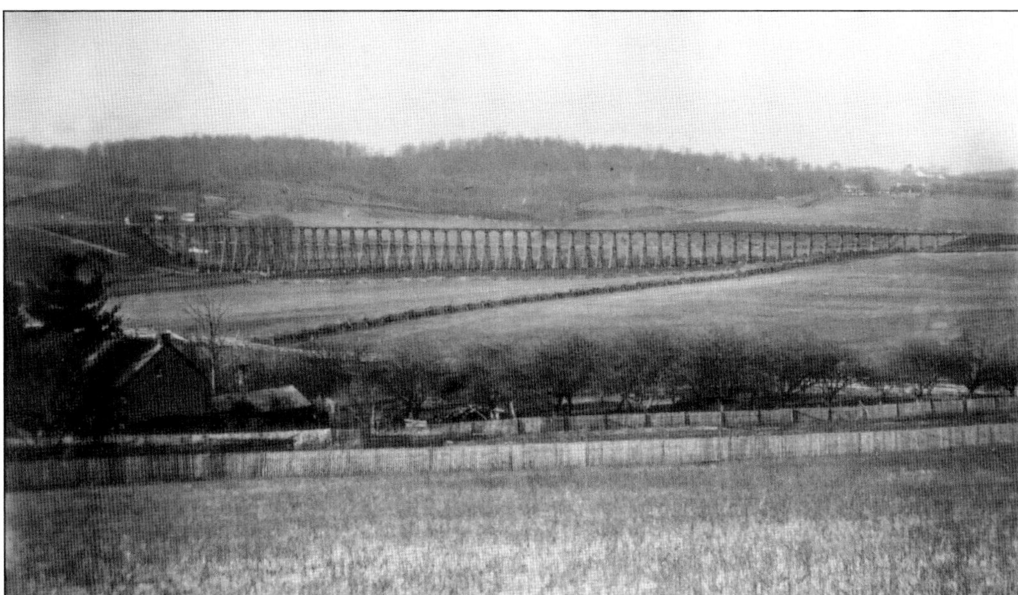

The Broad Run Trestle, which crossed the valley on David Brown's farm (east of Newark Road), was constructed for the Wilmington and Western Railroad. The trestle, standing over 40 feet high in places and about a third of a mile long, required 360,000 feet of lumber to construct. Built in 1873, it stood for 70 years until World War II, when the rails were removed for scrap metal. Its demise symbolized the end of industrialized Landenberg. (Courtesy NGTHC.)

Three

KAOLIN

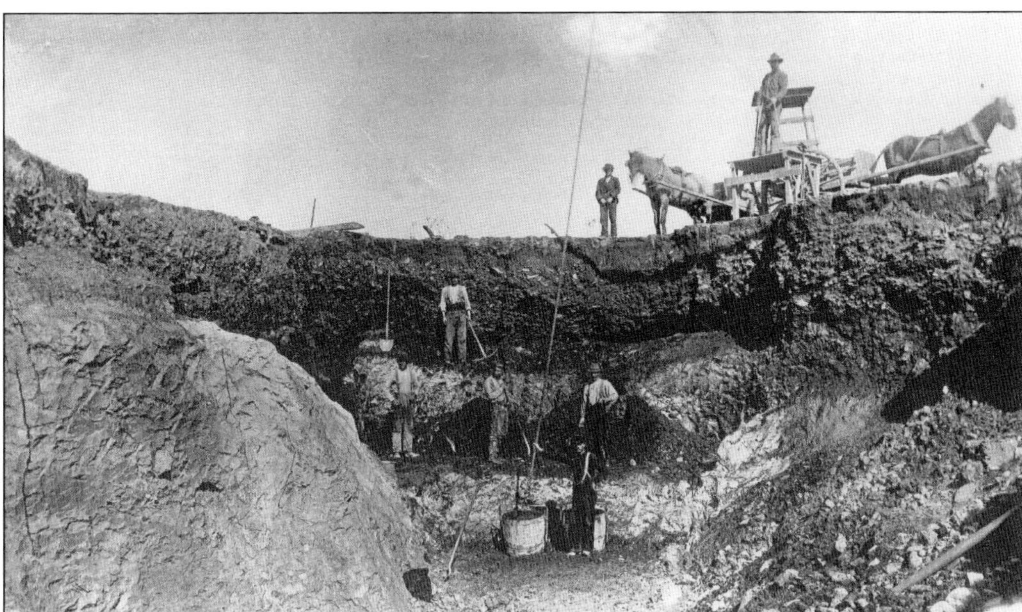

Kaolin, clay formed by the decomposition of feldspar, was known to lie under the soil in New Garden Township as early as 1802. Dug in open-pit mines, some as deep as 60 feet, there was always the risk of springs inundating a mine. Not until the coming of the railroads in 1863 was it economically feasible to ship the clay to city markets to make fine porcelain. (Courtesy NGTHC.)

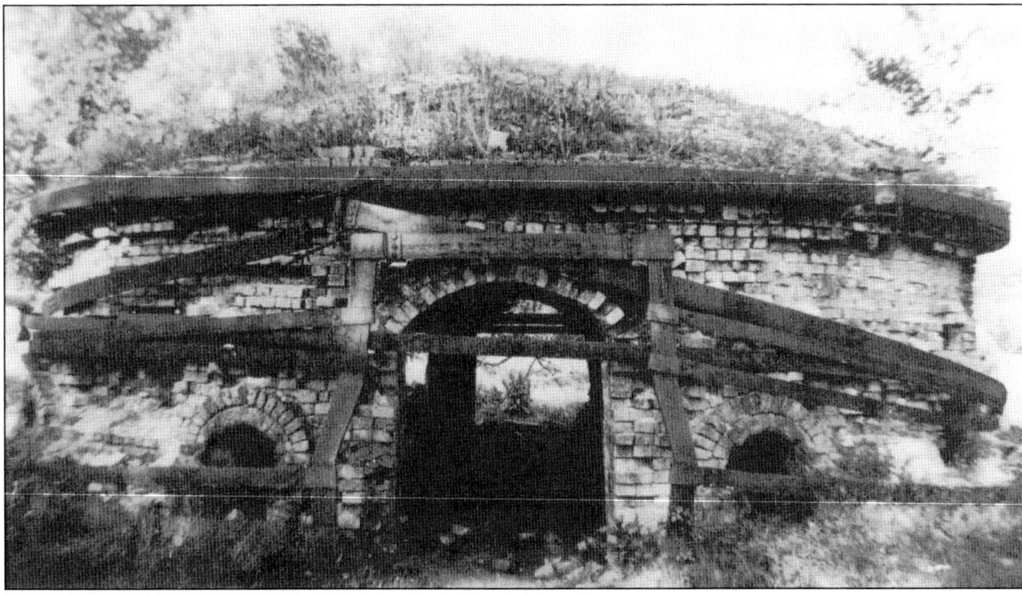

Manufacturing of firebricks was done on-site; producing firebricks for the Chester iron furnaces was a lucrative business. In 1874, a train car a day loaded with white firebricks was shipped to iron foundries from the Southwood station. Each year, more than 150,000 firebricks were purchased by foundries for furnace construction. (Courtesy NGTHC.)

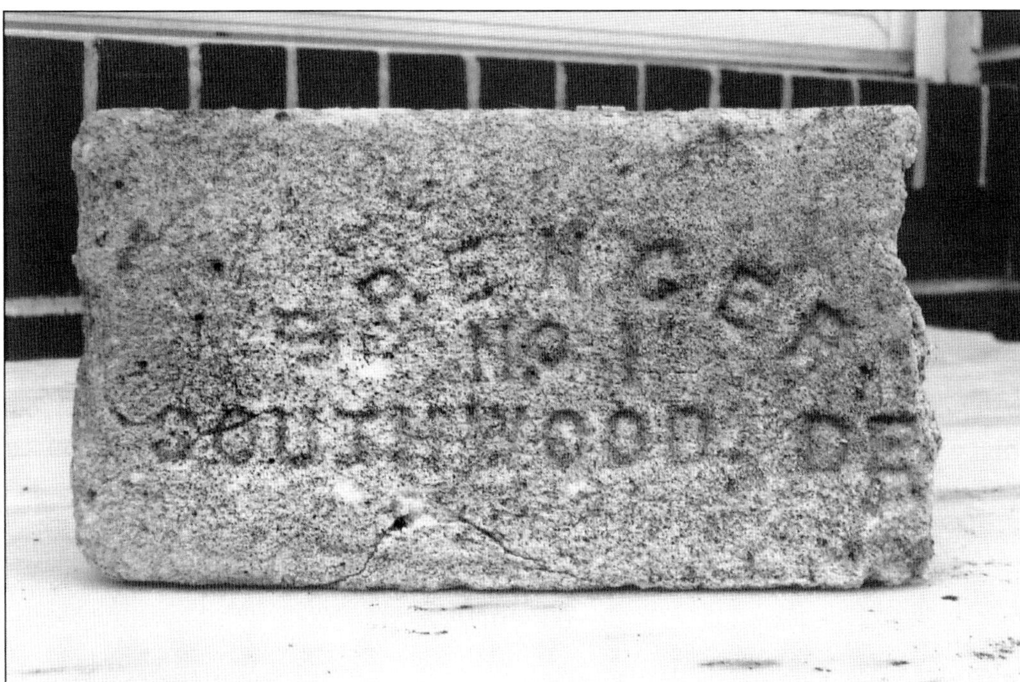

White clay firebrick was made by the American Kaolin Company and others. Names associated with the Kaolin industry were Graham, Spencer, and Marvel. The advantage of this brick over those made with other materials was that it could withstand exceedingly high temperatures, such as those found in blast furnaces. (Author's collection.)

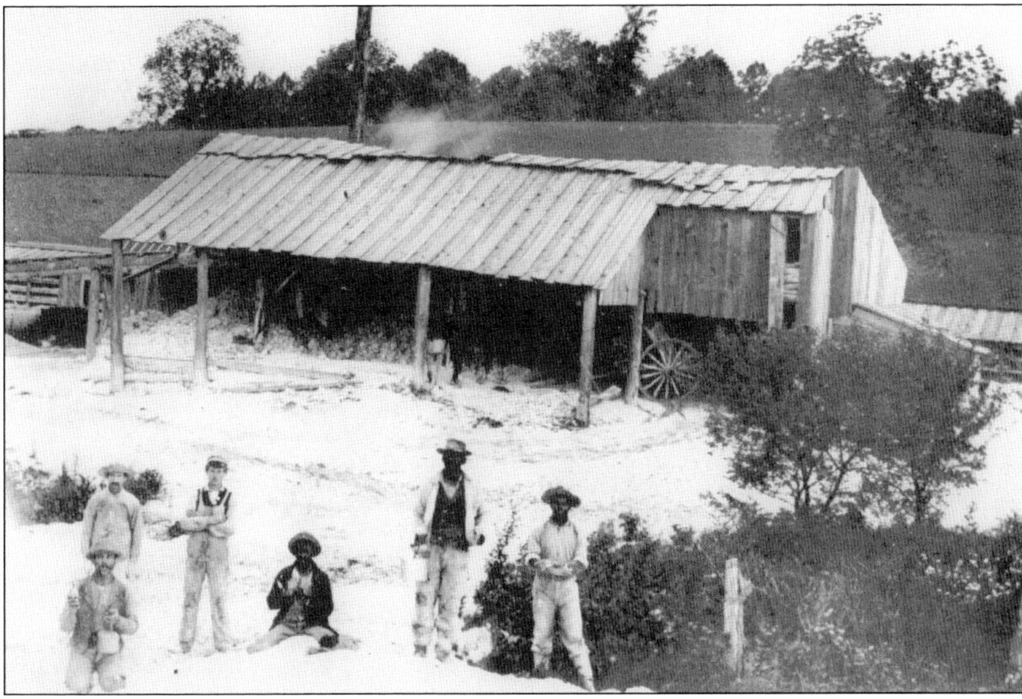

Buildings such as this housed the clay kilns. Kaolin production was labor intensive, with workmen working around the clock. In 1879, New Garden's several kaolin companies employed as many as 175 men with a payroll of about $5,000 a week. (Courtesy NGTHC.)

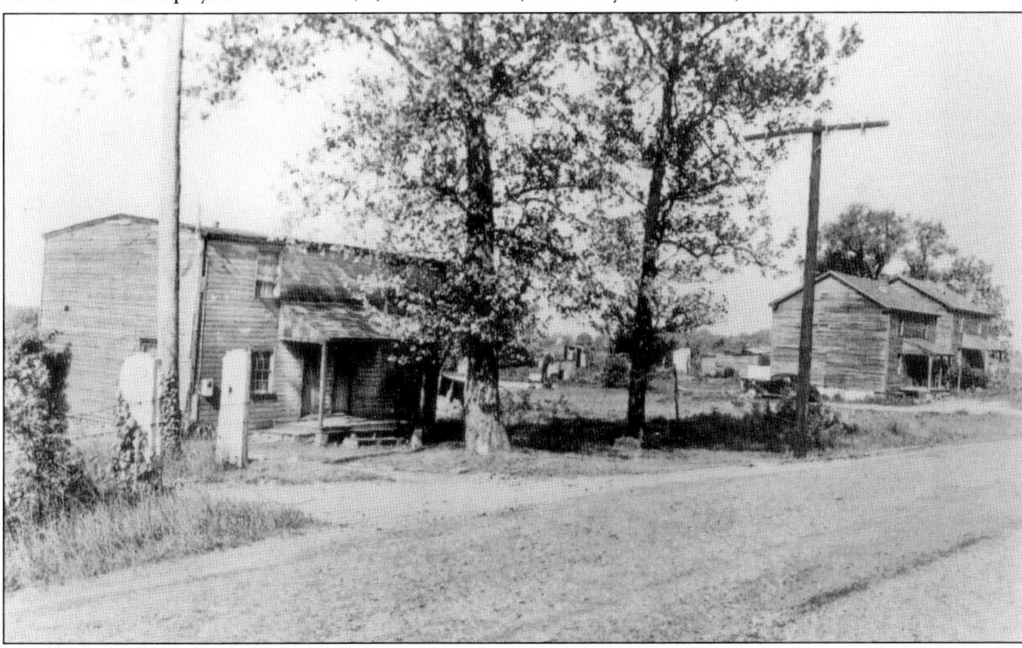

Deutsch Row was a series of eight or ten conjoined houses built for the families of the men who worked in the pits. A company store run by John Jefferis complemented the employee housing. In 1939, when the cloverleaf intersection of Route 41 and Route 7 was built, these houses were demolished to make way for the access ramps. (Courtesy Ed Lafferty.)

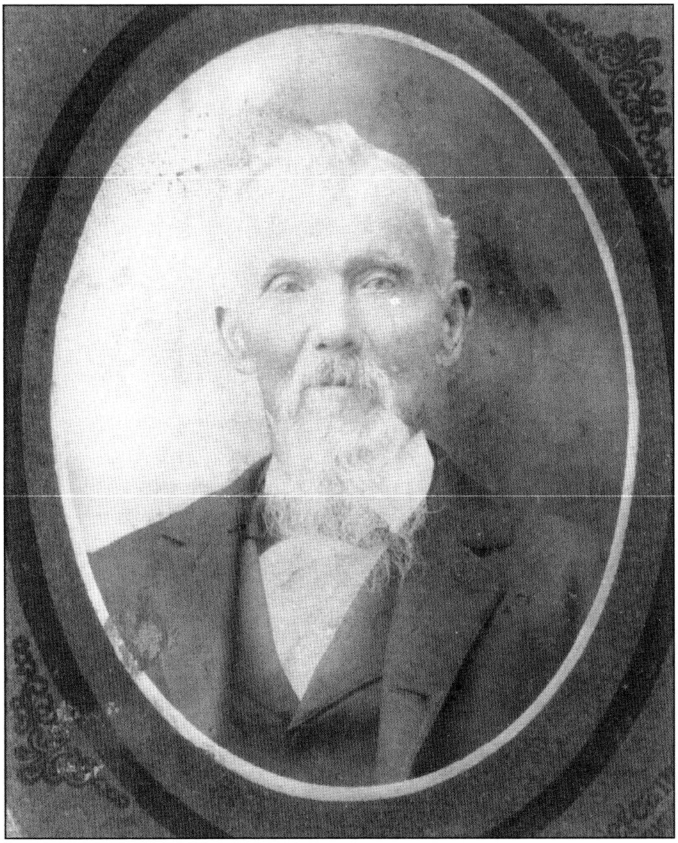

Michael Peter Lafferty arrived in Philadelphia from Desertmartin, Derry County, Ireland, prior to 1870. He was one of 15 Irish immigrants hired to work in the pits. They were clothed, shod, given money upfront, and put on a train for Southwood. Those that didn't skip out along the way replaced the Pennsylvania Dutch who were first hired to dig the clay pits. (Courtesy Ed Lafferty.)

Boyd's 1904 Directory lists Kaolin's population as 125. Businesses operating within the town's confines included American Kaolin Works, Graham Kaolin Company, Dan Sheehan's general store, William Haggerty's smithy forge, and J. W. Hoopes and Son, butchers. Sheehan's store, pictured below, also housed the post office. (Author's collection.)

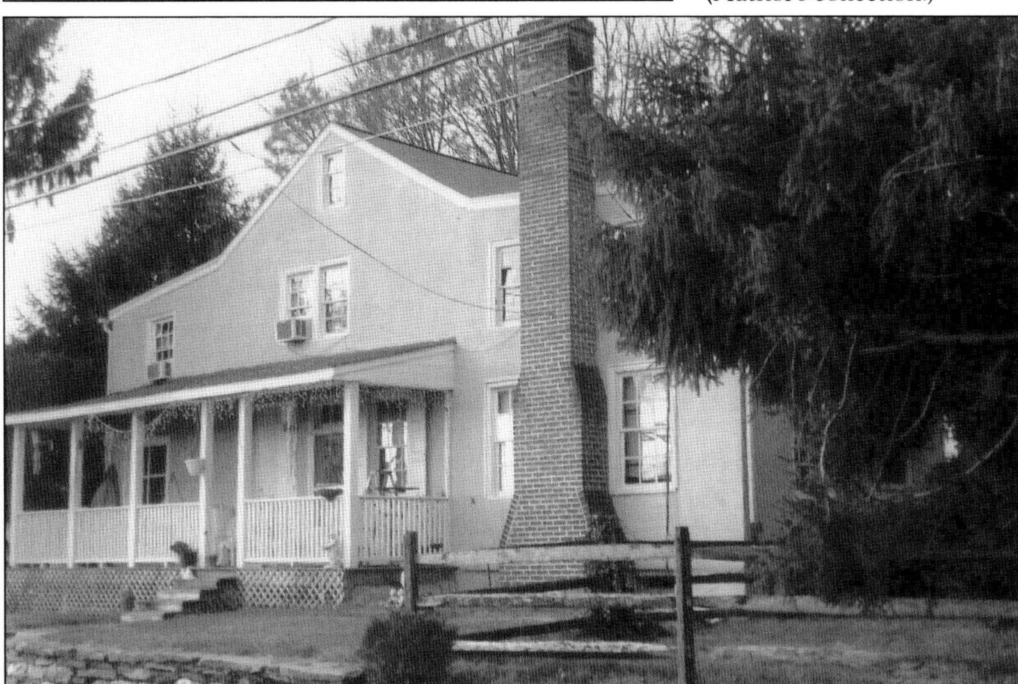

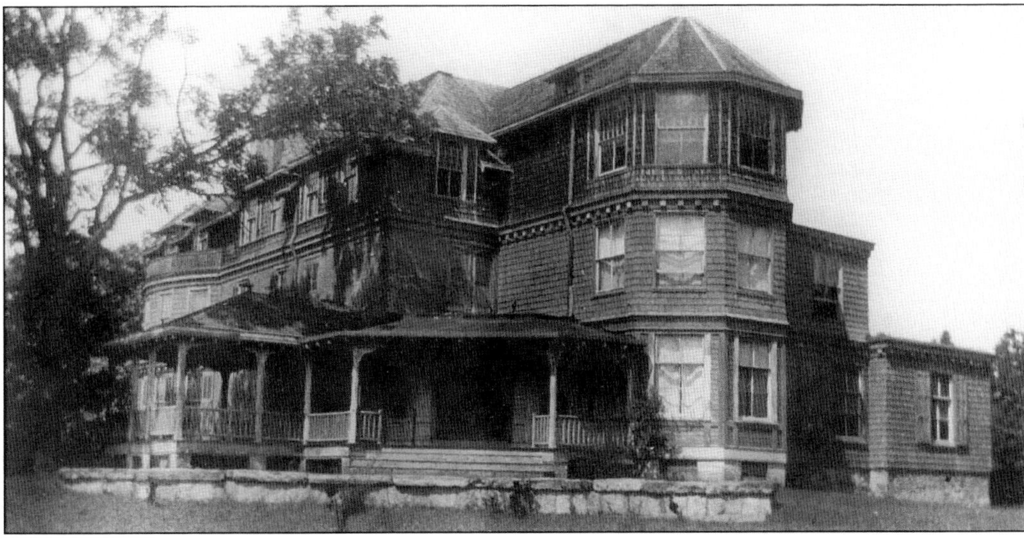

Hamilton Graham, a mining engineer and owner of a clay operation, built this palatial mansion of 32 rooms between Route 41 and his pits. Maintaining the enormous structure necessitated an army of workers; thus did the spouses and daughters of clay miners find employment. In 1885, Graham retired and sold his business to Howard Spencer's American Kaolin Company. (Courtesy James Lafferty.)

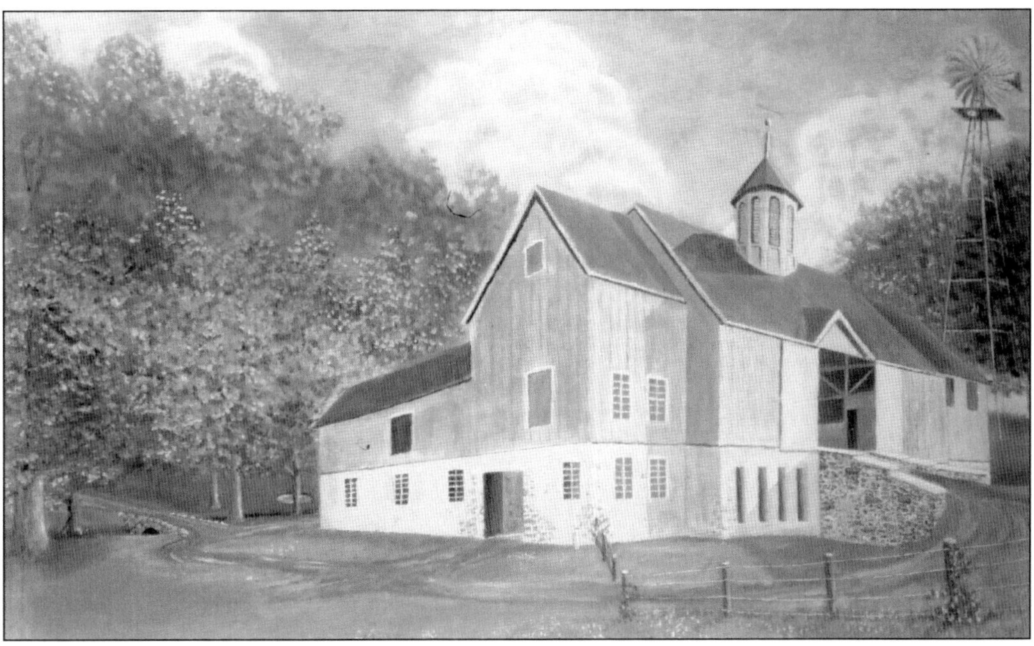

In 1900, Mrs. Howard Spencer built this stable for her private use at a cost of $5,000. Newspapers reported that the addition of this commodious stable would put the property on par with some of the residences near Philadelphia. James Lafferty, who grew up in the mansion and painted this rendition, remembers, "My brother and I used to go into the barn's ballroom in the winter to catch and play ball." (Courtesy James Lafferty.)

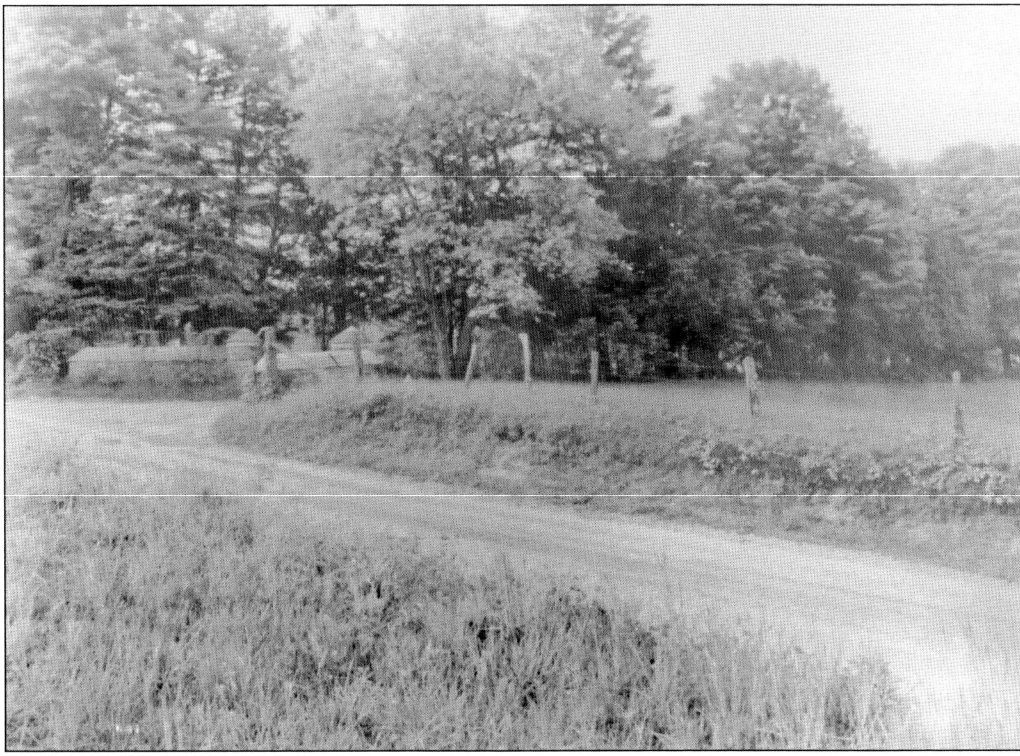

The lane to the Spencer mansion led off of the Gap-Newport Pike. Newspapers reported that in 1901 Mrs. Spencer was planting trees along the driveways and grounds as well as improving buildings on the property and building three new tenement houses. (Courtesy Ed Lafferty.)

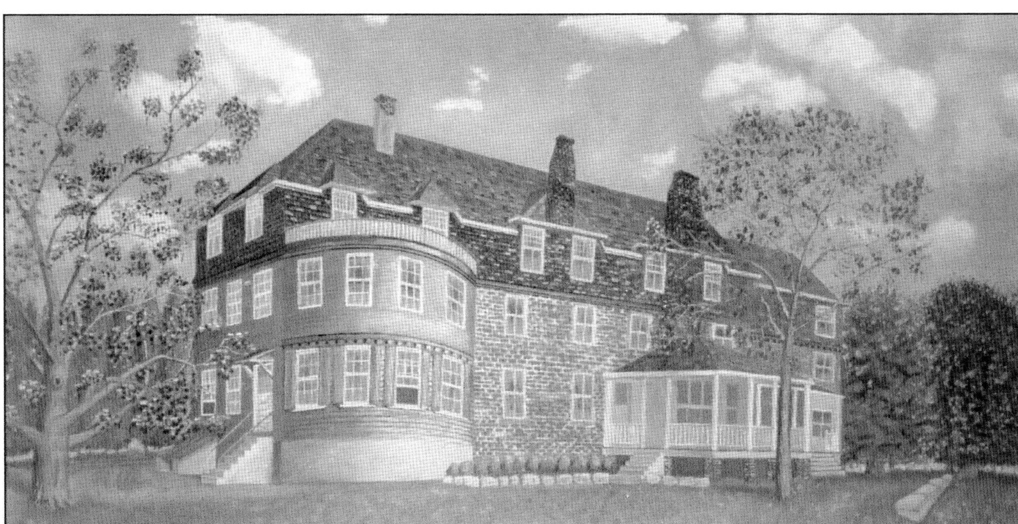

The clay market sank as deposits were discovered in Georgia, where cheaper excavation and processing glutted supply. In addition, many of the kaolin pits had breeched the water table and flooded. In 1908, the Graham-Spencer estate was sold at sheriff's sale. Michael Lafferty, the Irish immigrant who had worked the pits, had purchased the entire property by 1913. His grandson James Lafferty's painting shows the mansion's rear elevation. (Courtesy James Lafferty.)

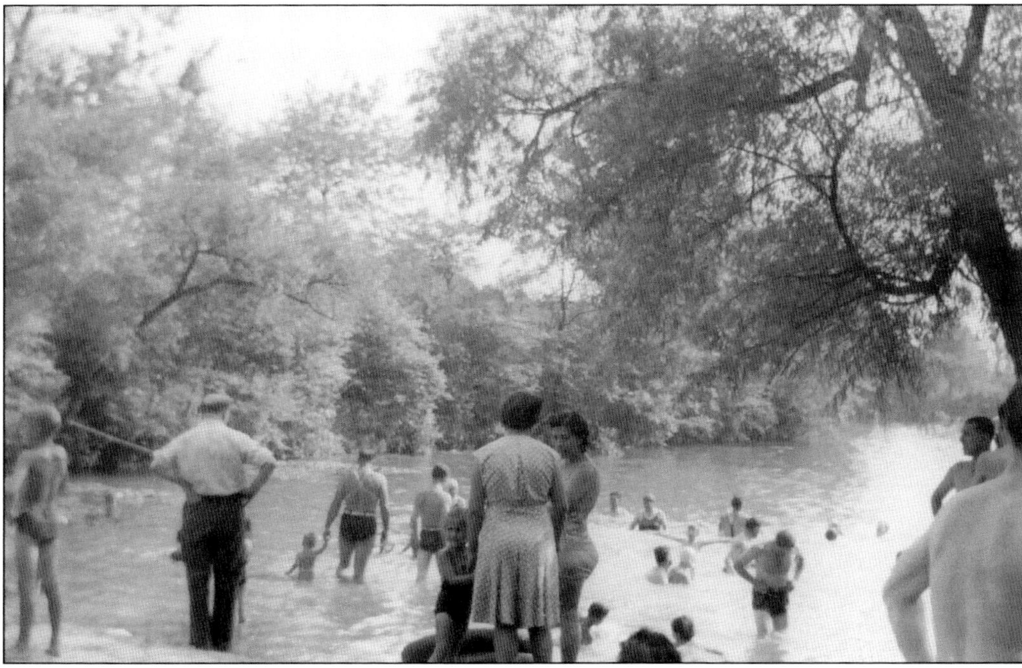

In many instances, mining companies lost all their equipment when workers hit springs in the bottom of the clay pits. Sometimes a pit would fill with water within a day. After the mines closed, these pits became popular swimming holes. Lewis Lafferty opened Kaolin Lake, the easternmost flooded pit, in the 1930s. Charging 25¢ to swim, he built changing rooms and a parking lot. The lake attracted visitors for decades. Farther west, the Marvel pit became a resort, surrounded by vacation cottages. These pictures, taken in 1940, show a typical summer day at the lake. Eventually, both lakes were condemned because of mushroom compost runoff. (Both courtesy James Lafferty.)

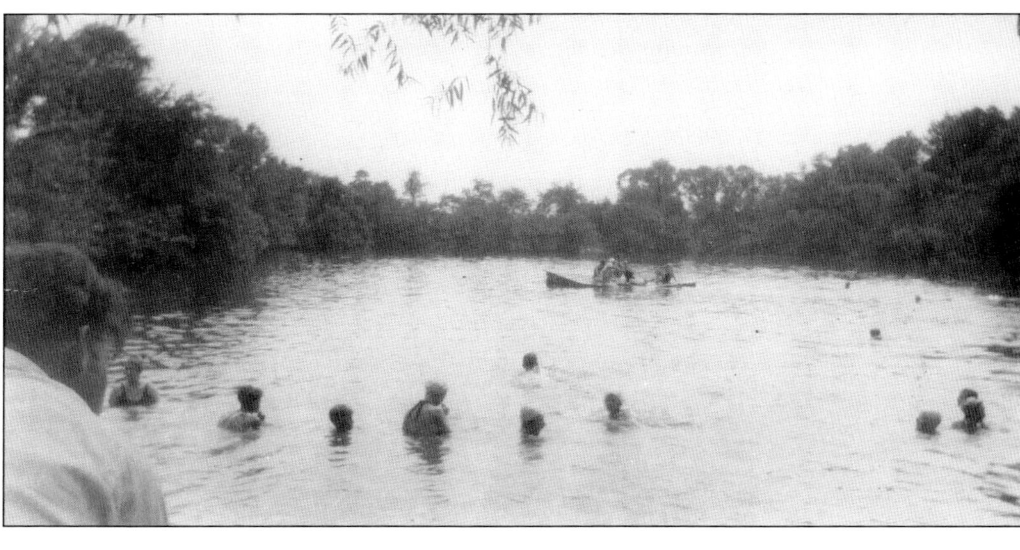

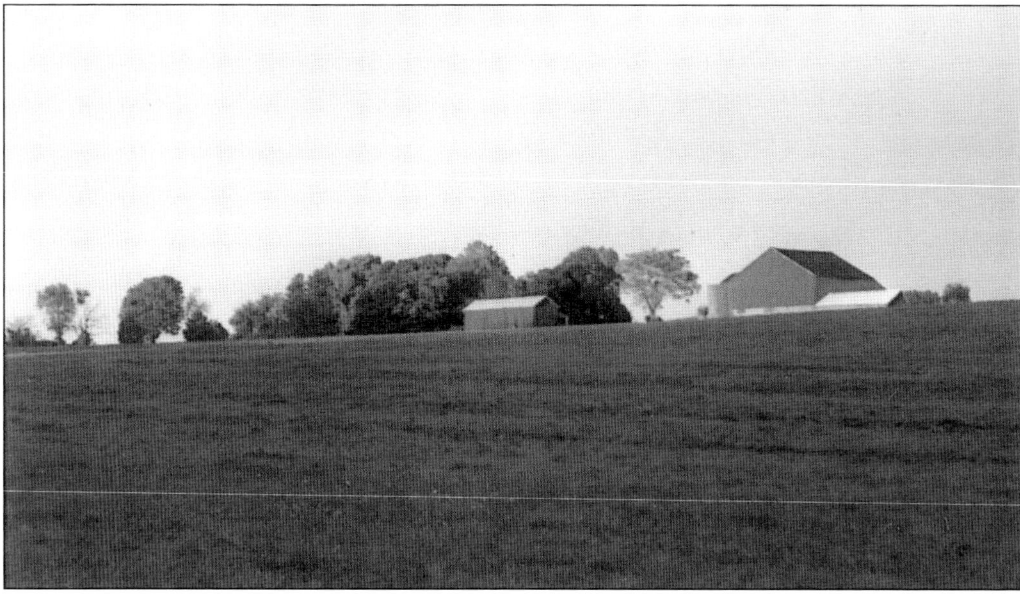

By the end of the first decade of the 20th century, the clay companies in Kaolin closed. Workers moved away, and Kaolin slowly disappeared. Reconstruction of Route 41 doomed the remainder of the buildings, Ray O'Neill's auction barn, and the baseball field. The Kaolin companies' land returned to agriculture. Pictured here is the so-called "Upper Farm" of the Michael Lafferty family. (Courtesy Ed Lafferty.)

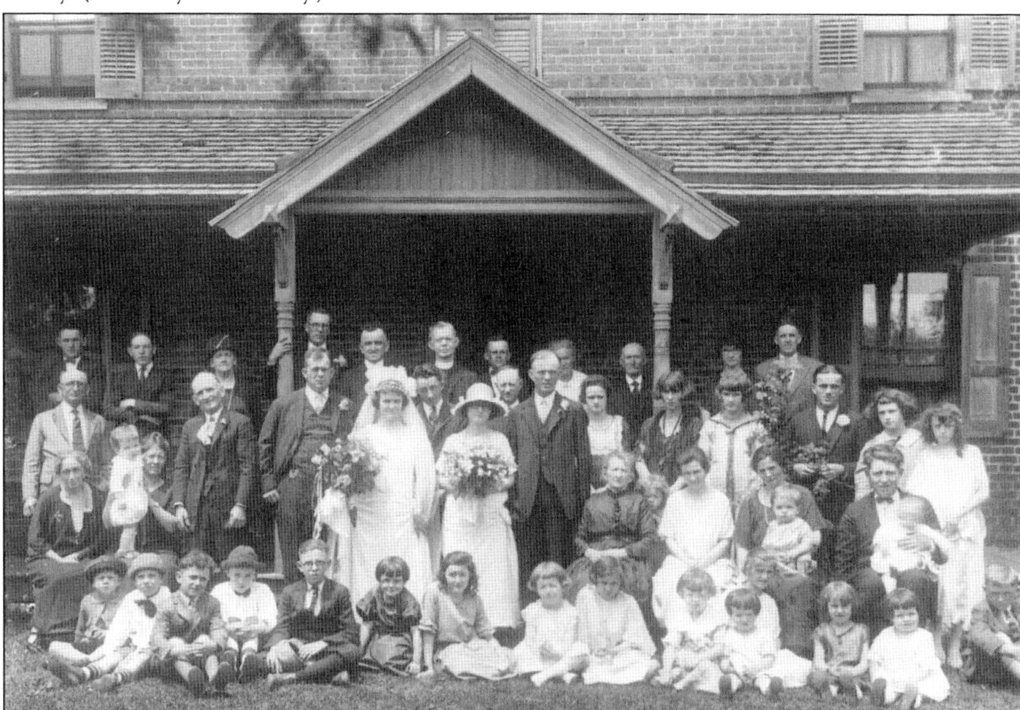

The wedding of Margaret Lafferty, daughter of Michael and Mary Lafferty, to Christopher Vandergriff was celebrated on the lawn of the Upper Farm in 1926. (Courtesy Ed Lafferty.)

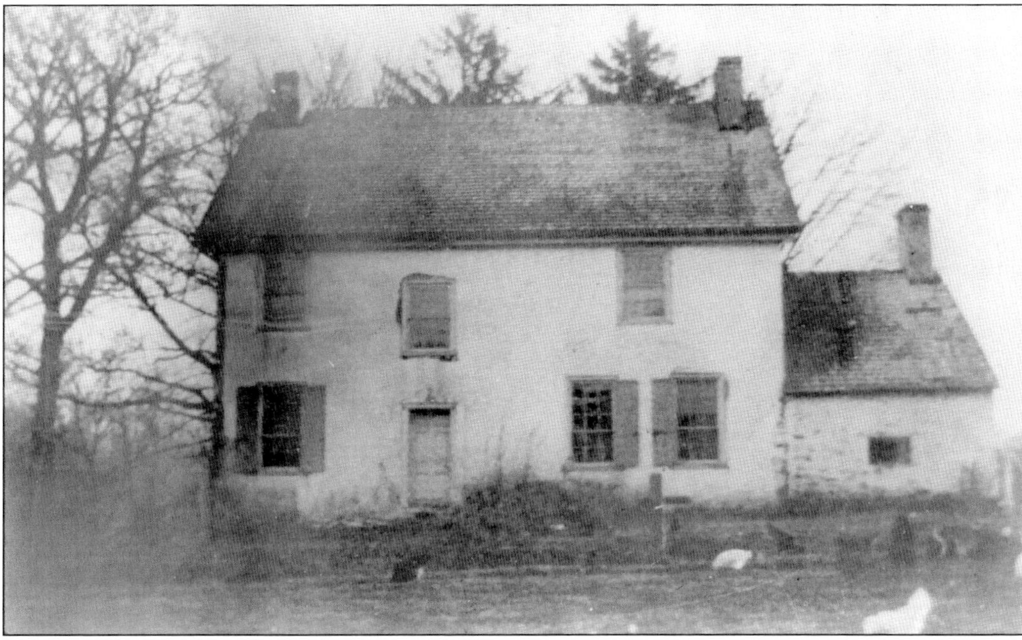

The tenant house where Frank and Anna Lafferty reared eight children remains on the St. Anthony's property. After Anna's death in 1928 and Frank's in 1930, the children moved in with their grandmother and aunts on the Upper Farm. (Courtesy Ed Lafferty.)

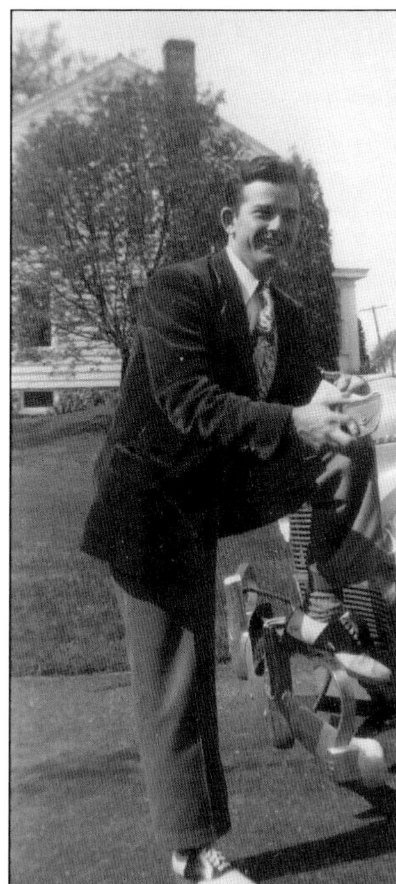

Eddie Lafferty was his most polished self when he posed for this picture sometime around high school graduation. Eddie graduated on June 15, 1943, and was in the U.S. Army by July 1. Lafferty served his country for 33 months, after which he attended Goldey-Beacom College and worked for General Motors before he began mushroom farming in earnest. (Courtesy Ed Lafferty.)

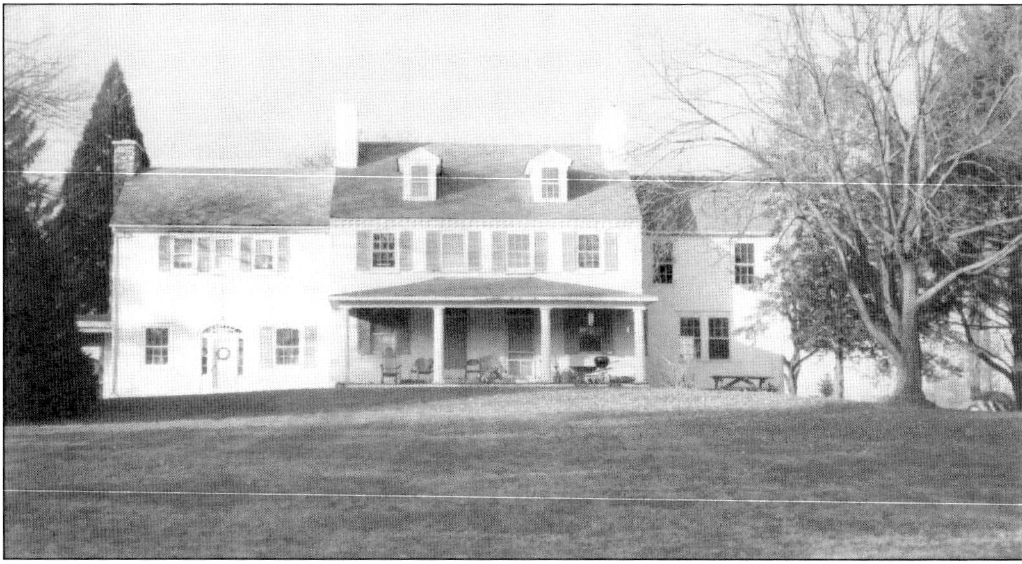

Capt. Charles Robinson bought the Kaolin farms of Charles Wilkinson and Jacob Taylor in 1918. Dubbed Colonial Farms by Robinson, the 135 acres consisted of the 1812 Wilkinson farmhouse, large bank barn, granary, 1790 Taylor farm house, Kaolin post office/general store, frame tenant house, and central garage/shop building. Robinson planned a working farm surrounding a village. A calamitous barn fire in 1927 brought an end to Robinson's residential farming concept. (Courtesy Joan B. Procino.)

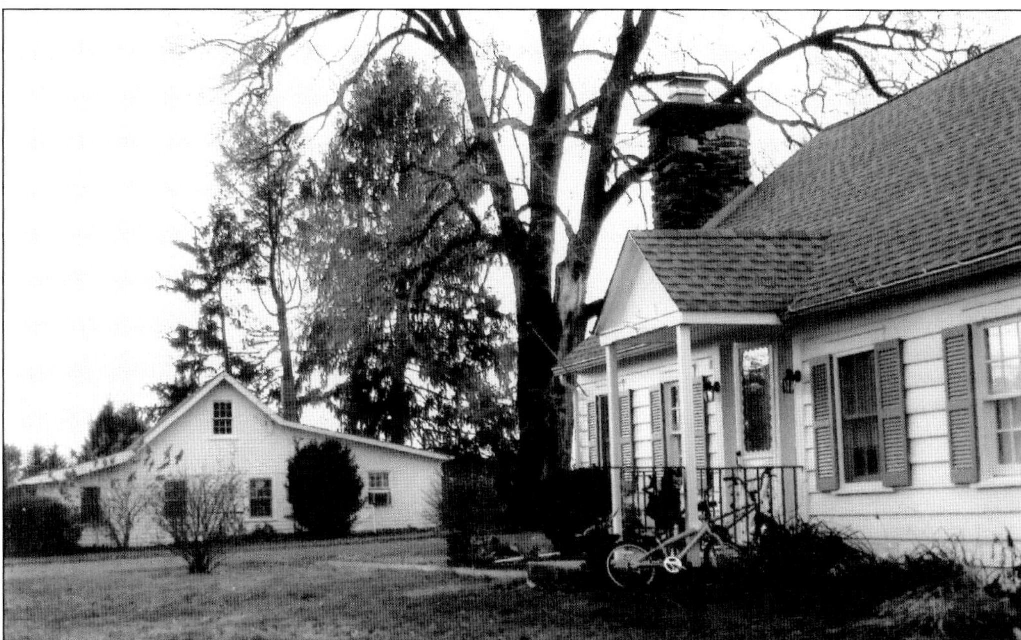

Beginning in 1940, under the stewardship of Captain Robinson's son, Charles A., and his wife, Josephine Raskob, the community tradition continued to provide young families affordable housing with an open-space atmosphere. These families, "Farmites," witnessed weddings, births, deaths, graduations, honors, land acquisition, new construction, special celebrations, Easter, Fourth of July fireworks, Halloween, Thanksgiving, and Christmas. (Courtesy Andrea Tauson.)

Four

TOUGHKENAMON

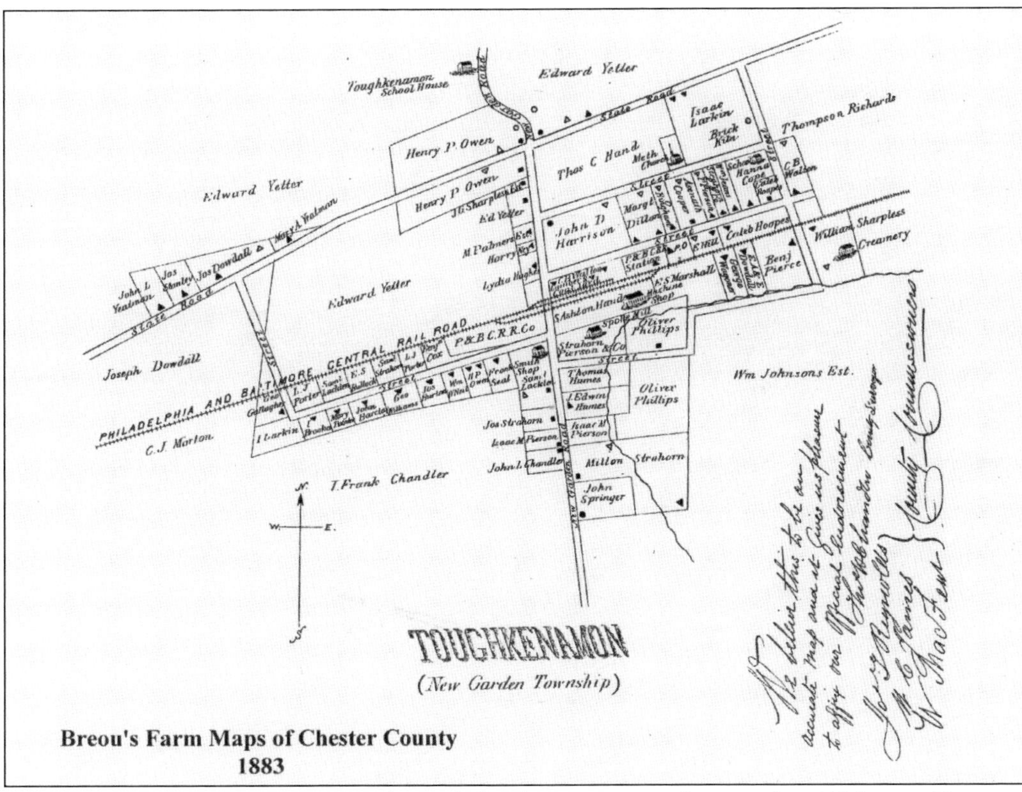

The height of Toughkenamon's industrial development is evident in this 1883 map. However, Toughkenamon's earliest recorded history dates to an 18th-century surveyor's map identifying the valley between two ridges as "Doch ran amon." Allegedly, "Dochranamon" is the literal representation of the Lenape word for "firebrand" and was attached to the area based on Lenni Lenape legends about repelling an invading tribe by using firebrands, or signaling allies on neighboring promontories using burning wood. The name may also have identified the tribe that inhabited the valley's northern high ground. (Courtesy NGTHC.)

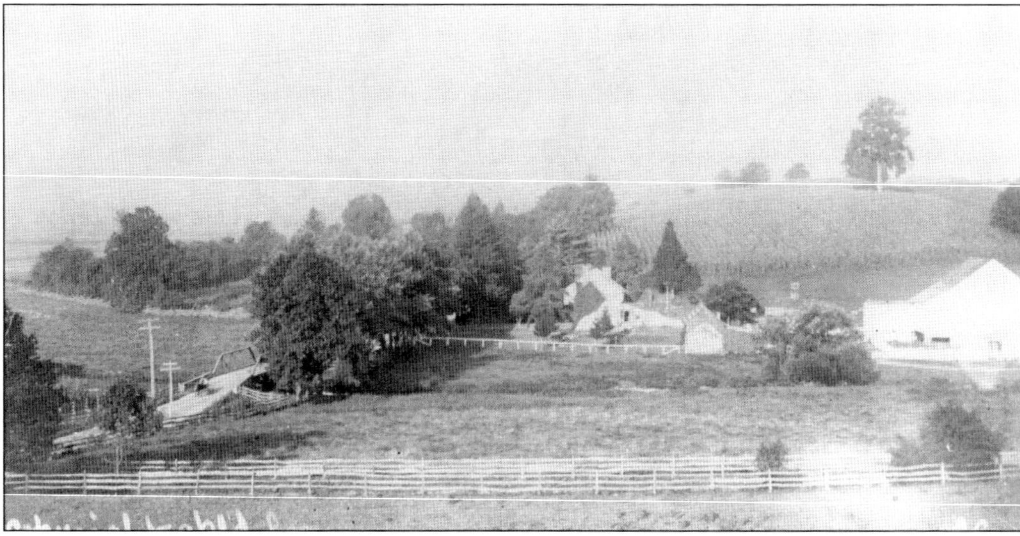

The Toughkenamon Valley stretches east and west for more than 2 miles between two promontories. Since Colonial times, there has been a main thoroughfare following the valley floor, a road ultimately known as the Baltimore Pike. As early as 1747, there was an inn or public house at the intersection of the Newark Road and the Baltimore Pike. The name Hammer and Trowel was given to this inn in 1786, and over the next century, a sequence of owners accommodated cattle drovers and teamsters hauling produce to market. In 1844, Sidney Marsh changed the inn into a temperance inn with disastrous results; his trade declined precipitously. Four years later, the inn was sold at auction. Bayard Taylor immortalized the Hammer and Trowel in his *Story of Kennett*. (Above courtesy NGTHC; below courtesy Jim Bertrando.)

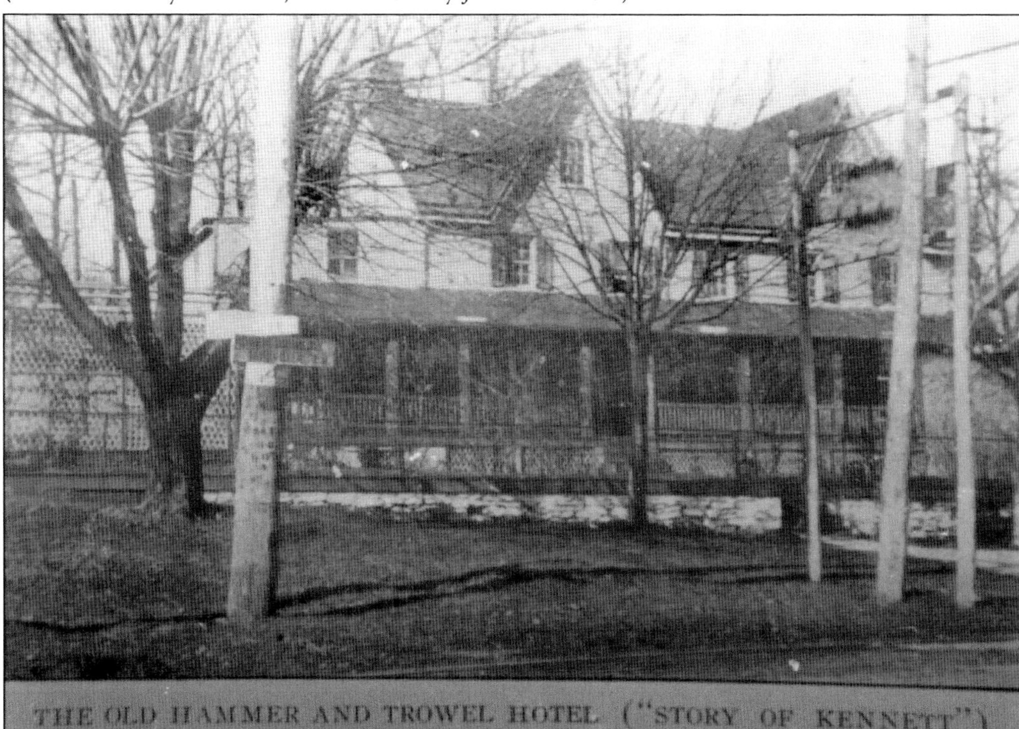

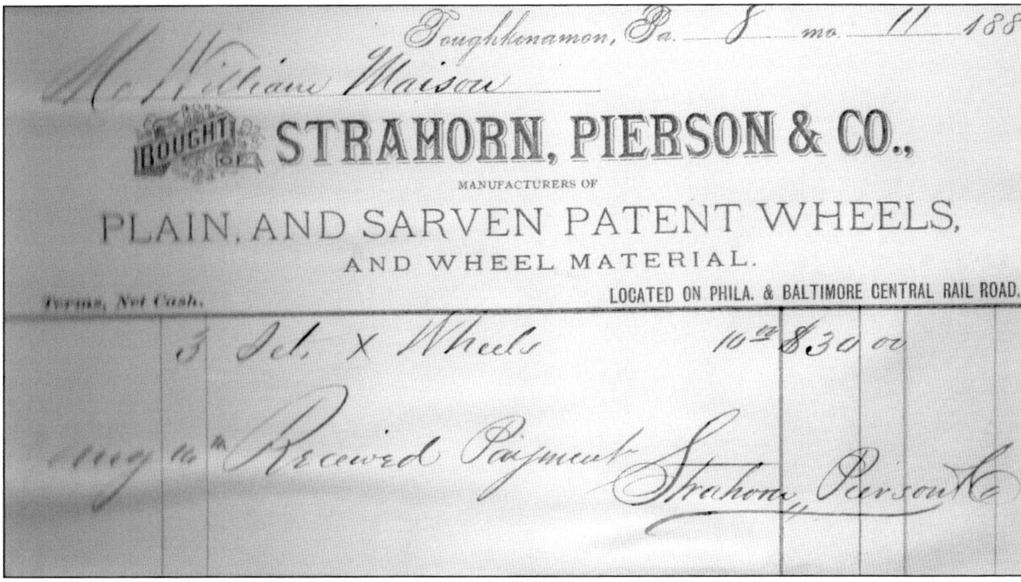

Toughkenamon, Pa. 8 mo. 11 1886

Mr. William Maison

BOUGHT OF STRAHORN, PIERSON & CO.,

MANUFACTURERS OF

PLAIN, AND SARVEN PATENT WHEELS,

AND WHEEL MATERIAL.

Terms, Net Cash.

LOCATED ON PHILA. & BALTIMORE CENTRAL RAIL ROAD.

3 Set. X Wheels 10^{00} $30 00

Aug 16th Received Payment Strahorn, Pierson & Co

Until about 1852, the village of Toughkenamon consisted of the inn, a store, and three houses. Samuel Strahorn, a Landenberg mill owner who owned a spoke factory, learned that a railroad route was planned for the Toughkenamon Valley. With steam power beginning to replace waterpower, he saw the potential for relocating his mill near a railroad. In 1864, Strahorn moved his business into a three-story brick factory built by his associate, Isaac Slack. Employing 20 to 30 men, the Strahorn Wheel and Spoke Works made wheel sets, hubs, and replacement spokes for wagons for the U.S. Army (Civil and Spanish-American Wars). Strahorn turned out as many as 400,000 spokes and 1,200 sets of wheels yearly, shipping them to markets in Philadelphia. Strahorn's mill, located about 150 feet east of Newark Road and south of the railroad track, was completely destroyed when it burned on Christmas Eve, 1903. (Both courtesy NGTHC.)

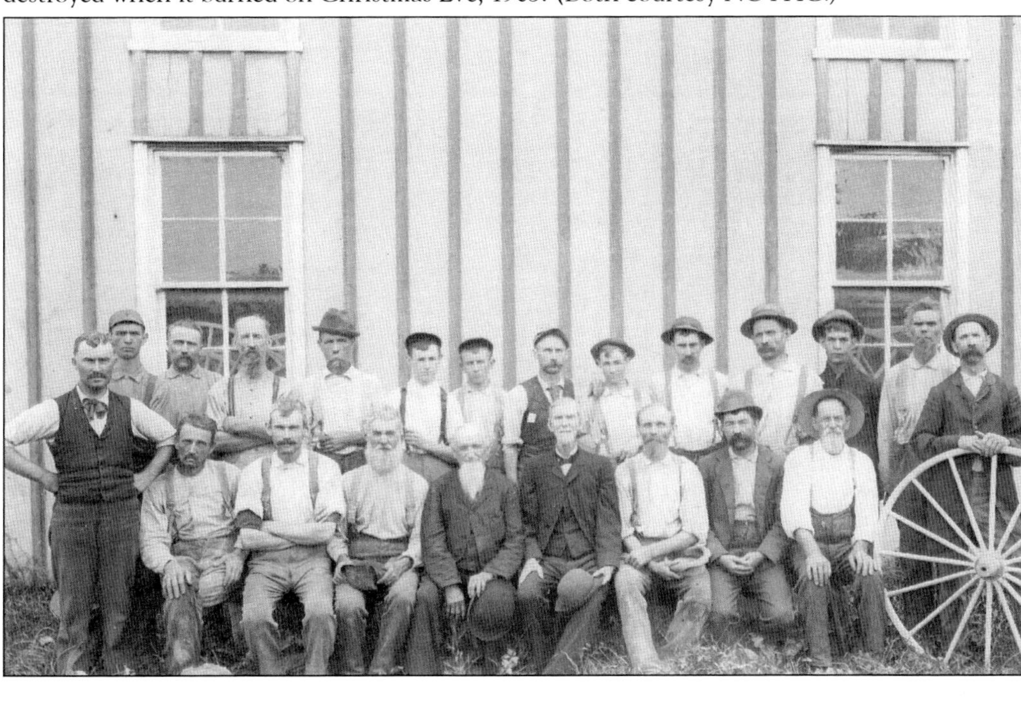

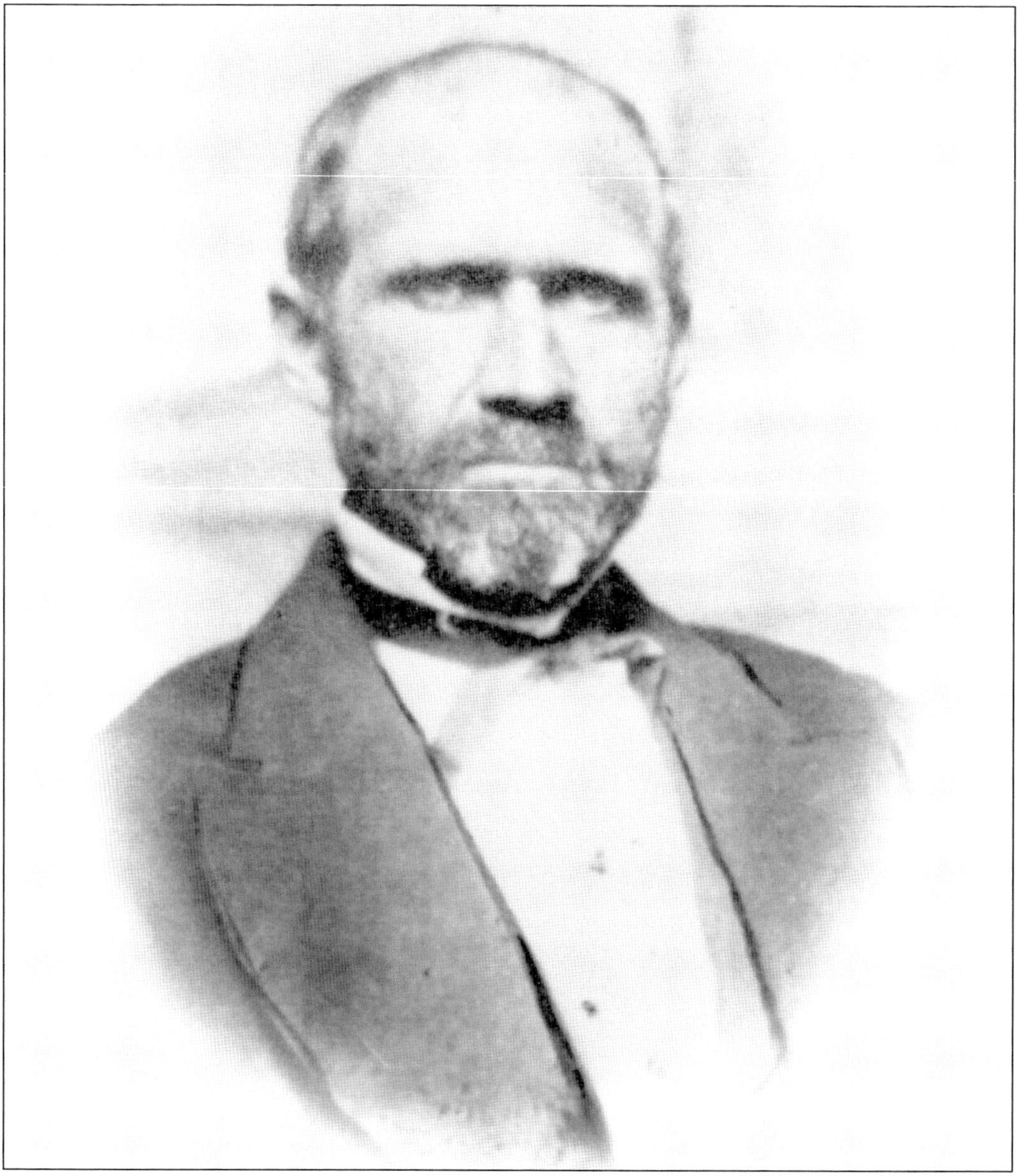

Isaac Slack is generally acknowledged to be the father of Toughkenamon. An enterprising carpenter, he worked for Samuel Strahorn in his Landenberg spoke factory. During this period, Slack went to the government patent office in Washington, memorized the plans for an efficient spoke-turning lathe, and returned to secretly build Strahorn a lathe, paying no royalties for many years. When Strahorn decided to move his business to the Toughkenamon Valley, Slack built his mill. He also built a stone grist- and sawmill for himself. Slack knew regular train service was necessary if their enterprises were to succeed. To encourage the railroad to make Toughkenamon a regular stop, he built a station, platform, and water tower, deeding them to the Philadelphia and Baltimore Railroad. In 1863, trains began to make Toughkenamon a regular stop where the steam engines could take on water. Business succeeded. In 1866 alone, the sawmill filled an order for ship timbers for Boston and another for thousands of axe, pick, and hatchet handles bound for Philadelphia. (Courtesy CCHS.)

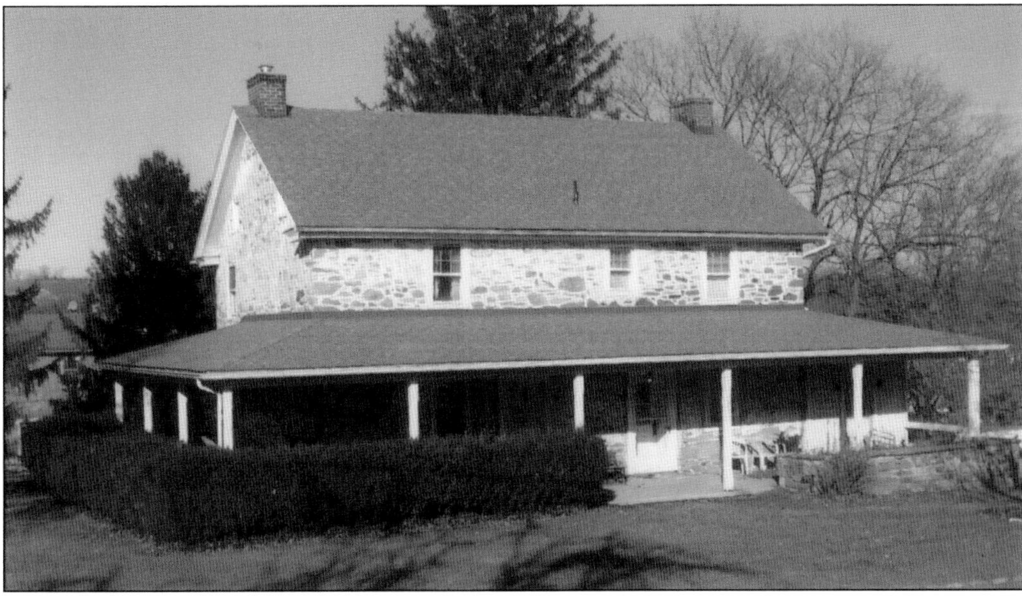

In 1855, Isaac Slack purchased a 132-acre farmstead, subdividing it into small tracts while reserving the 1746 stone house for his family. Slack's small tracts soon sprouted workers' houses, a blacksmith shop, a brick kiln, a wheelwright shop, a broom factory, a harness shop, and a creamery. While the boom lasted, the Slacks lived in this house; however, going bankrupt in 1866, Slack sold the house and moved to the village. (Author's collection.)

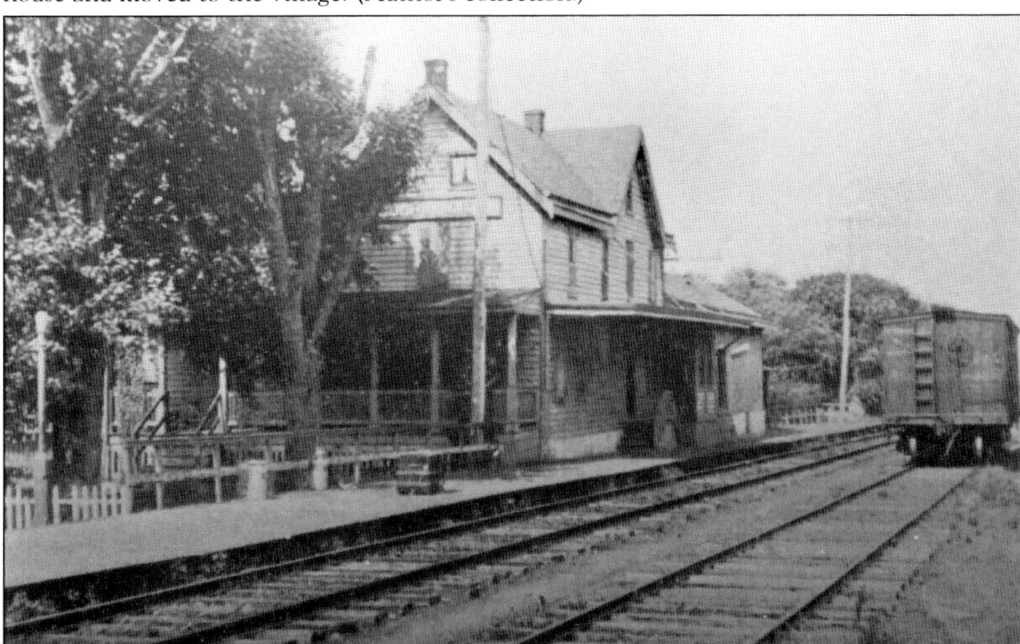

Initially the Philadelphia and Baltimore Railroad, although routed through the valley, did not plan a regular stop in the Toughkenamon village. Knowing that the fledgling industries needed a stop, Isaac Slack lured the railroad with the gift of a station, platform, and water tower. The name Toughkenamon became official in 1868, when a post office of that name opened in the railway station. (Courtesy Jim Bertrando.)

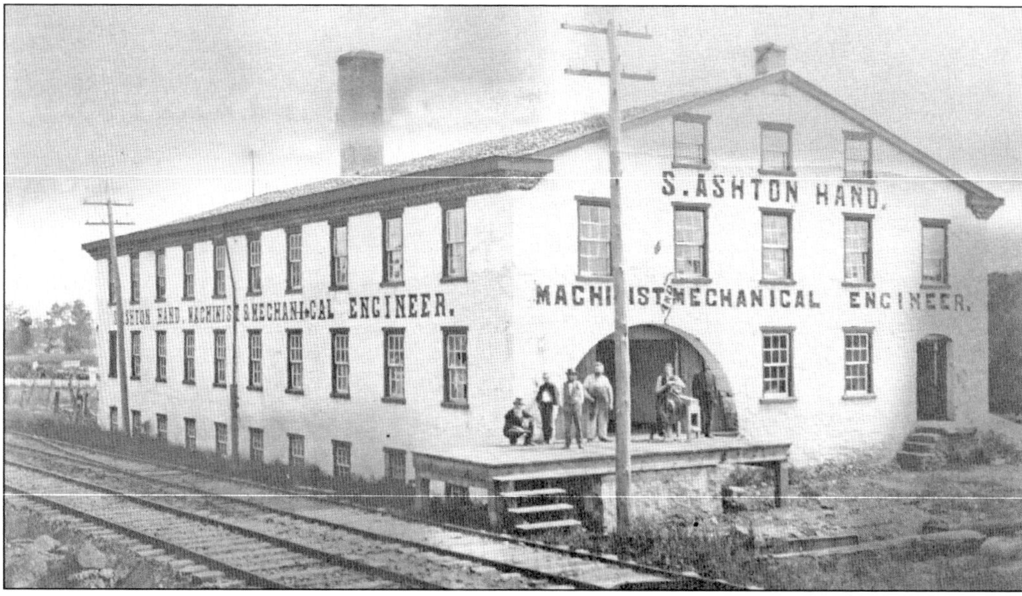

Isaac Slack, developer of Toughkenamon, built this stone mill for sawing timber and grinding flour. Measuring 90 feet by 45 feet, the building stood two-and-a-half stories high along the railroad track. Designed to saw large oak timbers for ship building, it had a capacity of 3,000 board-feet per day. With power supplied by a steam engine, the mill was later used for a machine shop and for grinding feldspar. The mill burned in 1928. (Courtesy CCHS.)

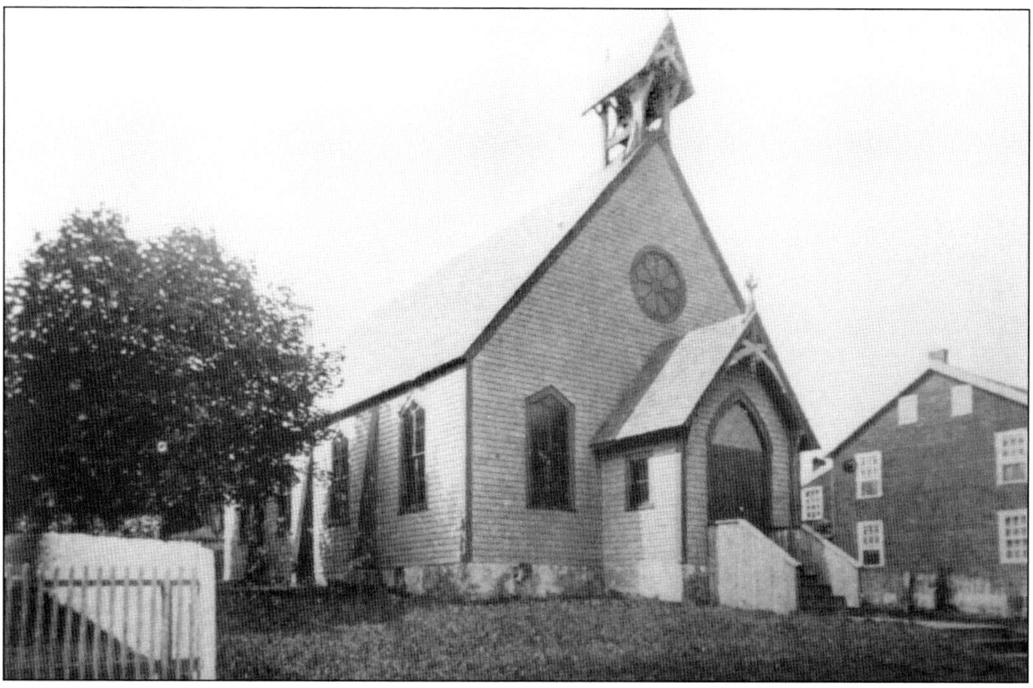

The Presbyterian church arose from a need for a village Sunday school in 1875. The first classes of this non-denominational school were held in Strahorn's wheelwright factory until Isaac Larkin completed the chapel in June 1877. After 11 years as part of Unionville Church, Toughkenamon's Presbyterian church formally organized in June 1888. (Courtesy Jim Bertrando.)

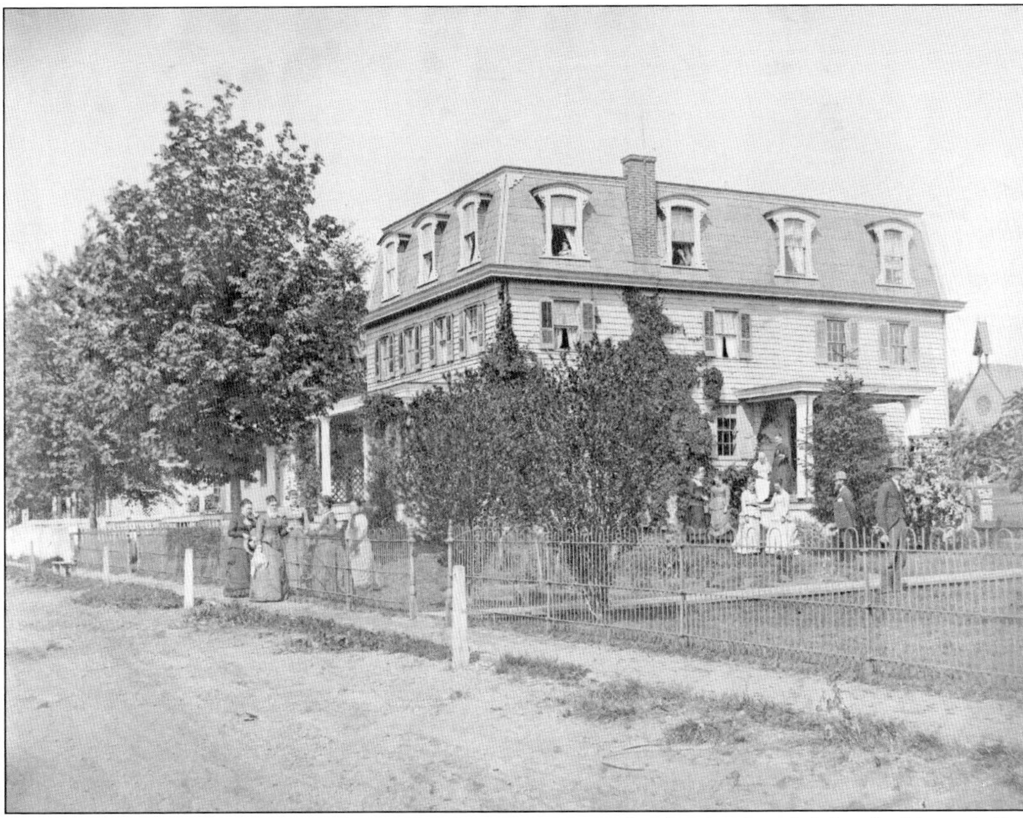

Hannah Cope opened her boarding school in 1867, soon after her husband, John, had been killed working on the railroad as an assistant superintendent. For 30 years, Cope and her daughter Lucy instructed girls on decorum, comportment, and academic disciplines. Pictured below are Hannah Cope's dwelling on the left, her school (center), and the girls' boardinghouse. The buildings faced Center Street. (Both courtesy CCHS.)

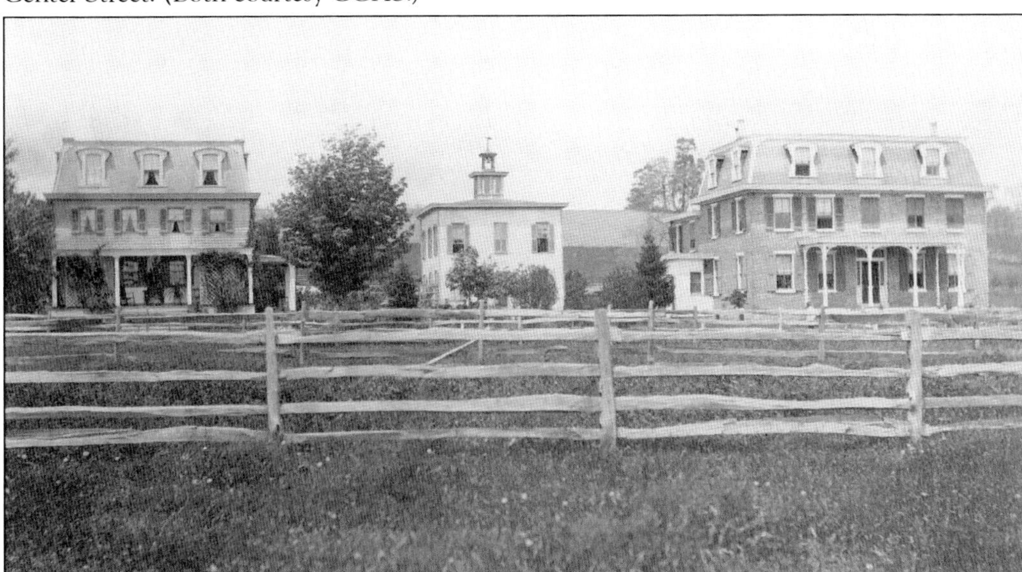

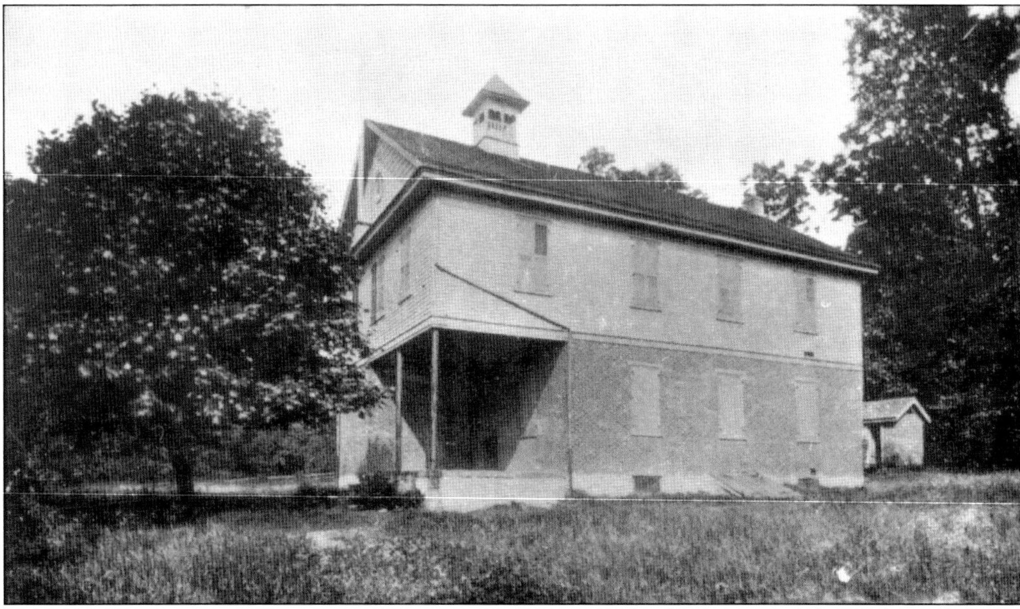

The public school along Newark Road on Toughkenamon Hill, built in the mid-19th century, had a second floor added in 1897. Jim Bertrando, remembering the 1920s, recalled, "One of the teachers at school had a wagon spoke and when you got out of line, she'd take care of you with it." Writing in 1930, John Cloud recalled that punishment was meted out by five raps across the knuckles with a ruler, which one ducked if one could. His memory also included freezing trips to the "backhouse" and the warmth close to the stove. The Toughkenamon School, like all the other New Garden schools, closed in 1932 with consolidation. The picture below shows a teacher in the early 20th century with her students ranging from first graders to eighth graders. (Above courtesy Jim Bertrando; below courtesy CCHS.)

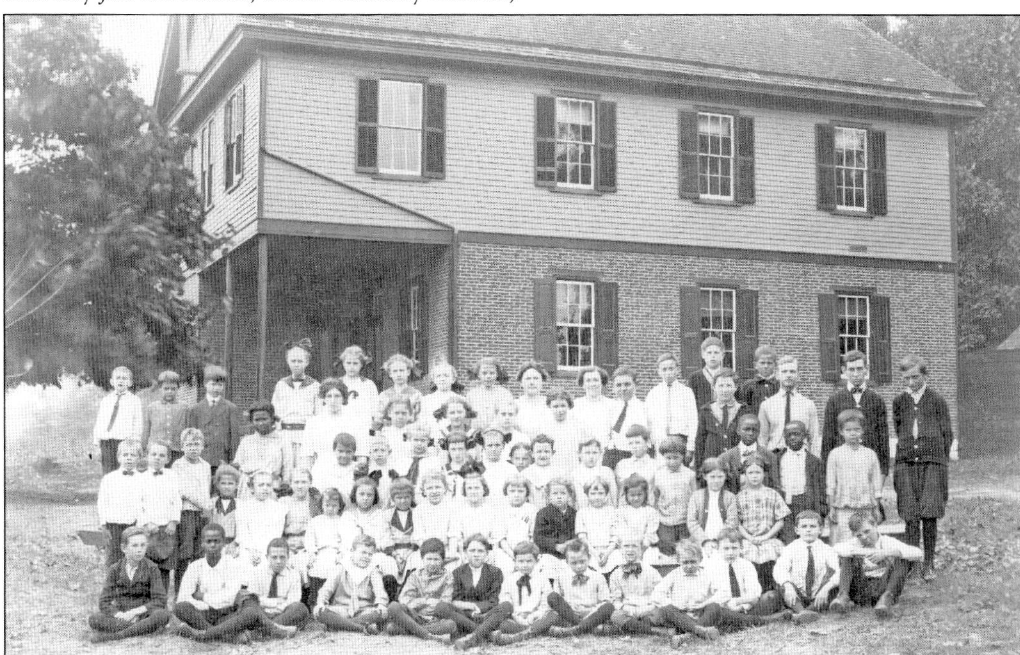

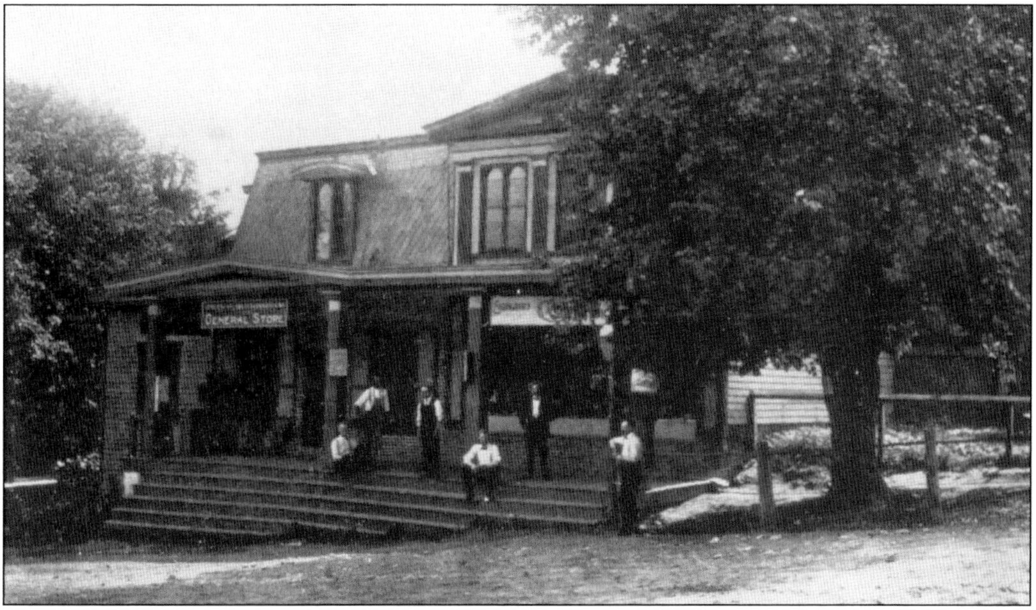

It is assumed that the southwest corner of Baltimore Pike and Newark Road was the site of a general retail store from as early as 1828, when the property was offered for sale as part of the estate of Anthony Paxson. Eli Bullock operated a general store at the location until 1872, when Harry P. Owen assumed proprietorship and sold items ranging from horse blankets and boots to wallpaper, fruit, produce, fabrics, and appliances. (Courtesy Jim Bertrando.)

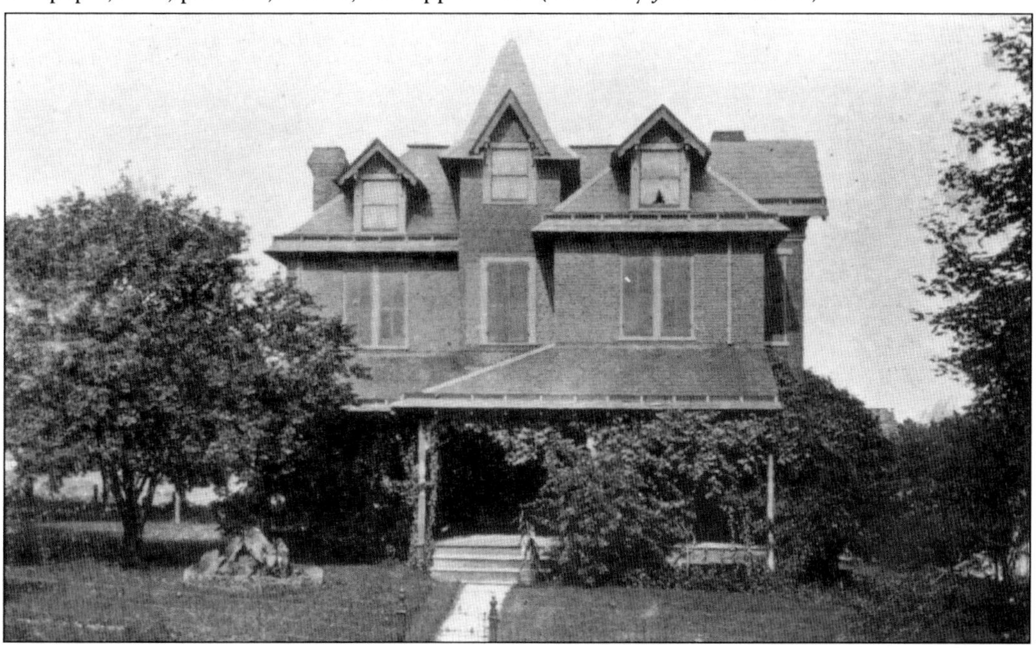

Harry Owens was not only the storekeeper in Toughkenamon, he was also a builder; newspaper accounts refer to his building three houses in the village. In order to build a house for his family across the road from his store, in the early 1880s Owens demolished "an old house." Given its location across from the Hammer and Trowel, this house he razed may have been one of the original three houses standing prior to 1850. (Courtesy CCHS.)

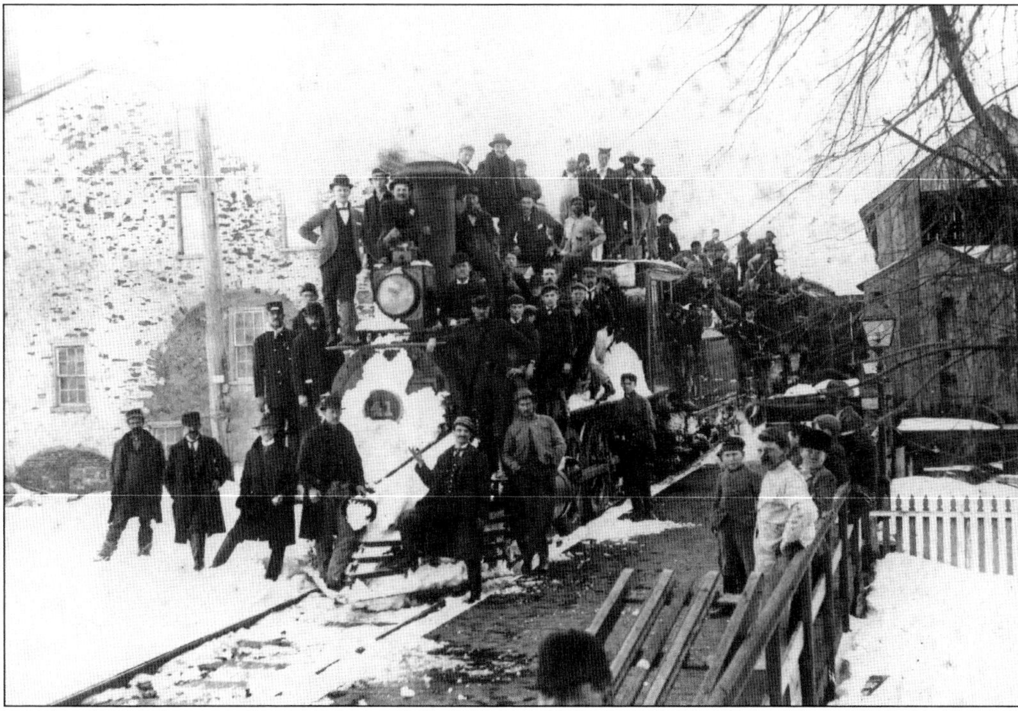

In March 1888 there was a blizzard, described as a nor'easter, that raged for two days; the drifts brought train traffic to a standstill. This picture was taken from the station platform looking east. On the left is Isaac Slack's sawmill and on the right the feed mill and lumberyard. (Courtesy NGTHC.)

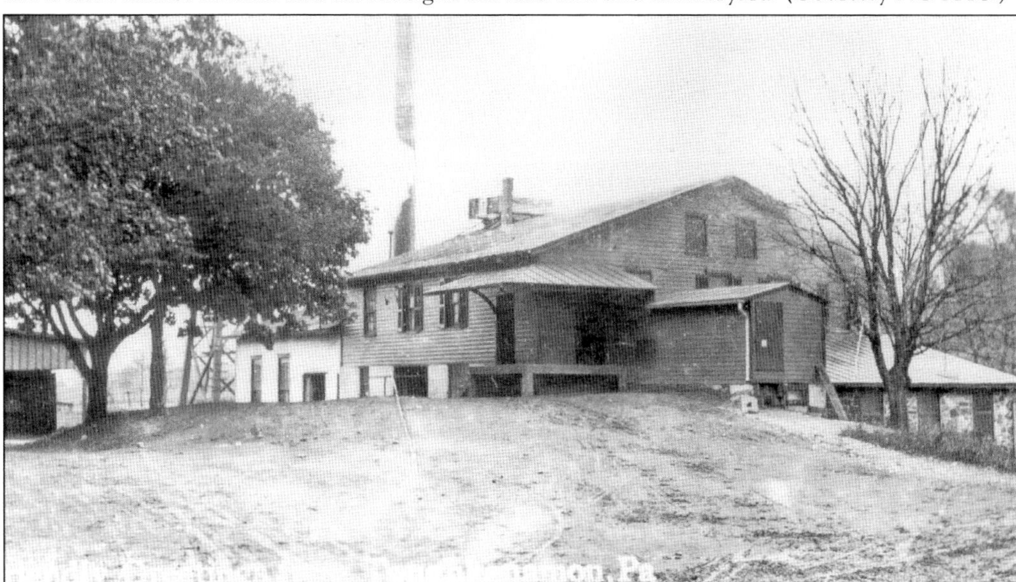

Over the last quarter of the 19th century, Toughkenamon was a thriving country town with many small businesses supported by the farming community. By 1900, the Sharpless Creamery, east of the depot along the railroad tracks, was the largest employer in town. The creamery, which opened in November 1881, received nearly 5,000 pounds of wholesale milk per day from which it produced butter and cottage cheese for city markets. (Courtesy NGTHC.)

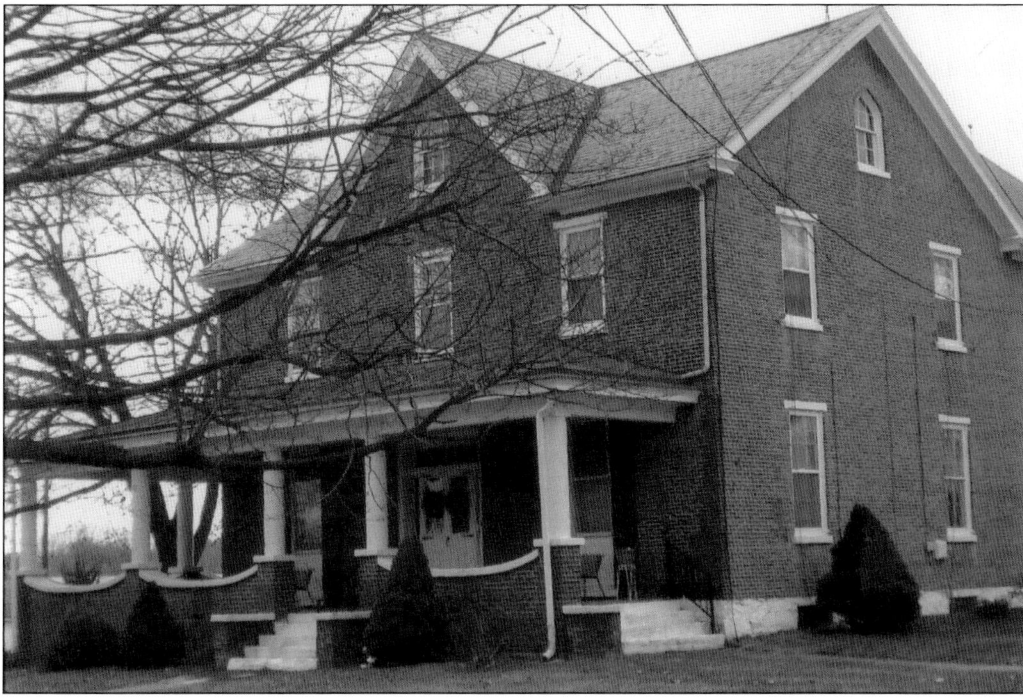

In the mid-1870s, Dr. Edward Yetter built this substantial brick house and eventually a racetrack to the west of the house. Cocochetti Bertrando purchased the entire property in the early 1900s and added the porch on the front. His sons—Angelo, Bill, and Jim—grew up in this house, trained racehorses, and raised mushrooms. For decades, the Bertrando brothers grew mushrooms in the 10 "doubles," or mushroom houses, behind the house. (Courtesy Andrea Tauson.)

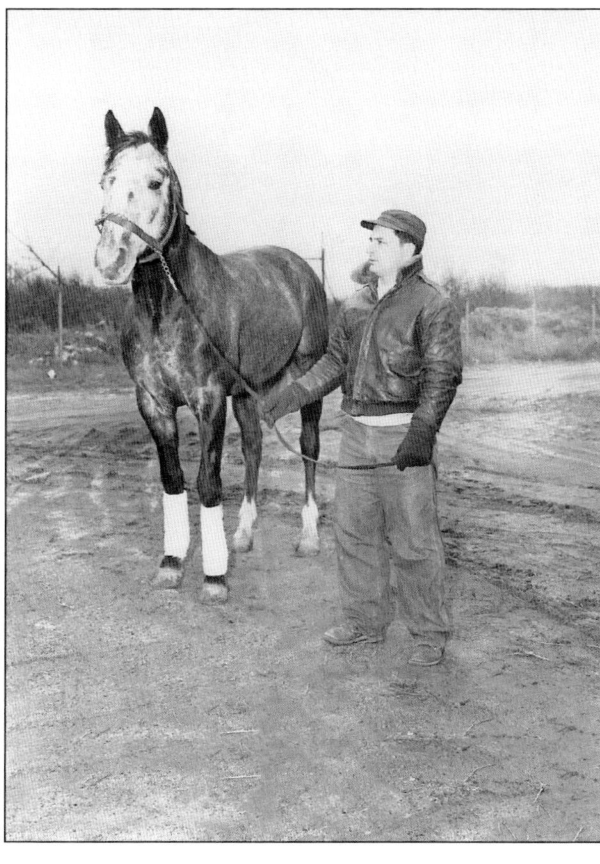

The Gentlemen's Driving Park, a half-mile oval built by Dr. Edward Yetter south of Baltimore Pike and north of the railroad, opened in the summer of 1875. Here Jim Bertrando, the youngest son of Cocochetti Bertrando who eventually bought the Yetter property, trains one of the Bertrando brothers' mounts on the oval in the late 1940s. (Courtesy Jim Bertrando.)

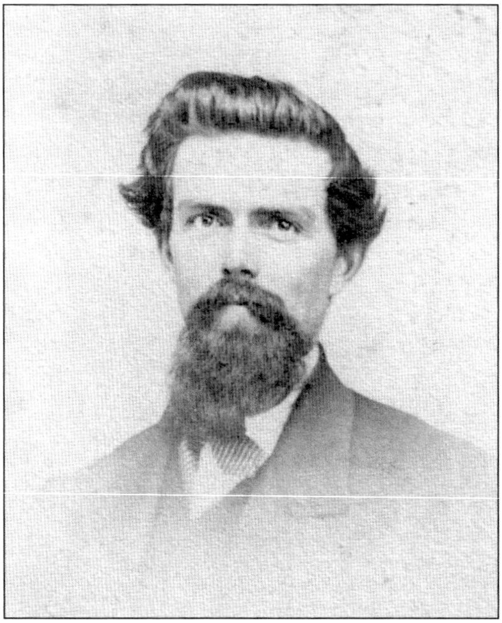

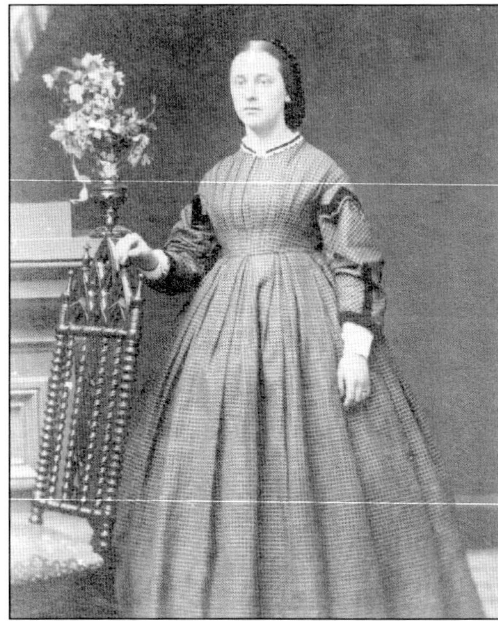

On the evening of January 27, 1912, the home of Thompson and Anna Mary Scarlett Richards exploded. Richards (above left) was killed. His wife (above right) and daughter were seriously injured. Newspaper accounts called it "a singular and complete ruin" never seen before in Chester County and "an appalling scene of calamity." An acetylene gas plant that operated the home's lighting was suspected of causing the destruction. Quickly, neighbors were on the scene, trying to rescue the wounded and retrieve family papers, which had been shredded and scattered to the wind. People came from as far as Philadelphia to view the destruction, and a special train was put on from Oxford. (All courtesy Ruth Richards.)

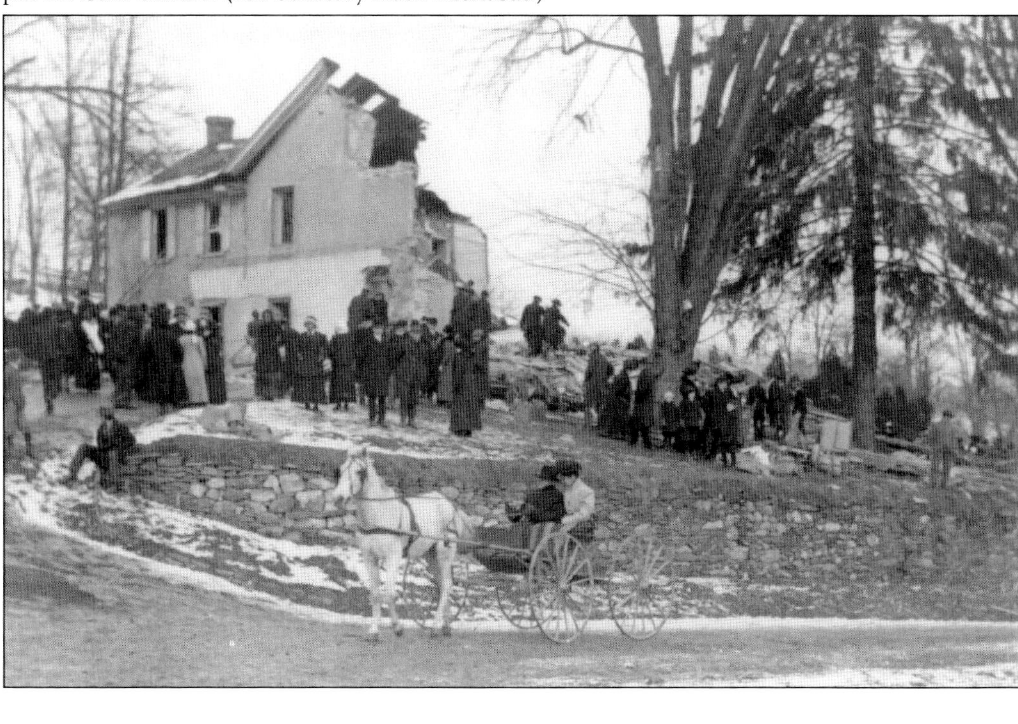

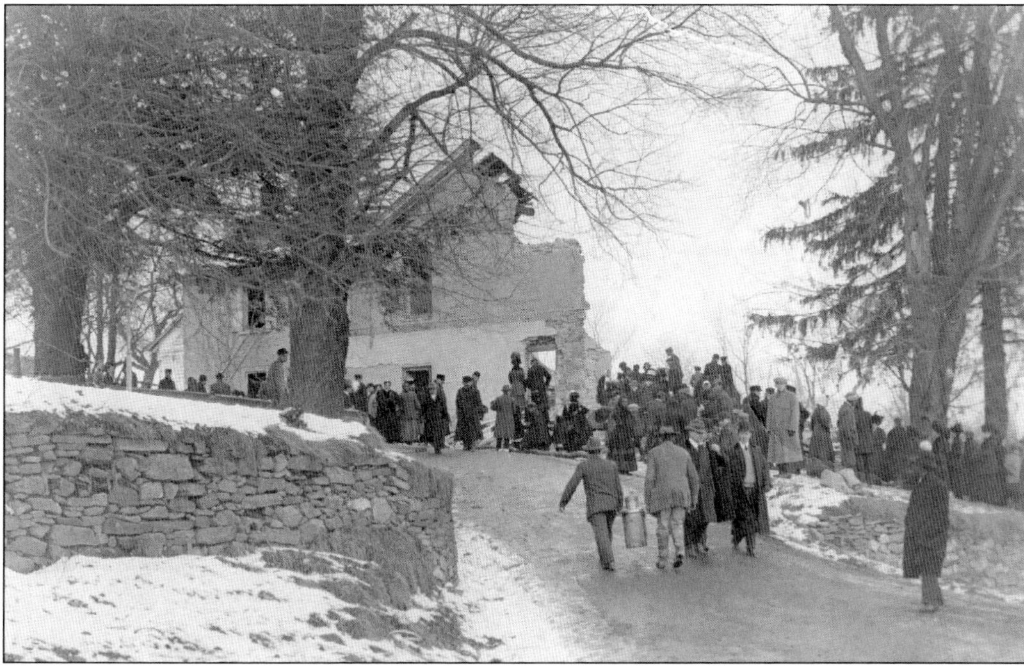

Thompson Richards, born February 11, 1842, was a descendant and farmed the land of Mary Rowland Richards, who received the first Penn patent in New Garden Township in 1708. Thompson Richards was a Civil War veteran and prominent member of the community. A member of New Garden Meeting, he had been township supervisor, a school director for many terms, and a director of the National Bank of Kennett Square. At the time of his death, Richards, a successful farmer, had been planning to retire to Kennett. (Both courtesy Ruth Richards.)

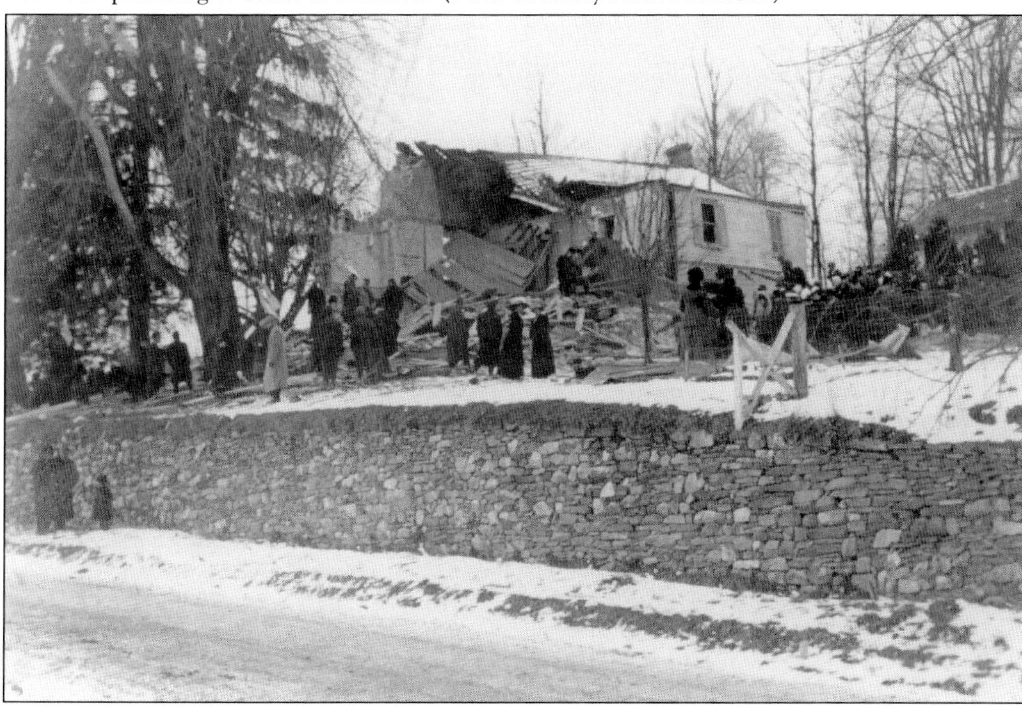

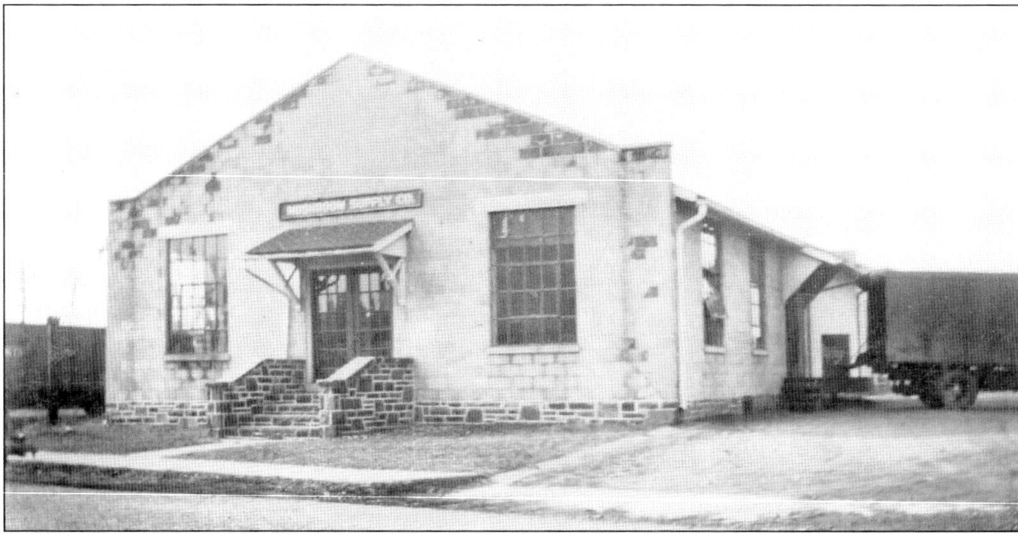

Mushroom houses began to dot the landscape before World War II, and Toughkenamon's economy changed to support this developing industry. Mushroom Supply Company, established in the mid-1920s, sold myriad supplies for the mushroom growing industry, ranging from spawn to forks, shovels, and insecticide, and manufactured mushroom baskets. The business stood west of Newark Road, along the railroad tracks; the top picture shows the original building, often expanded to accommodate the burgeoning agribusiness. Losito's cannery, which served growers with a way to preserve the always perishable mushrooms for later sale, was located east of the railway depot. Toughkenamon's railroad siding south of Mushroom Supply formed an integral link in the mushroom business. It was here that hundreds of cars of horse manure from Philadelphia stables and racetracks were unloaded. The manure, mixed with straw, formed the basis for mushroom compost, the medium in which mushrooms were grown. The Martelli Building, below, was the original spawn plant. (Above courtesy CCHS; below courtesy Andrea Tauson.)

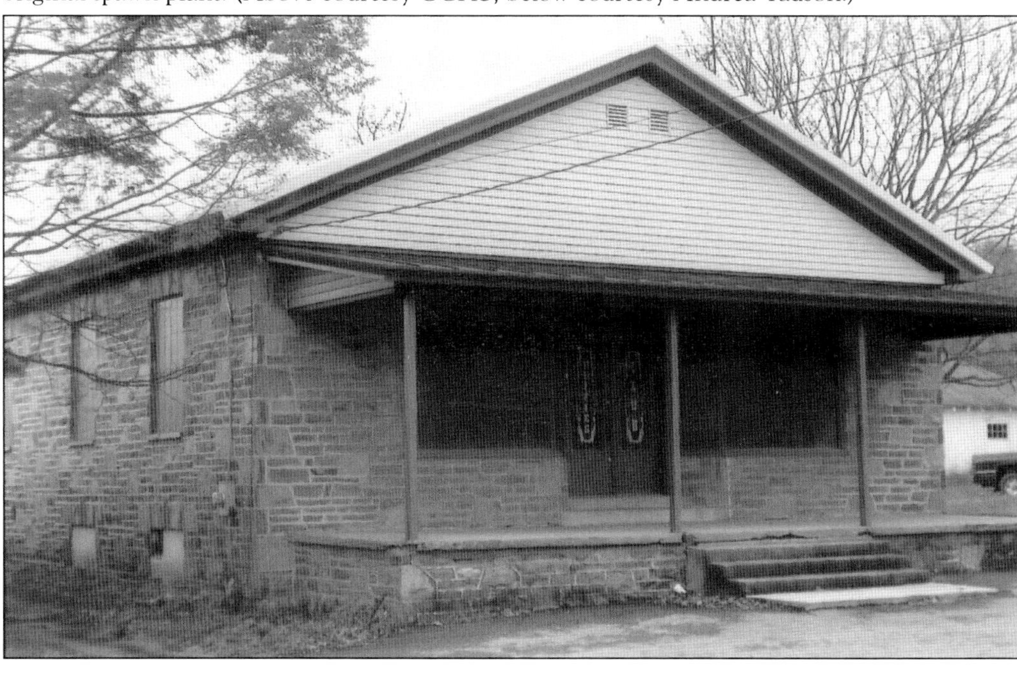

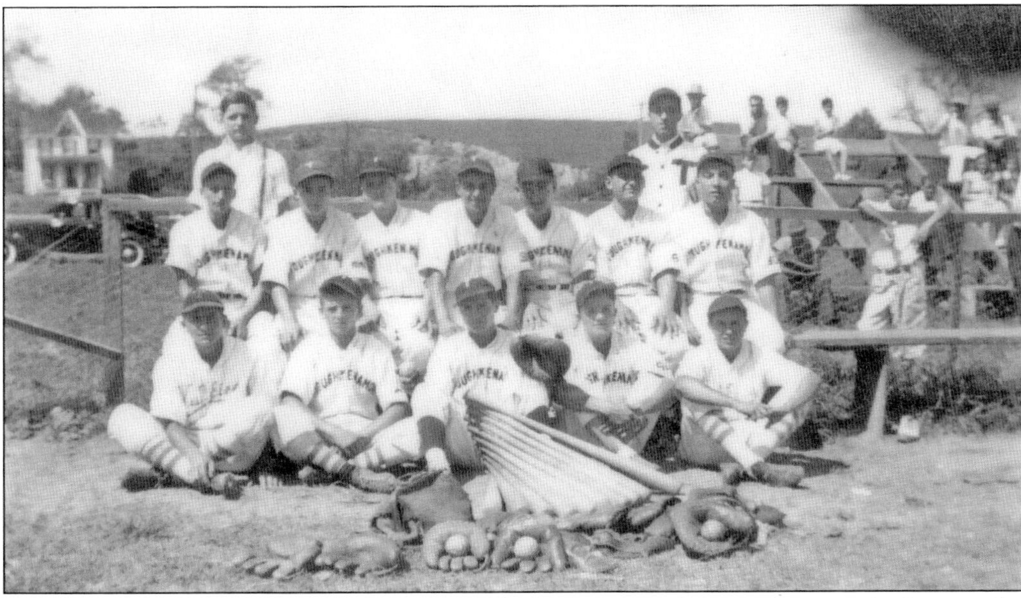

Recreational venues in the late 1800s included Morton's Woods, west of town, which catered to camp meetings and picnics. By the early 1900s it had become Reynolds Park, and hosted rifle team competitions and concerts from both the orchestra and United Cornet Band. Since the 1870s, baseball stirred local passions. For many years, semi-pro teams battled on Sunday afternoons. This team photograph from the 1940s was taken on the home field, west of Reynolds Park and south of Baltimore Pike. (Courtesy Lenny DiFilippo.)

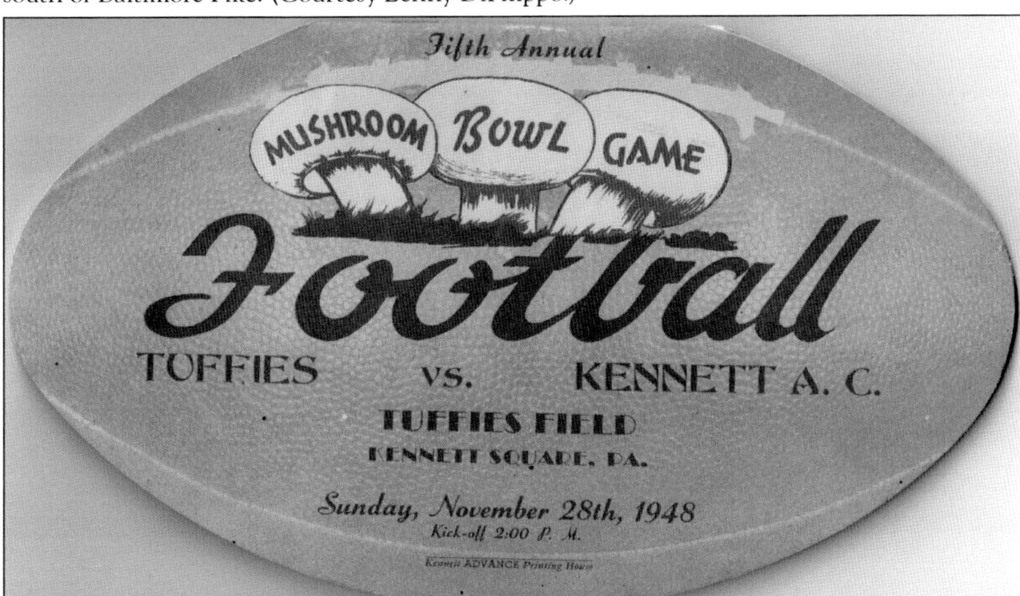

Tuffies Club began in 1944. With older teens off to war, Lenny DiFilippo proposed to start a club to host dances every Sunday night. Eventually, floor shows were added, beer was sold without a license, and three slot machines tempted weary mushroom farmers. After World War II, the club sponsored teams, the culmination of which was the Mushroom Bowl between Tuffies and Kennett Square. This program is from the 1948 contest. (Courtesy Lenny DiFilippo.)

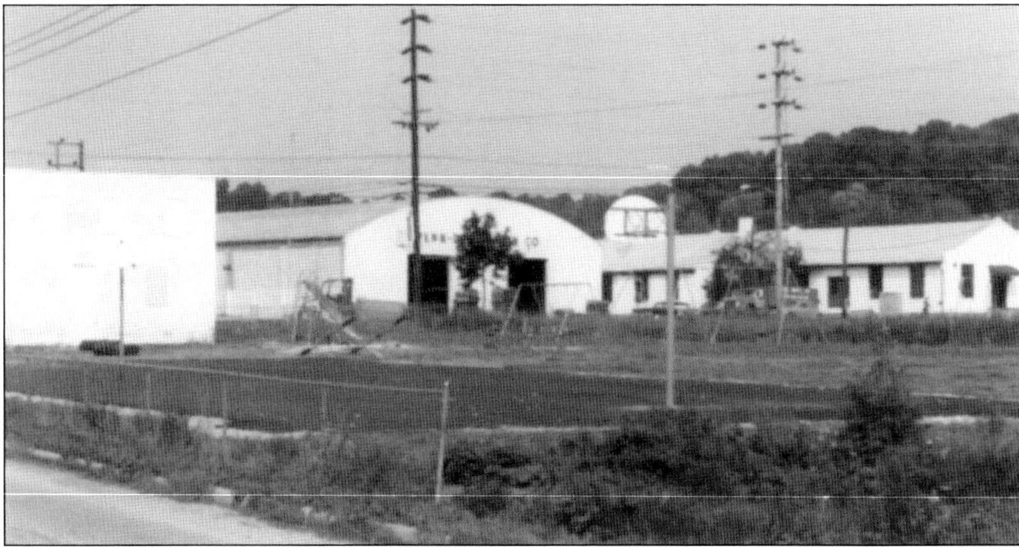

Toughkenamon native and shipping/warehouse entrepreneur Frank Manfredi described growing up in Toughkenamon during the mid-20th century. "You could walk to see your friends. You could ride your bike. You could play out in the yard, the front yard, the side yard. You knew your neighbors; you knew them well." This playground provided one place where young people at mid-century could gather. (Courtesy NGHC.)

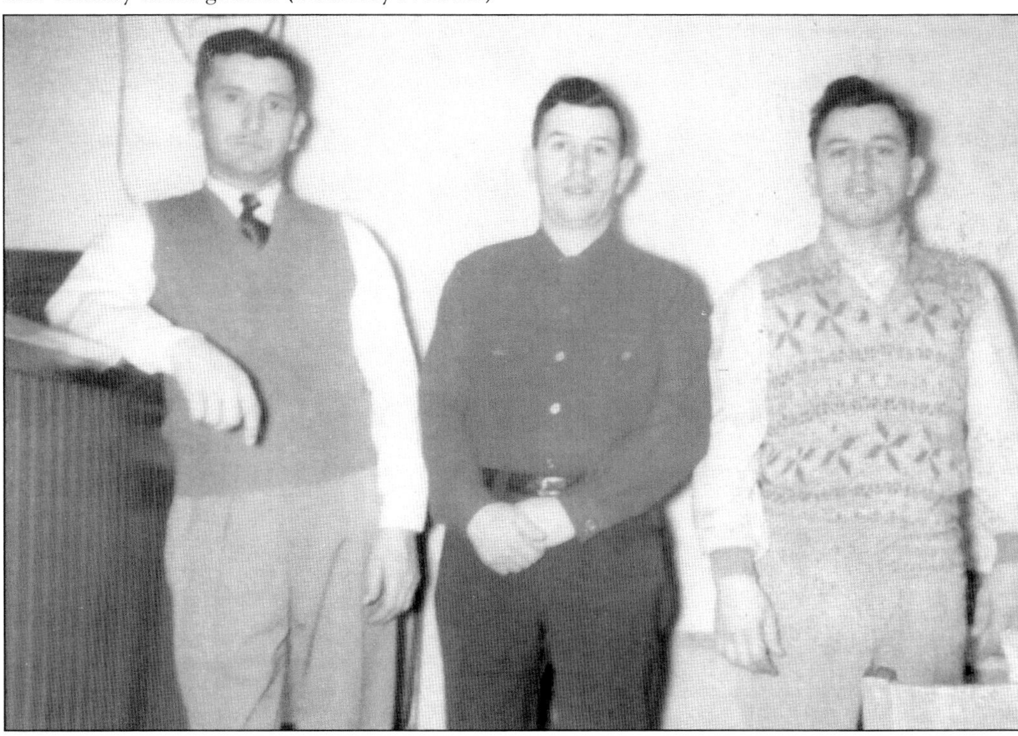

Jim Bertrando, right, remembered some of the pranks he and brothers, Angelo, left, and Bill, center, played in their youth. Returning from the movies in Kennett, "Mr. McCluskey drove the trolley car. Coming back, we'd all pile on the back of the trolley. Up front, he'd stop the car. We'd all run. We'd keep hopping on, just to get back home, and we did." (Courtesy Jim Bertrando.)

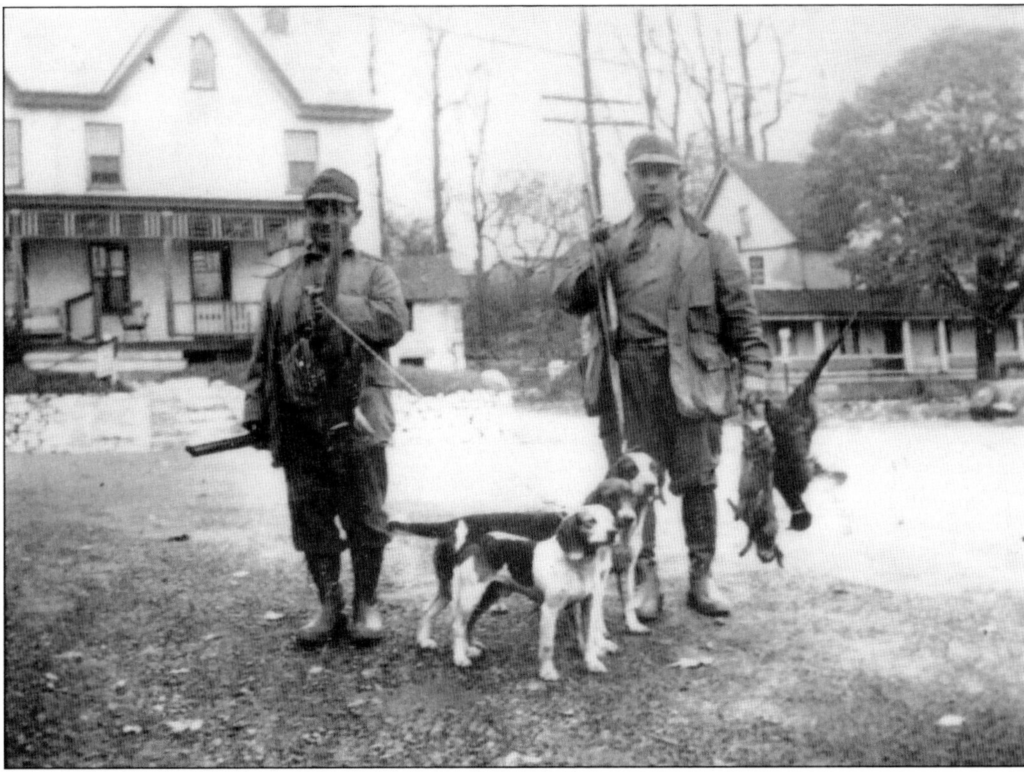

Eugene DiFilippo, right, and Rocky Manfredi pose with their hunting trophies; behind them to the right can be seen the Hammer and Trowel Inn. DiFilippo purchased Harry Owen's store in 1921, and the store remained "DiFilippo's Store" until 1999. Jim Bertrando said, "Uncle Gene's was a general store. He sold groceries, nails, shoes, pants, everything." (Courtesy Lenny DiFilippo.)

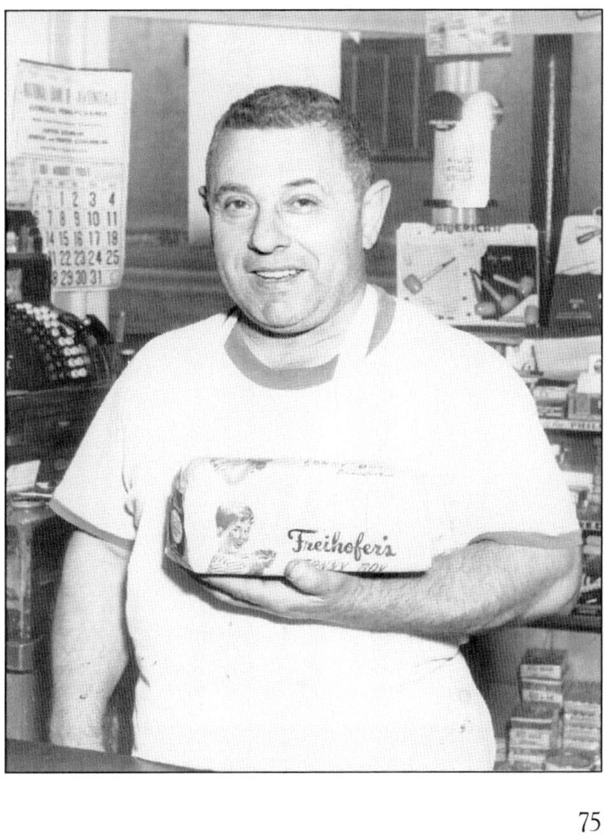

Eugene DiFilippo was more than Toughkenamon's premier storekeeper. He was also the keeper of joys and sorrows in the village. An example of his altruism was how, in collaboration with the postmaster, he created a job for a disabled man, Herford Nemo, who would go each day to the post office, collect a wheelbarrow of mail, and bring it to the store, where customers could collect their letters without a trip to the post office. (Courtesy Lenny DiFilippo.)

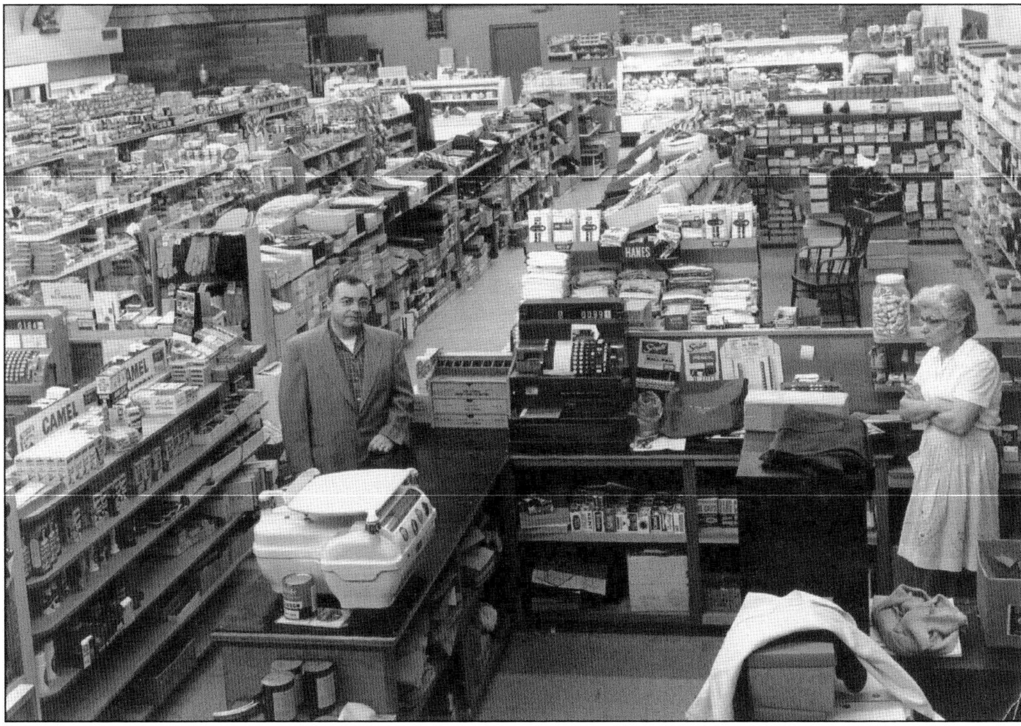

Mary DiFilippo was usually to be found behind the cash register of DiFilippo's store, which was a family enterprise. In this picture, elder son "Junior" (Eugene) is standing at the counter. Gene would be everywhere, stocking shelves and greeting customers. Younger brother Lenny delivered groceries to those who had called in their orders. Later, as store butcher, he trimmed meat on a block and ground sausage in a grinder, both devices from the 19th century. (Courtesy Lenny DiFilippo.)

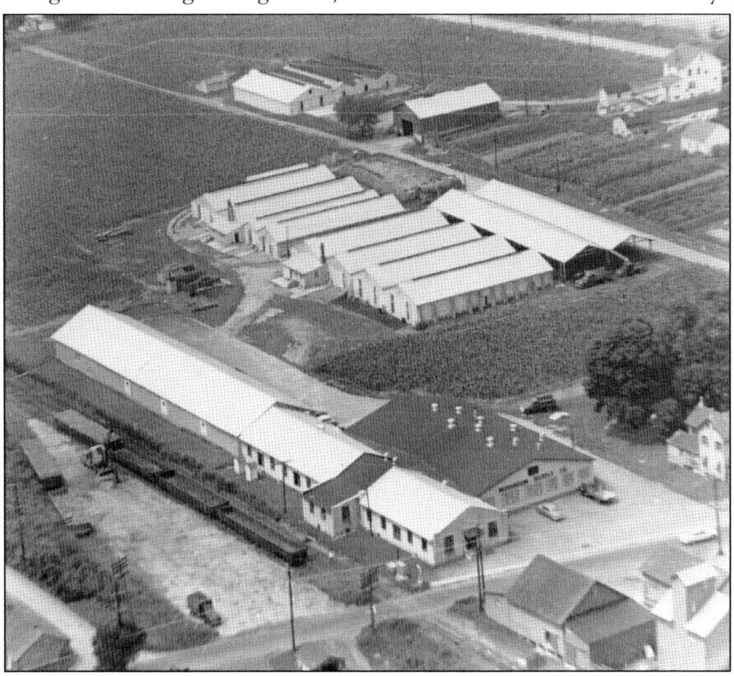

A 1940s view of west Toughkenamon shows Baltimore Pike at the top, Mushroom Supply Company in the foreground, and south of it, the railroad siding where gondolas of horse manure (for compost) were unloaded. Bertrando's mushroom plant sits north of Mushroom Supply; close inspection reveals the outline of Ed Yetter's race track circling the mushroom houses. To the east of Newark Road is Wilson and Brosius's feed mill, lumber, and coal yard. (Courtesy NGTHC.)

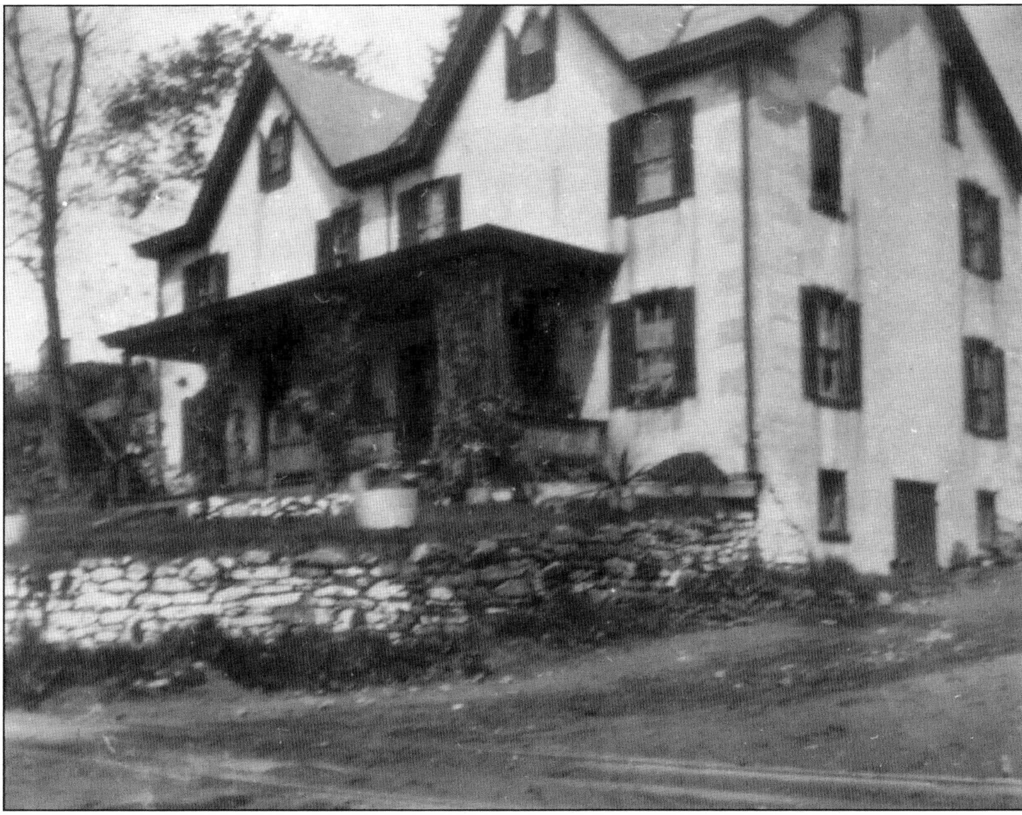

This stone house stood in Toughkenamon on the northwest corner of the intersection of Newark Road and the Baltimore Pike. Early records note that before 1850, Toughkenamon consisted of three houses, a store, and the Hammer and Trowel; this house was probably one of those buildings. During much of the early 20th century, Benny LeCourte owned and lived in the house, maintaining a barbershop in a downstairs front room. (Courtesy NGTHC.)

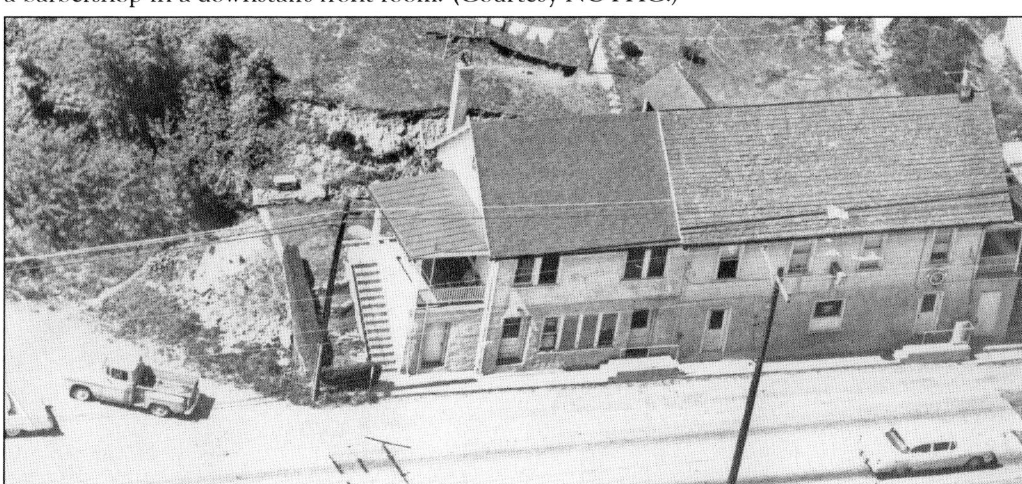

This aerial shot of Baltimore Pike west of Newark Road shows a building Harry Owens owned in 1883. At that time it was described as a barn, but by the early 20th century, it had become an ice cream store. Later it became a taproom, with apartments above, owned by Nick Piergiovanni. (Courtesy NGTHC.)

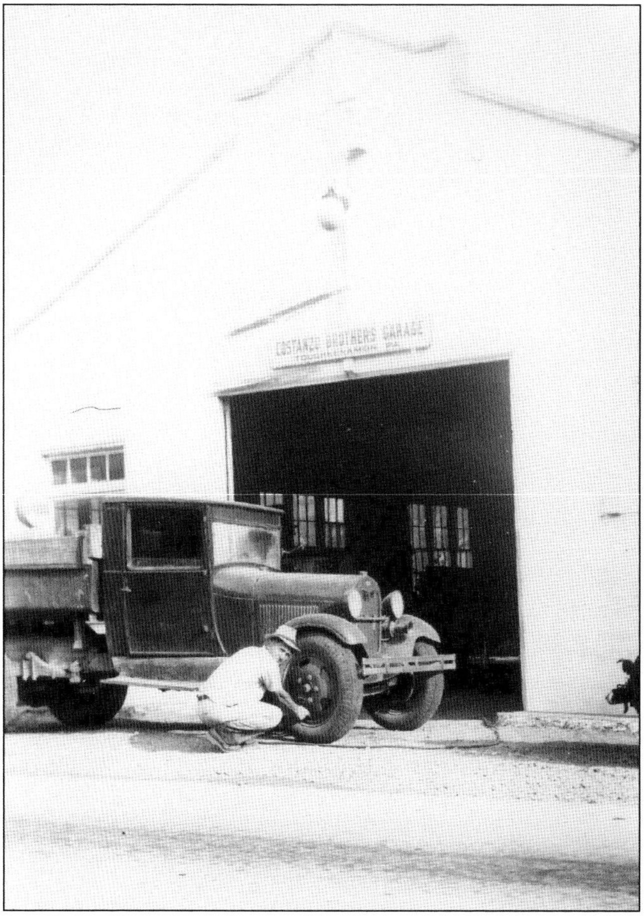

The coming of the automobile eclipsed the services of the livery stable and created the need for gas stations and garages for servicing cars. The Costanzo brothers' garage was located west of Toughkenamon's main intersection on Baltimore Pike. Long after its gas station function ended, the building continued to be used for auto and tire repair. (Courtesy Jim Bertrando.)

Another garage and service station, located on the east side of Toughkenamon along Baltimore Pike, was remembered for its distinctive roofline. Owned in the 1920s by Frank Vattilano, the garage also housed a Hudson automobile dealership. By the mid-20th century, the building was known as Wayside Market, selling fruit and vegetables. (Courtesy Steve Allaband.)

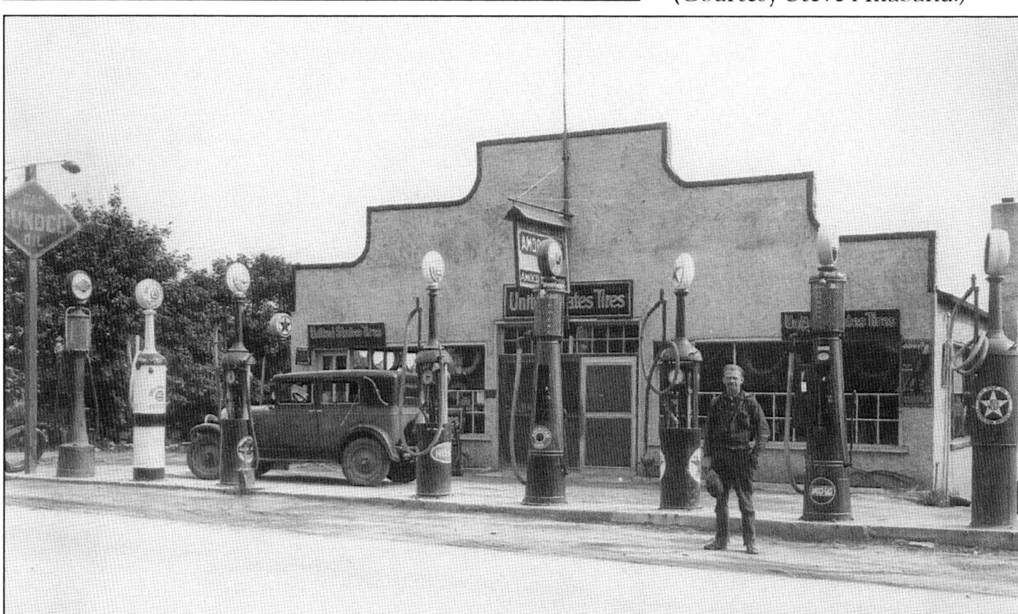

Five

Rural Life

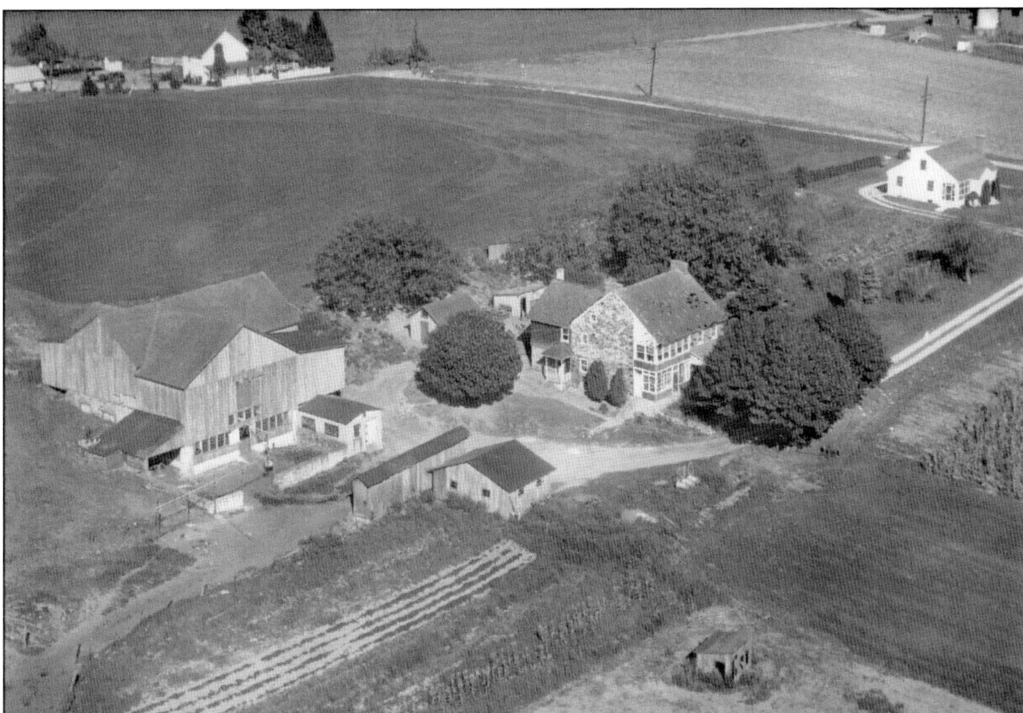

This aerial photograph of the Barclay Hoopes farm shows a typical New Garden dairy farm with many single-use buildings—dairy barn, bull barn, chicken house, corncrib, machinery shed, and dwelling house. The dairy industry did not develop until the later part of the 19th century, when creameries were built in both Landenberg and Toughkenamon and the railroads could carry milk to city markets. By 1900, there were about 100 small dairy farms in the township; each dairy might have 10 to 20 milking cows. Farmers diversified; they would milk cows, raise chickens and hogs, and grow a variety of field crops. Before mechanization, farming was labor intensive. A typical 80-acre farm would require several hands in addition to the farmer. Often large families contributed to this need for farm labor. (Courtesy Barclay Hoopes.)

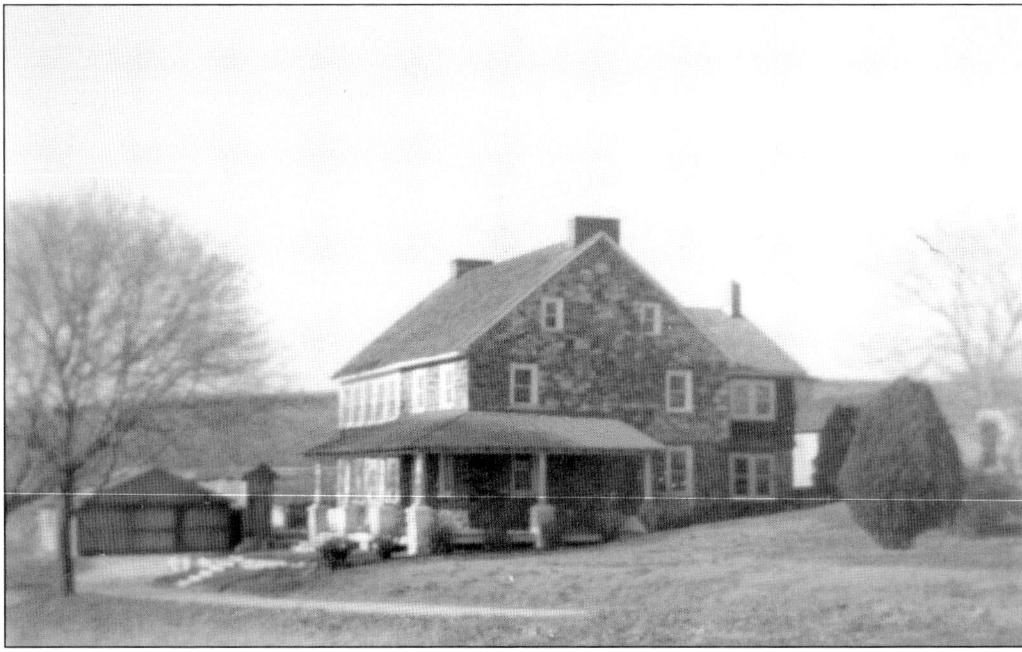

The Hoopes farm, on Walnut Run Road near Landenberg, was created in 1803, when Swithin Shortlidge assembled several small tracts; around 1811, he built his stone house. In 1854, the farm was purchased by David Owens, father-in-law of the first Barclay Hoopes. Throughout the 20th century, the farm remained in the Hoopes family. (Courtesy Barclay Hoopes.)

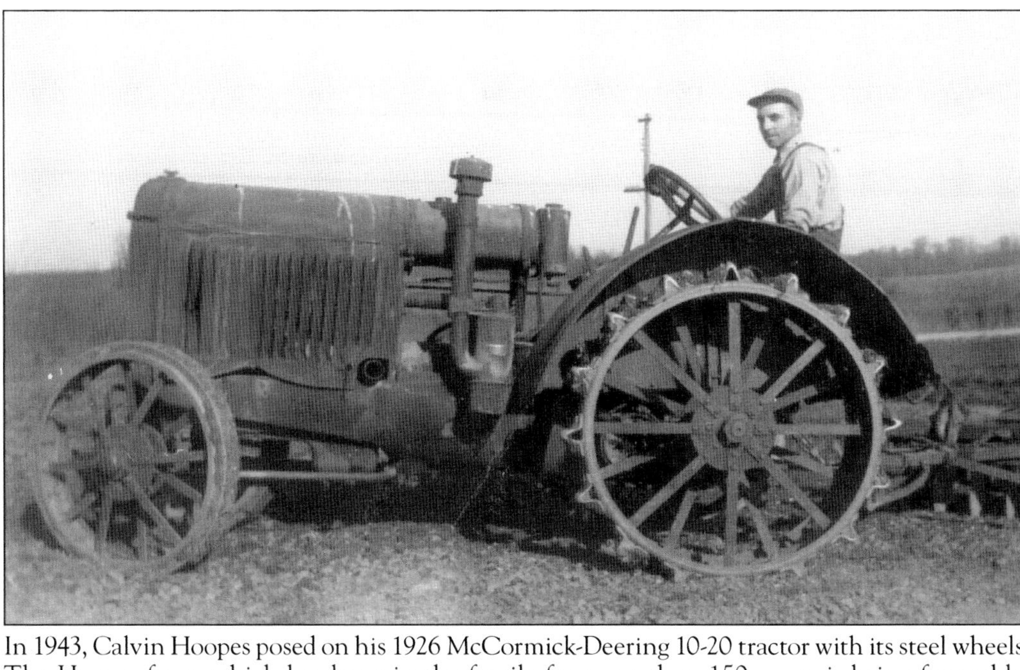

In 1943, Calvin Hoopes posed on his 1926 McCormick-Deering 10-20 tractor with its steel wheels. The Hoopes farm, which has been in the family for more than 150 years, is being farmed by the sixth generation. Preserved in an agricultural easement, the land will forever be farmland. (Courtesy Barclay Hoopes.)

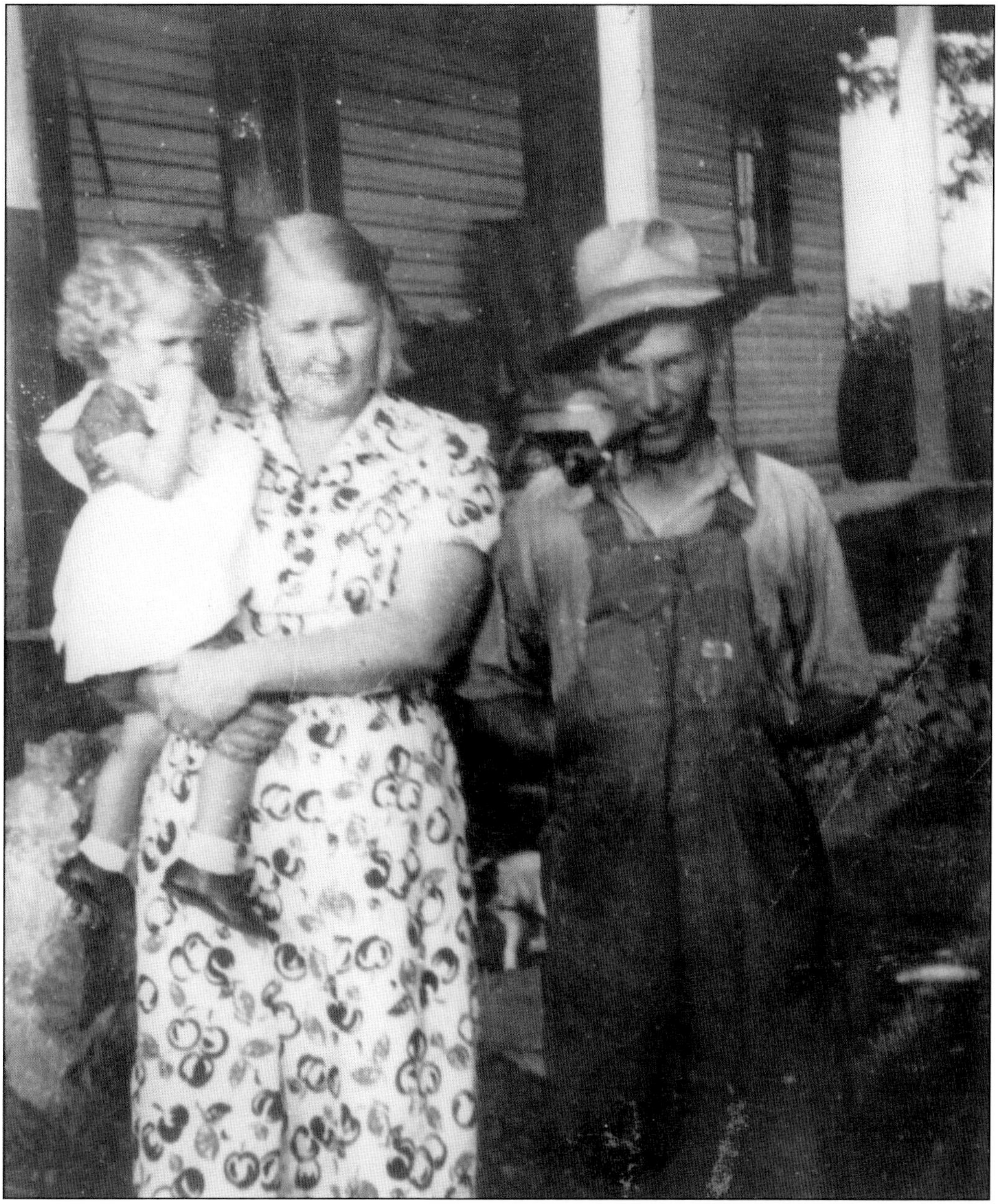

Most farms had one or two tenant farmers whose labor would supplement that of the farmer and his sons. Here George Robbins, who worked for Cornelius Quill, poses with his wife, Fanny, holding their niece, Joan Bitler. The couple reared her as their own daughter. In the days before agricultural mechanization, when farm equipment was horse-drawn and cows were milked by hand, tenant farmers like Robbins were a vital part of the farm economy. In return for everyday year-round labor, a farmer would supply a house, garden, and chicken yard, plus usually coal or wood for heating and cooking, and sometimes food, like a winter's supply of potatoes, in addition to a weekly salary. The tenant's wife might receive the farmer's printed chicken feedbags for dressmaking. Tenant farmers sometimes remained on a single farm all their working days; others moved frequently. April 1 was always designated moving day. (Courtesy Joan B. Procino.)

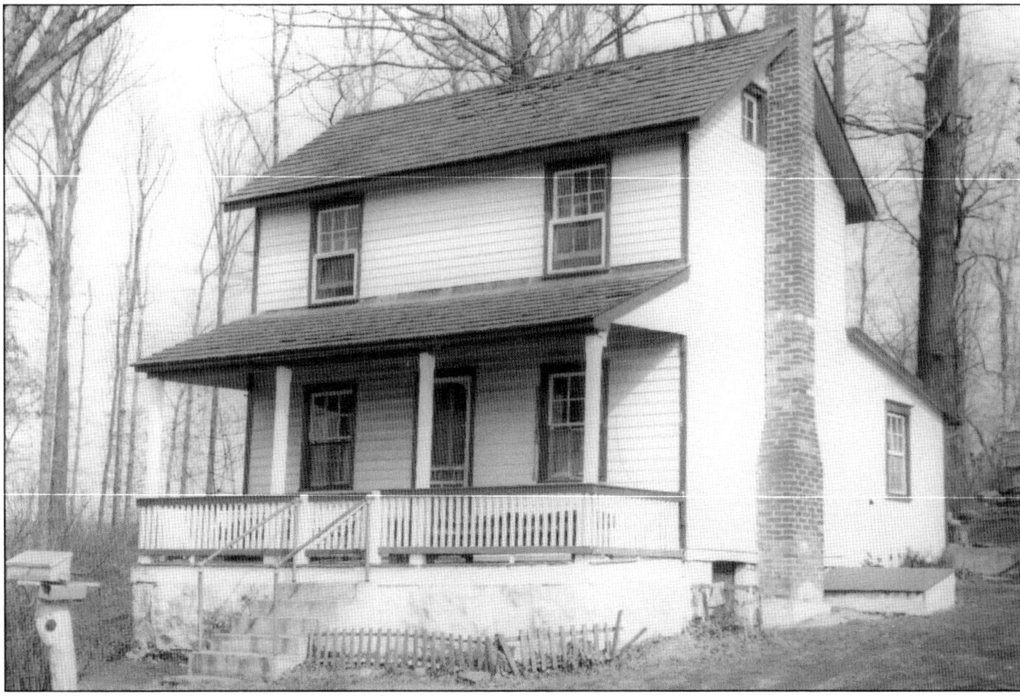

James Mendenhall built his new tenant house along Newark Road in 1879. Typical of tenant houses, it had four rooms and a lean-to kitchen. (Courtesy Margaret Jones.)

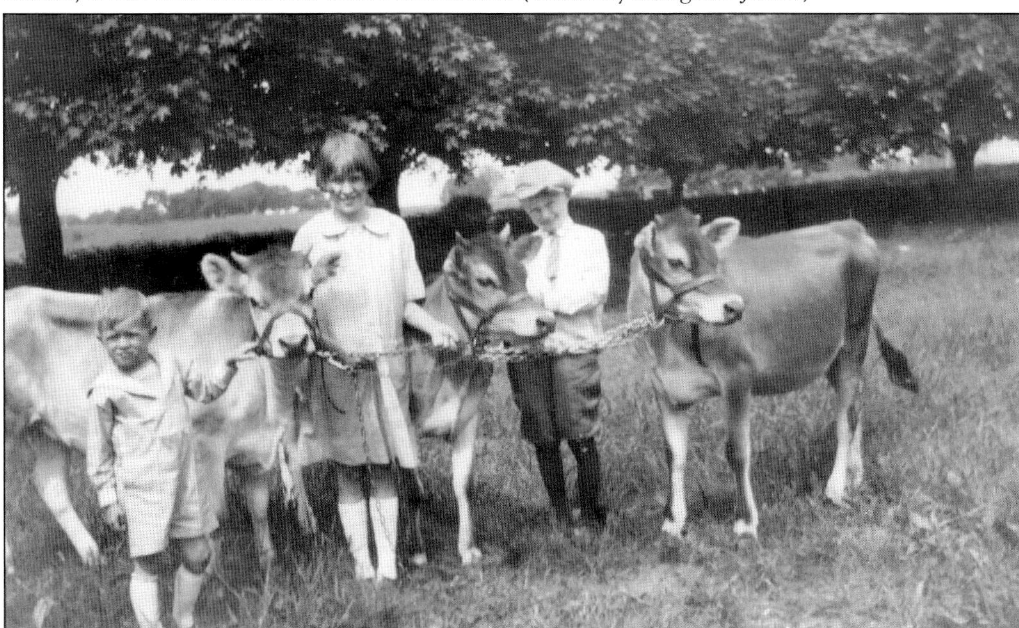

Dairy farming was very restrictive; cows needed to be milked twice daily. Frequently activity in the barn was the center of family life, with calves becoming family pets. Here about 1930, Charles, Eleanor, and Paul, children of Howard and Ellen Wollaston, pose with their Jersey calves. The Wollaston family had Jersey cows for almost 100 years, for three generations of dairymen and women. (Courtesy Peggy Empet.)

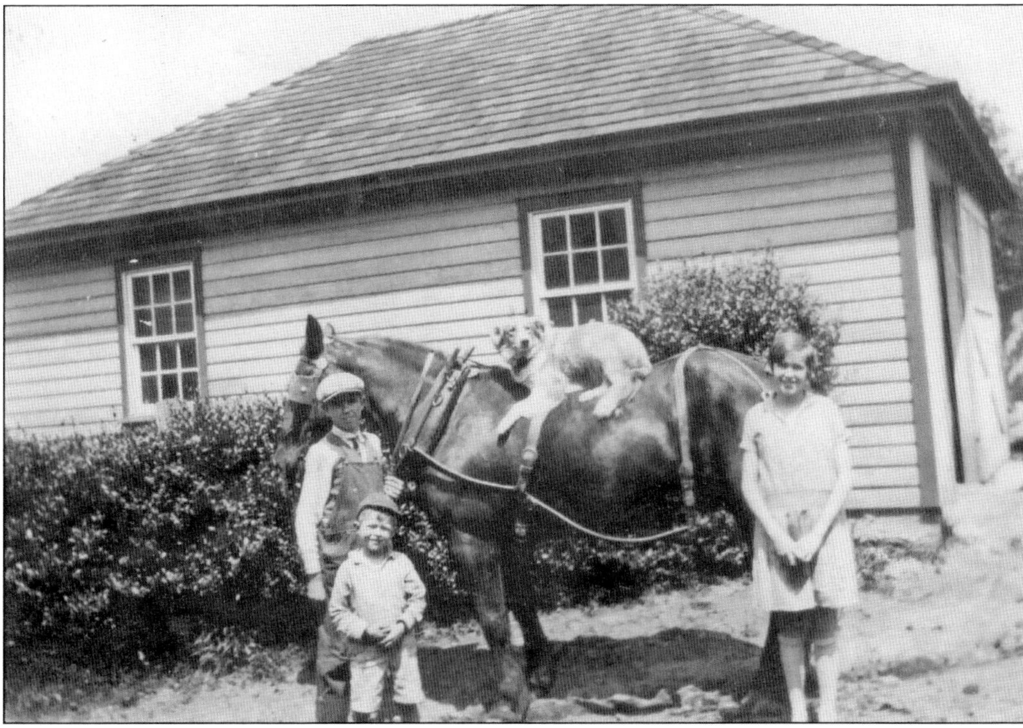

Until the late 1930s, most farmers used horses and mules. Only with the coming of tractors and other mechanized equipment did the dray animals gradually disappear. Like the cows, these became pets, playmates for children whose horizons did not extend much beyond the farm. This picture from the 1930s shows the Wollaston children of Maple Lawn Farm posing with their pets. (Courtesy Peggy Empet.)

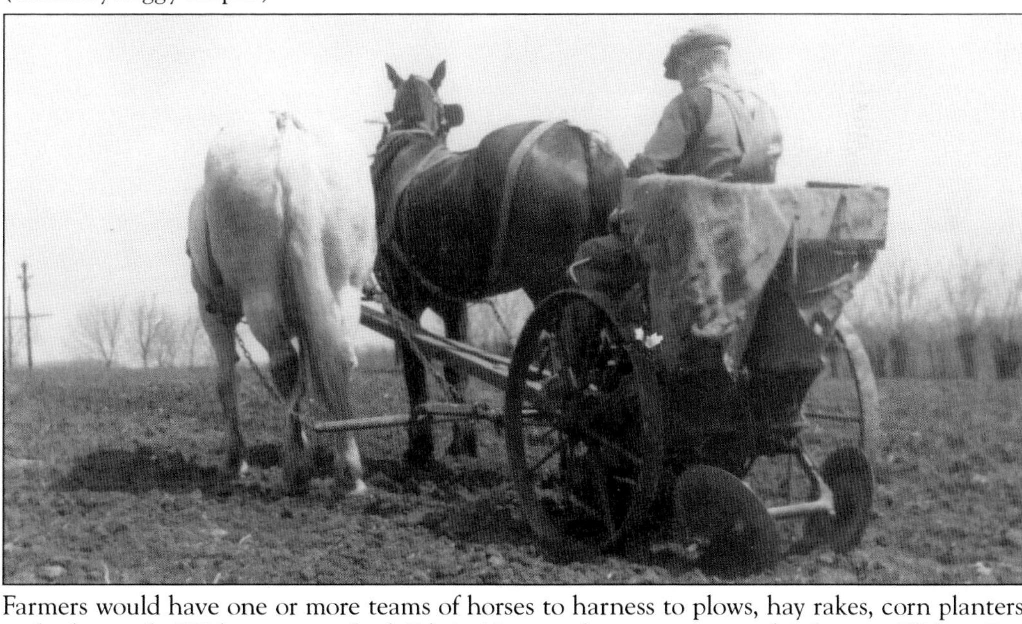

Farmers would have one or more teams of horses to harness to plows, hay rakes, corn planters, and other tools. With team attached, Edwin Hoopes plants potatoes on his farm on Walnut Run Road around 1930. (Courtesy Barclay Hoopes.)

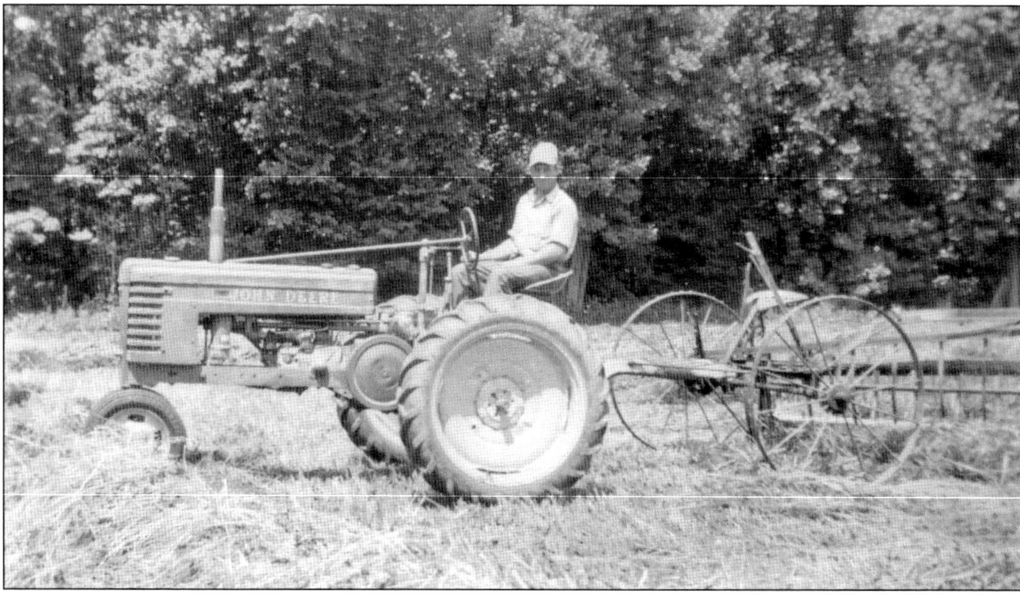

Charles Sproat of Bancroft Road rakes hay with his John Deere tractor. Sproat was not only a farmer but in the 1930s–1940s was also supervisor and road master for New Garden Township. (Courtesy Mary Sproat.)

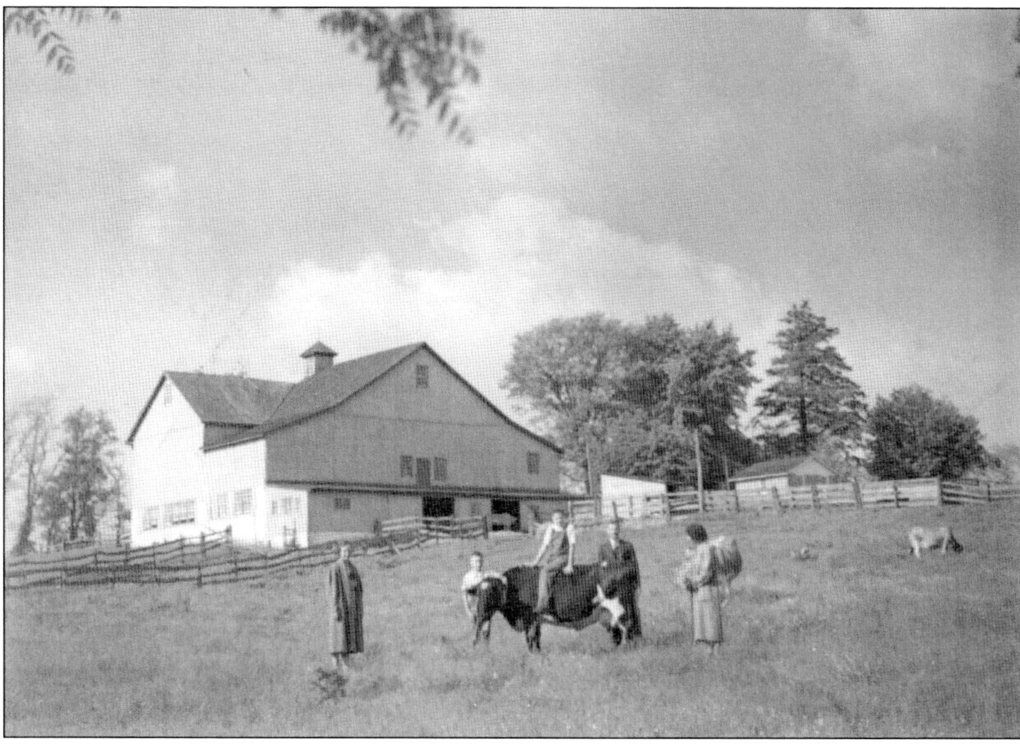

In this 1933 picture of the Gordon Jones family, son Pownall is astride a cow while his parents and guests admire his skill. The Jones bank barn on New Garden Road was typical of township dairy barns of the 19th and 20th centuries—stone walls with frame siding. The upper structure of these barns was storage for hay, straw, and grain. (Courtesy Margaret Jones.)

Farm children felt lucky if they had access to a stream in which to play on hot summer afternoons. Here, about 1928, Frank and Anna Lafferty's children stop their play in one of three streams that crossed their property to pose for the camera. (Courtesy Ed Lafferty.)

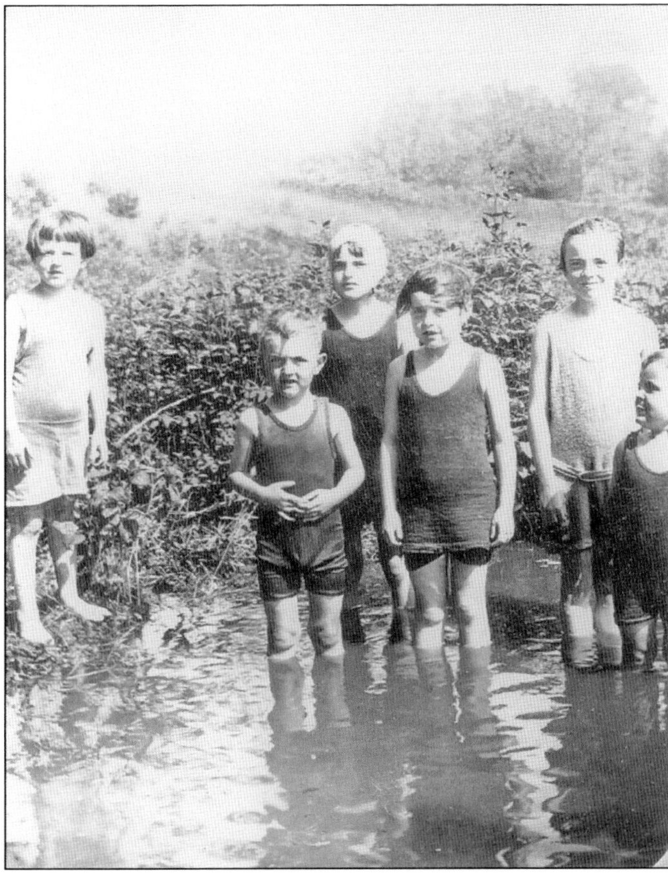

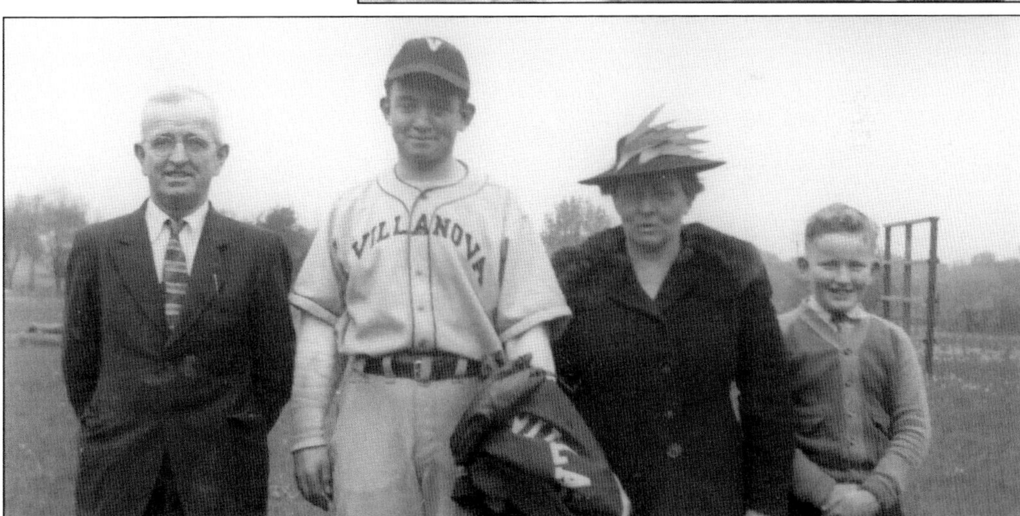

Baseball was a favorite sport among rural families; the boys played on teams while parents and siblings cheered. Many locals spent Sunday afternoons at the diamond watching fierce competitions. James Lafferty, all suited up as a freshman pitcher at Villanova University, walks off the field with his parents, Louis and Mamie Lafferty, and little brother William. The Yankees offered Lafferty a tryout. He joined the navy instead. (Courtesy James Lafferty.)

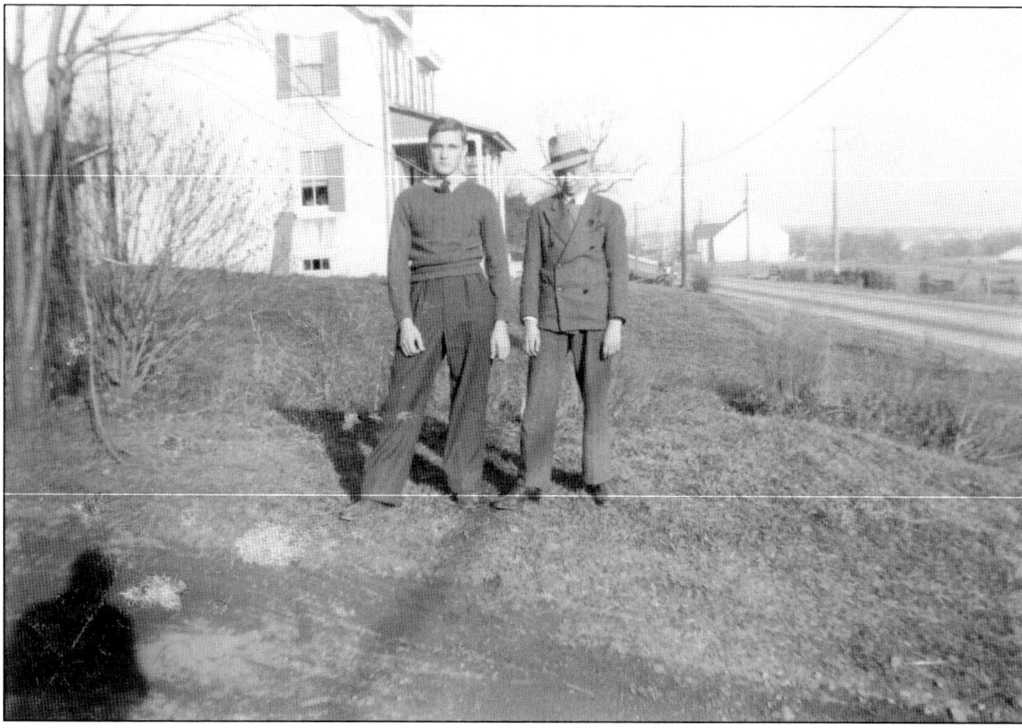

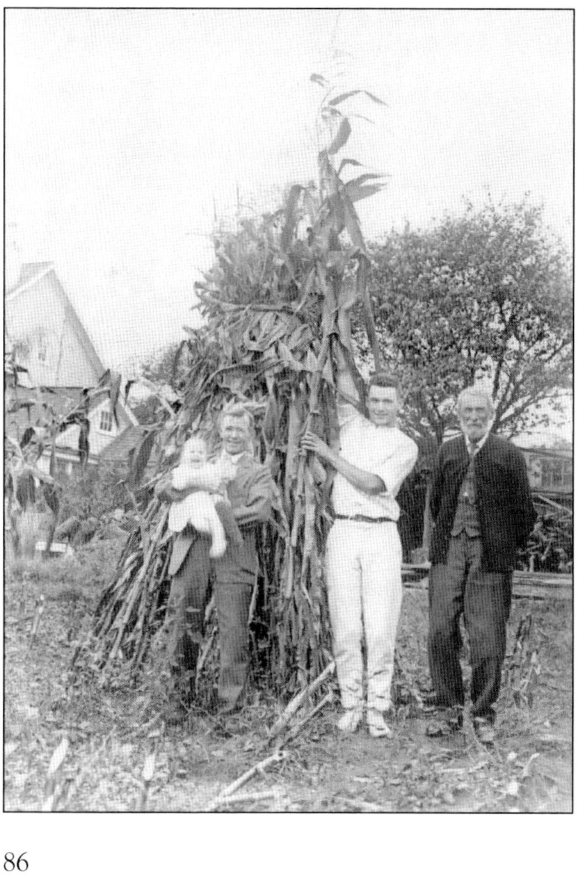

In the 1940s, Toughkenamon teenagers Lewis Taylor (right) and Ike Smith pose in front of the Taylor home along the empty Baltimore Pike. The Taylor home was a tenant house on the Richards farm, whose immense barn can be seen in the background. (Courtesy Lewis Taylor.)

Corn clubs, the precursor of 4-H clubs, provided opportunities for farm boys to learn farming techniques in a spirit of camaraderie. Here about 1918, Gordon Jones shows off his tall stalk of corn next to his father, Charles Jones, who holds granddaughter Ethel. On Gordon's left is his maternal grandfather, Benjamin H. Pownall. (Courtesy Margaret Jones.)

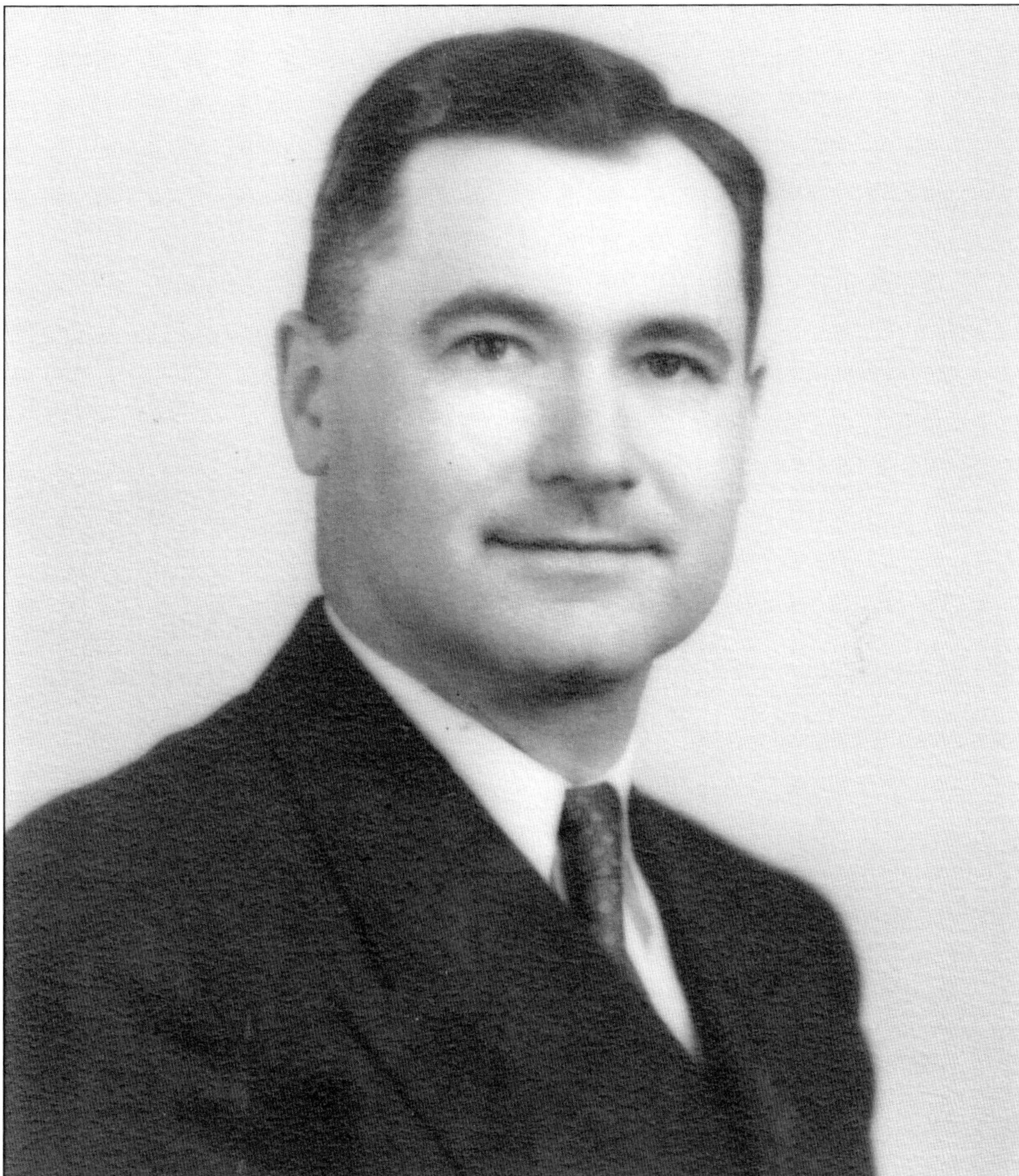

Gordon P. Jones (1900–1988) was a leader in both the agricultural and in the wider Quaker communities. Instrumental in establishing a chapter of the Future Farmers of America (FFA) at Kennett High School, he sponsored the local 4-H club, which met at New Garden Meeting House. Believing that the cooperative movement could increase farmers' purchasing and marketing power, he devoted his life to that end. He was a founder and, for 40 years, secretary-treasurer of the Chester County Dairymen's Cooperative Association, helping farmers as a group to negotiate the price paid for their milk. Jones also served as director and secretary of the Chester-Delaware Farm Bureau Cooperative Association, which bought farm supplies in bulk and passed the savings on to its membership. A member of New Garden Meeting, he was known for his leadership role and for his oral ministry. From 1942 to 1949, he was clerk of the Philadelphia Yearly Meeting of Friends. Gordon Jones wrote a book, *Christian Living in Rural Communities*, which elaborated on his belief that farming the land and caring for livestock was God's work. (Courtesy Margaret Jones.)

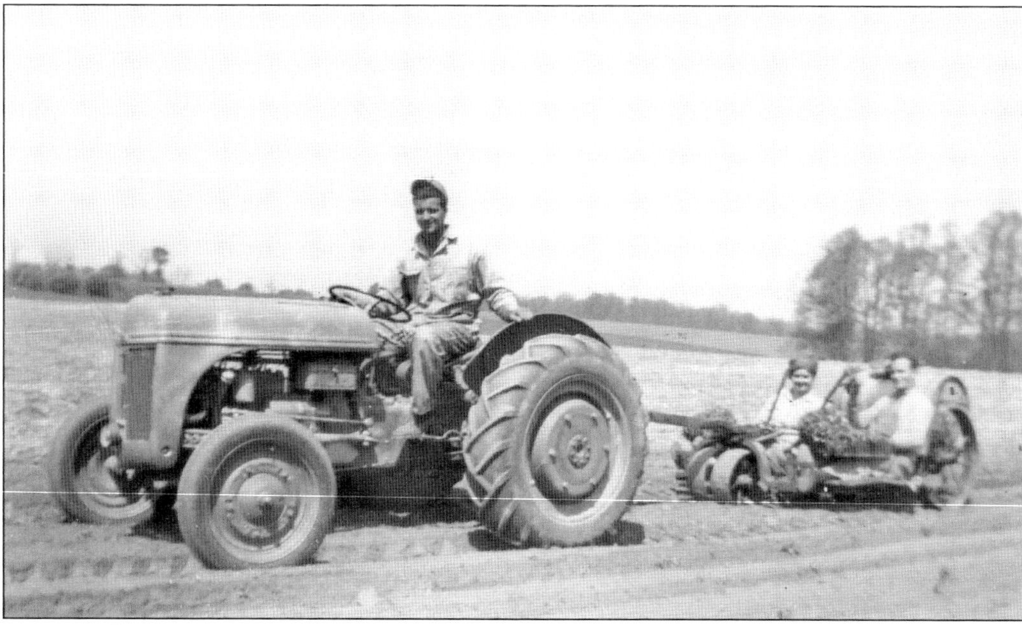

In 1941, John Pia planted 44,000 tomato plants to supply the Campbell Soup Company. The trip to the Camden cannery was long. Delivery hours were limited to between 8:00 a.m. and 4:00 p.m. To spare his father the constant round-the-clock routine of picking tomatoes, loading, traveling, and delivery, 13-year-old Lou drove the route. In later years, Lou said, "I was very careful. I didn't get out of the truck. I didn't have a driver's license." (Courtesy Lou Pia.)

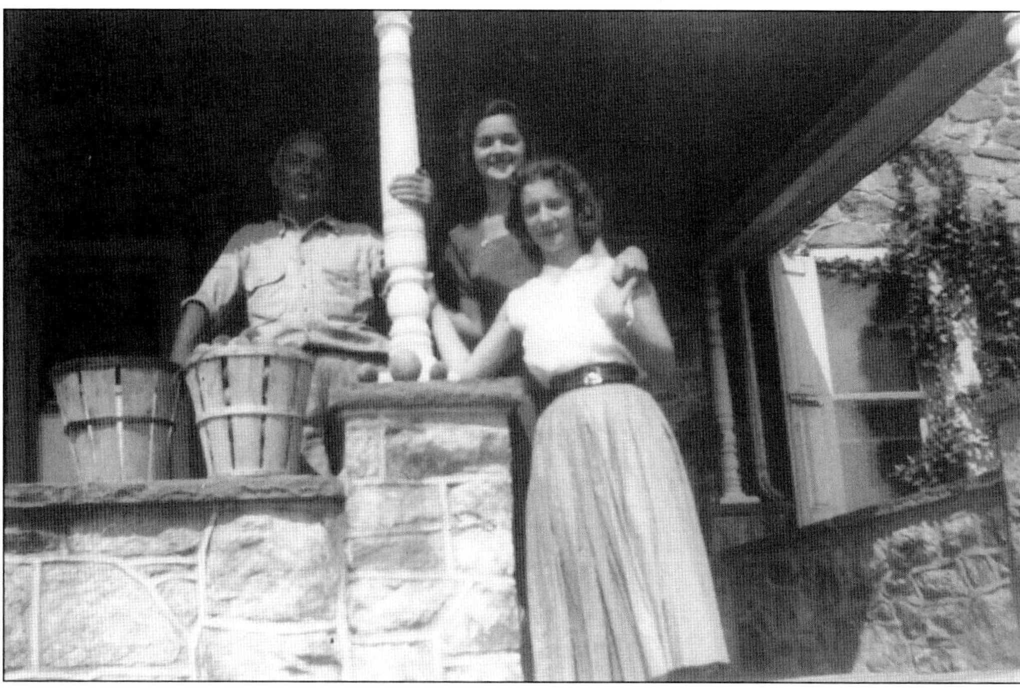

Before raising mushrooms, John Pia took pride in his smooth, round tomatoes. Standing on his front porch with his daughter Joan and daughter-in-law Norma (on the steps), he shows off the produce soon headed for Campbell's Soups in Camden, New Jersey. (Courtesy Lou Pia.)

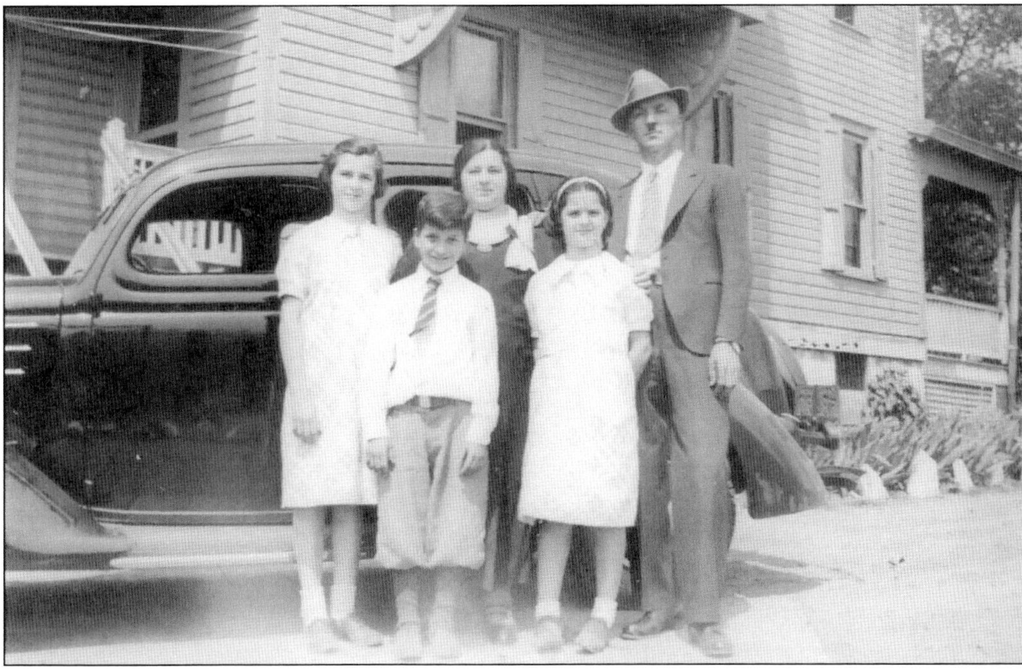

In 1940, John and Josephine Pia purchased the old Taylor farm and moved their family—Joan, Yolanda, and Louis—into the big stone house built by George W. Taylor. Initially, John Pia housed a dairy in the stone barn along the highway, but in 1941, when Route 41 was being rebuilt, crossing construction became such a nuisance that he sold the cows and concentrated on farming and growing mushrooms. (Courtesy Lou Pia.)

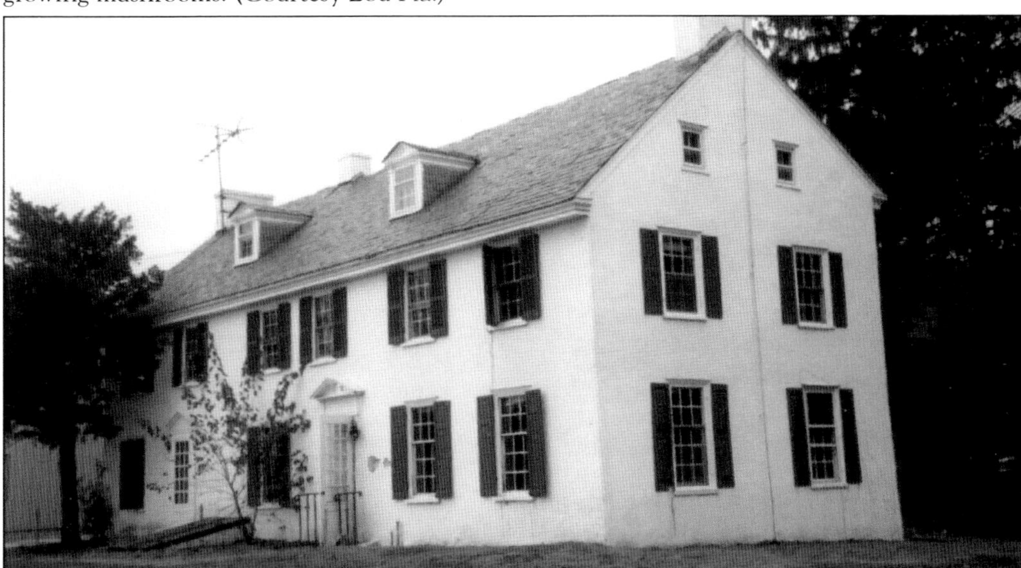

This house, owned by the Brown family from 1811 to 1883, stood at the intersection of Limestone and Southwood Roads, the township's Delaware border. Built by David Hoopes in 1770, the original small stone house withstood a British threat when troops camped nearby enroute to the Battle of Brandywine in 1777. Legend holds that Hoopes and other farmers offered the soldiers cattle in exchange for the safety of their buildings. (Courtesy Margaret Jones.)

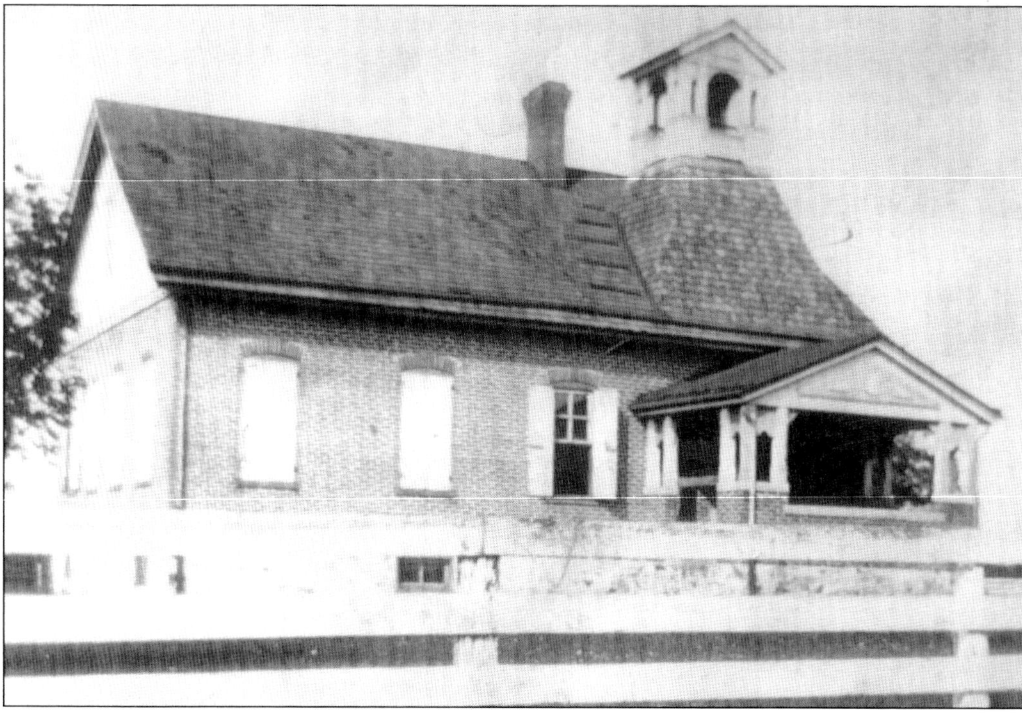

The Central Grammar School, sometimes called the New Garden School, was located at the corner of New Garden Road and Route 41 next to the Lyceum House. Built in 1900 when the Lyceum House schoolroom became too crowded, it extended to the 10th grade. Only in use for a decade, the building was sold in 1911 to Benjamin Walton, who remodeled it into a dwelling. (Courtesy NGTHC.)

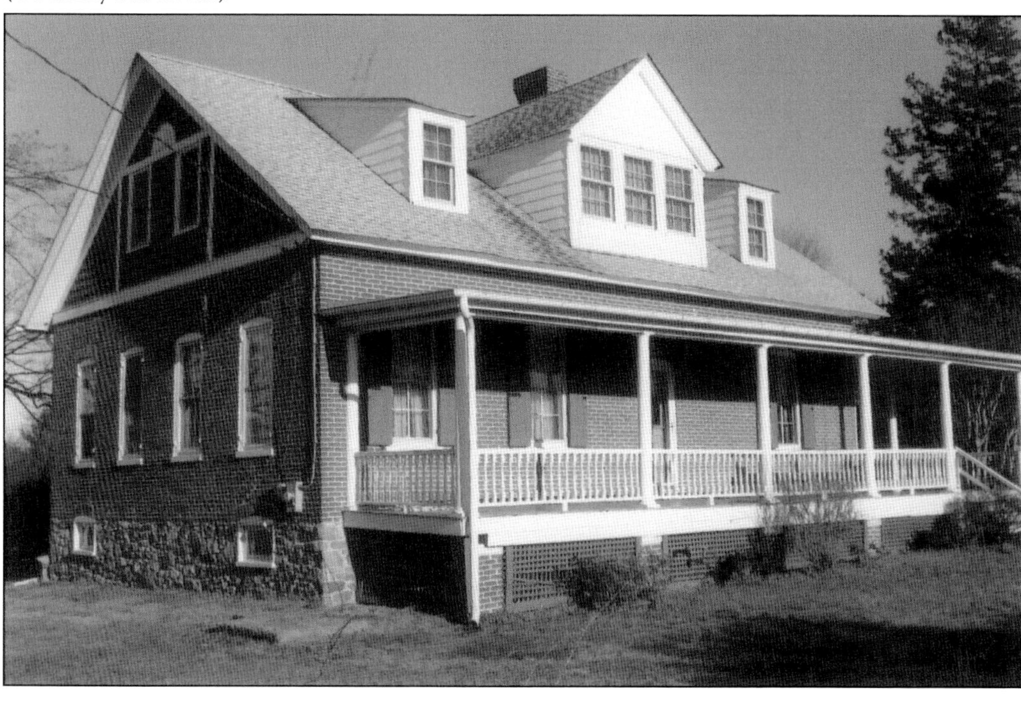

In the early 1930s, Pownall Jones takes his cousin, Barbara, for a ride in his pony cart on the Jones family's Crestfield Farm, just west of New Garden Village. (Courtesy Margaret Jones.)

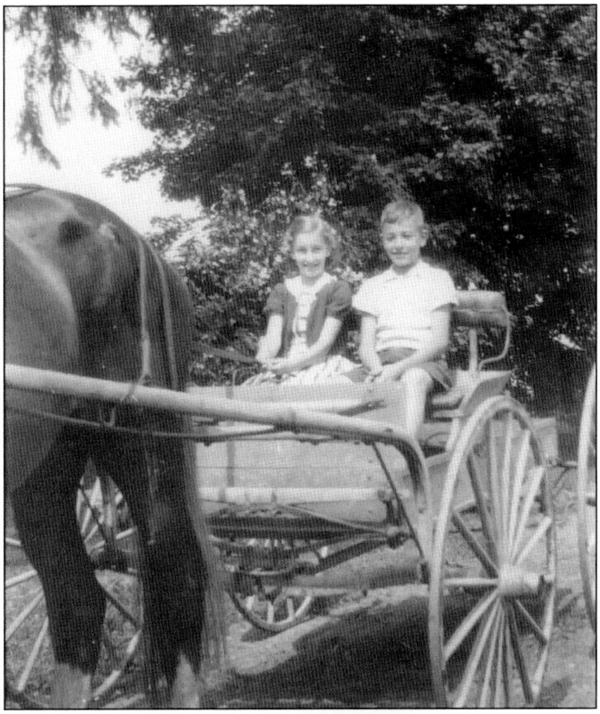

Charlie Wollaston stands with his dog in front of the sloping barn bridge, which led into the haymow of the barn on Starr Road. The barn was built about 1905 by his grandfather, Thomas E. Wollaston. (Courtesy Peggy Empet.)

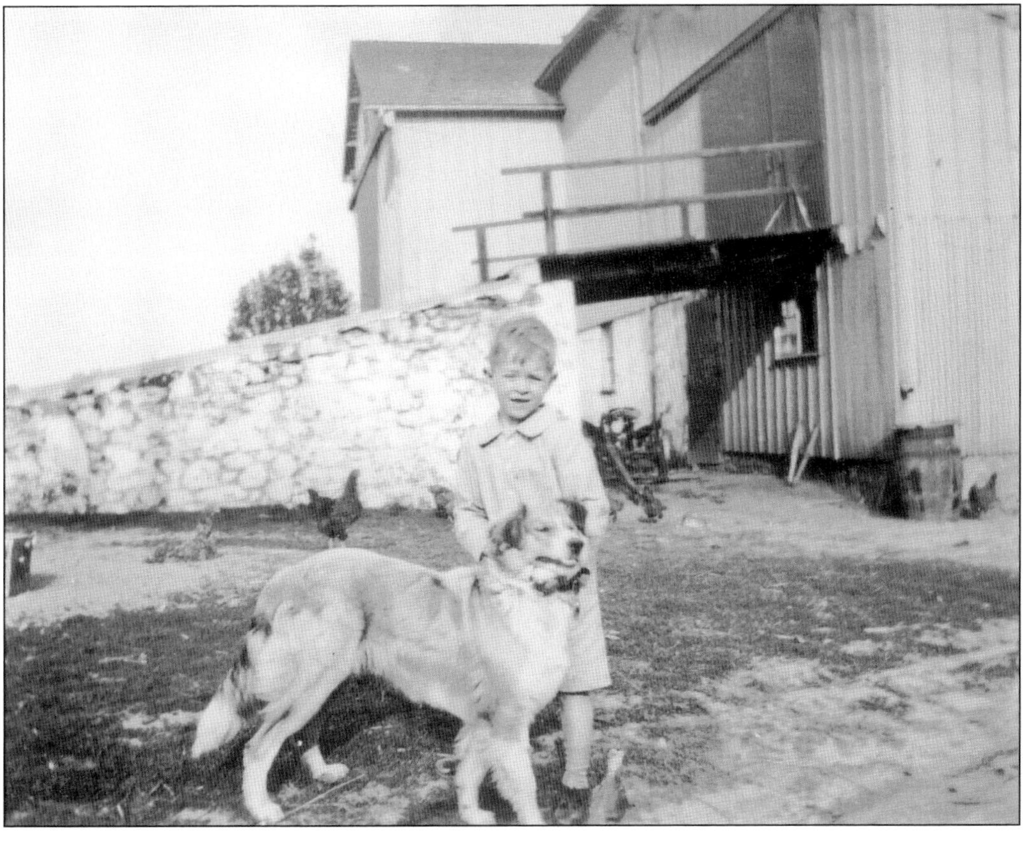

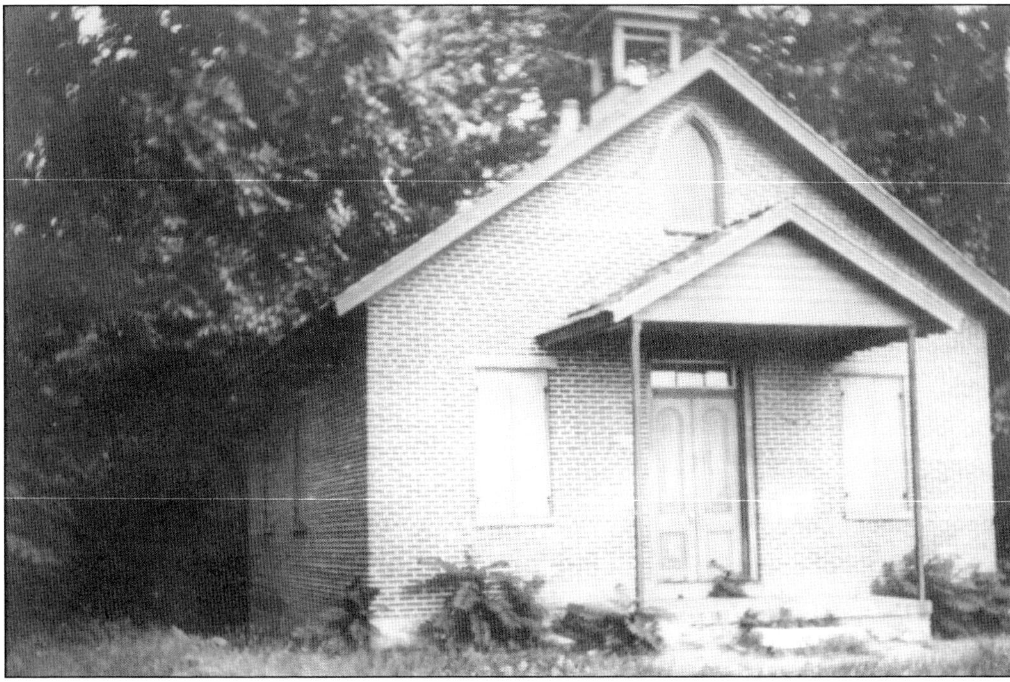

Greenwood Dell School, located on Hillendale Road just west of Thompson Road, was built in the 1860s. Typical of the one-room schoolhouses in New Garden Township, it served children who could walk 1 to 2 miles to school. Closed in 1932 when the Kennett consolidation occurred, it was renovated for a dwelling. (Courtesy CCHS.)

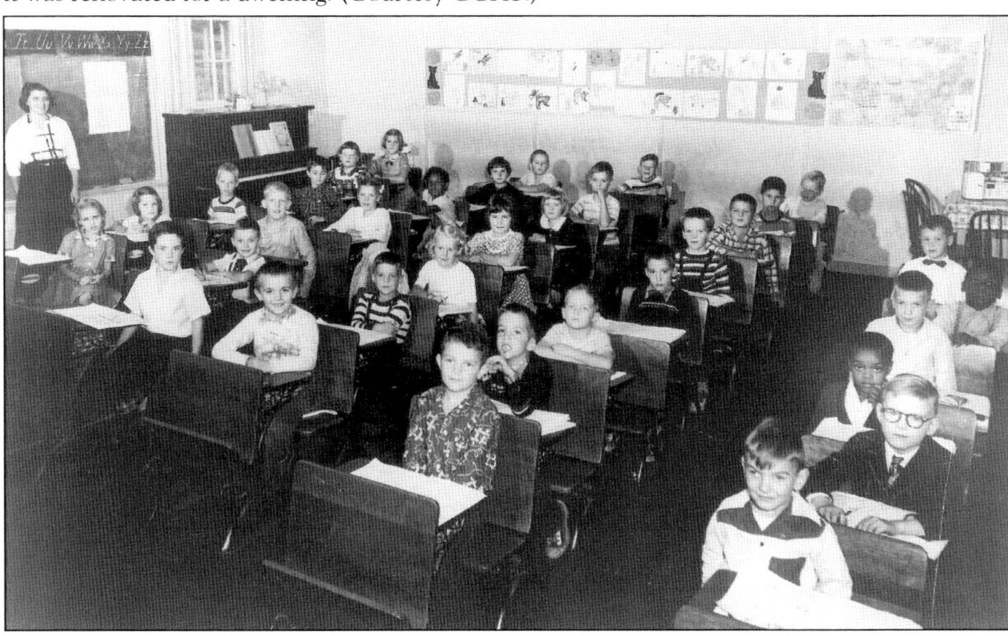

New Garden had a number of nearly identical one-room schools dating from the early 1800s. Students clustered by grade from first to eighth and shared one large classroom, a cloakroom, and an outside privy behind the building. Teachers taught all grades; older students helped younger ones. (Courtesy Alma Rigler.)

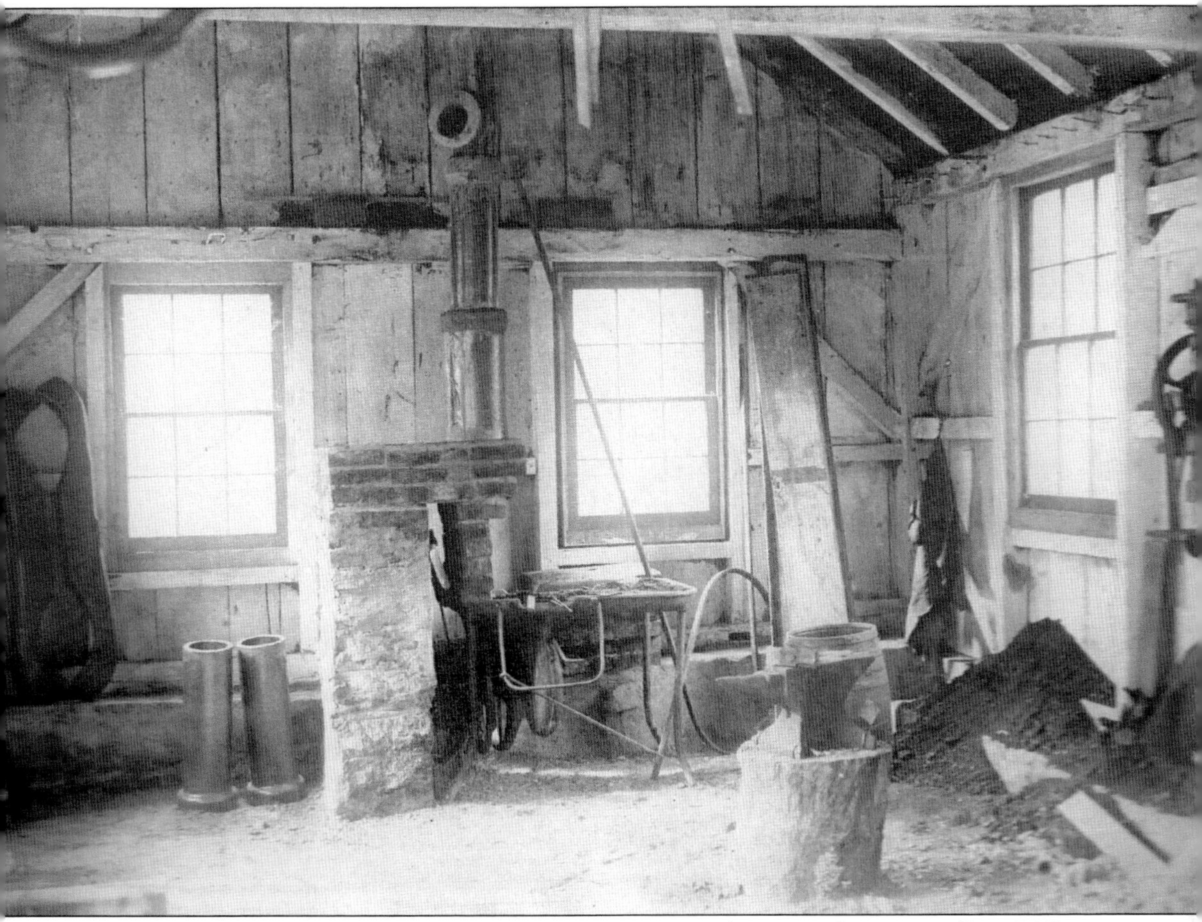

In 1799, the first blacksmith recorded on tax rolls in New Garden Township was William Miller. Miller's smithy was located west of the New Garden Crossroads. Of Miller, the story is told that when the time came to roll and scrape the roads, it was he with his muscular shoulders and strong arms who was chosen to drive the team of huge oxen. Blacksmiths formed an important part of the farm economy. It was they who made hoes, shovels, and digging irons. It was the blacksmith who fitted iron rims onto wooden wagon wheels and produced hinges and latches for buildings, fittings for horse tack, and, of course, mended broken tools and shoed horses. The blacksmith shop that lasted into the 20th century was that of Maurice "Johnny" Richardson, located on Broad Run south of Landenberg. (Courtesy Alma Rigler.)

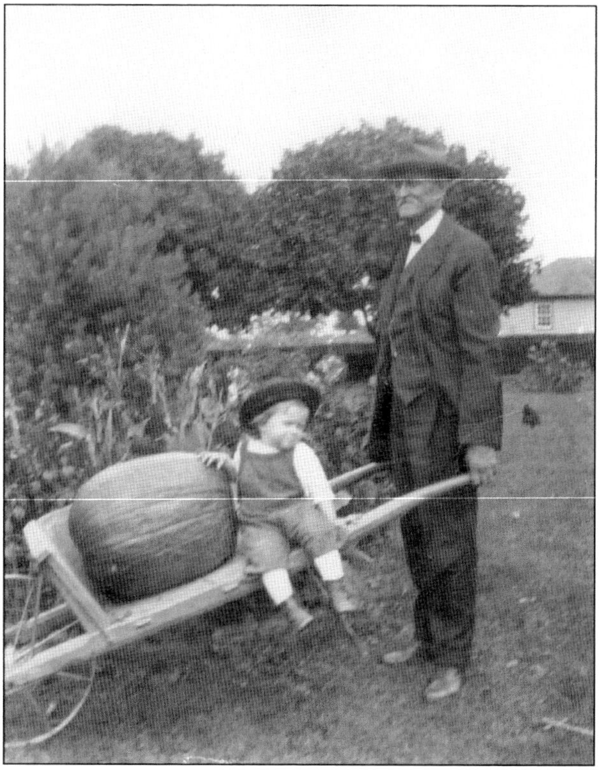

Farmers were justly proud of huge pumpkins. In this picture, Thomas E. Wollaston has both a monstrous pumpkin and a grandson, Charlie Wollaston, to tote around the Starr Road farm in his wheelbarrow. (Courtesy Peggy Empet.)

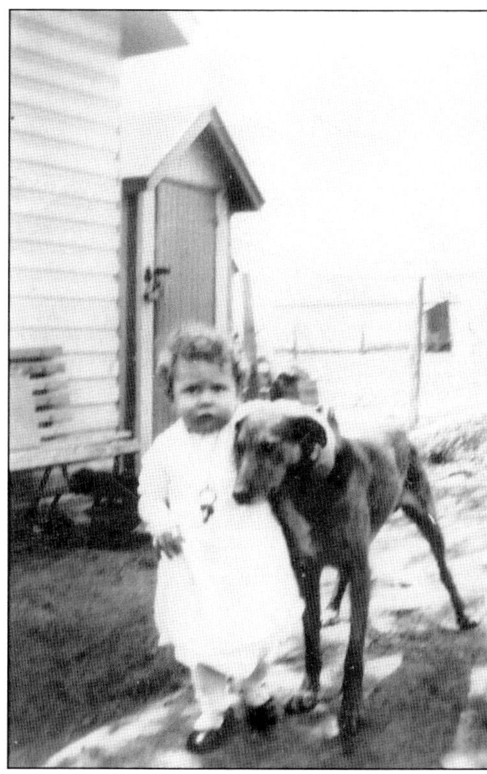

Faithful pets are the best friends. Here Lenny DiFilippo tries to harness the family dog before it makes a break for downtown Toughkenamon. (Courtesy Lenny DiFilippo.)

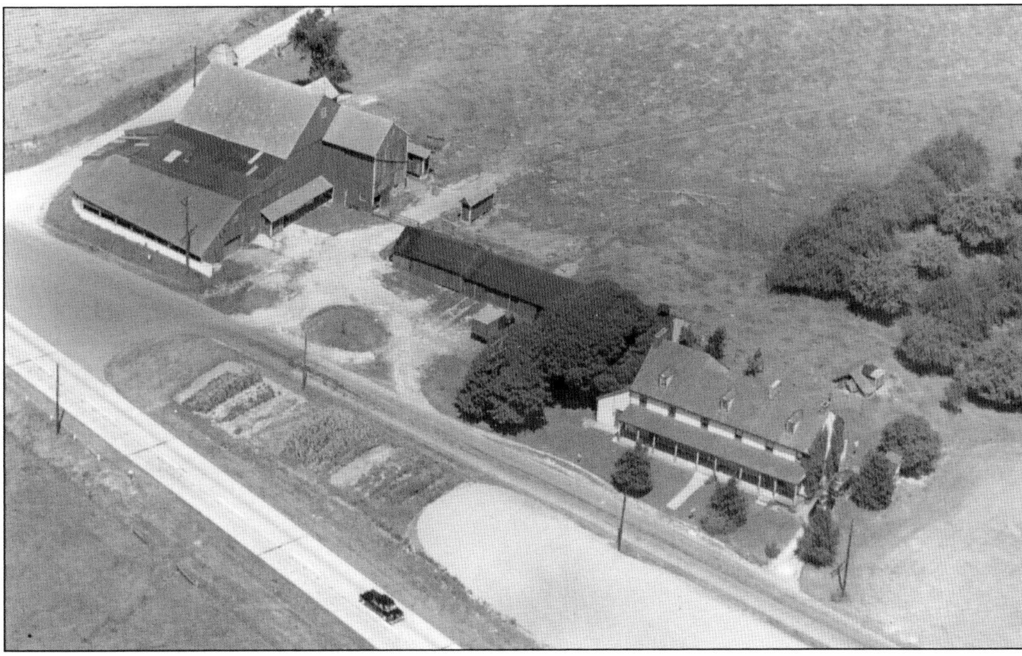

This aerial view shows the Quill farmstead sprawling alongside the intersection of Sharp and Sheehan Roads and Gap-Newport Pike. Purchased by Cornelius Quill and his brothers from the Schrader family in 1922, the barn, outbuildings, and tavern (far right) greeted travelers for more than 100 years as they crossed into Pennsylvania from Delaware. (Courtesy Joan B. Procino.)

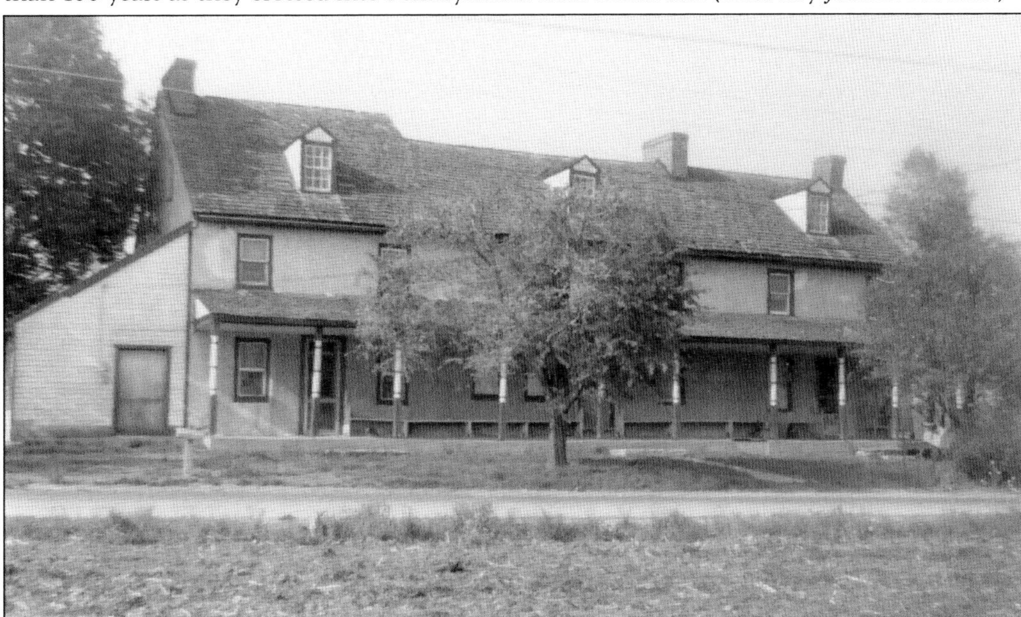

The center of the Quill farmhouse was the original log tavern built by Isaac Allen about 1750. In 1777, Hessian soldiers en route to the Battle of the Brandywine camped around the tavern and foraged in the surrounding countryside. By the 1850s, the tavern was the site of large livestock auctions and served as an election site, a post office, and a horse-changing spot for the U.S. Post Office Department. (Courtesy Joan B. Procino.)

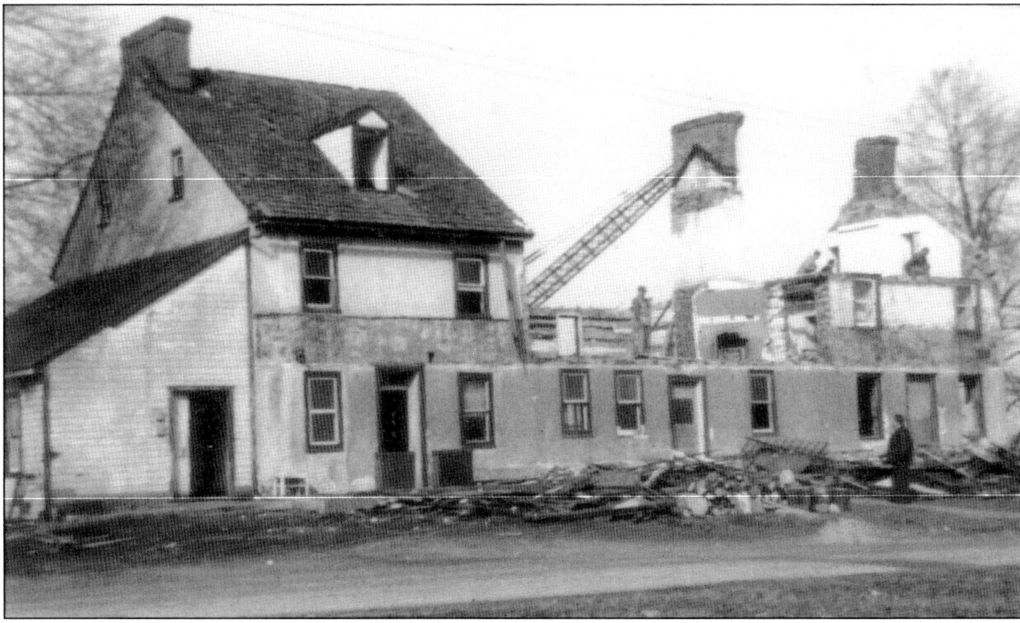

The tavern known variously as Allen's Tavern, the Sign of the Conestoga Wagon, Chandler's Inn, and the New Garden Inn, was sold to W. L. Gilbert in 1882. For 80 years thereafter, the 180 acres were farmed first by Gilbert's son-in-law, John Schrader, and then by the Quill brothers. In 1966, Louis Pia purchased the property, razed the house and barn, and disassembled the log tavern to be reconstructed in Chadds Ford. (Courtesy Joan B. Procino.)

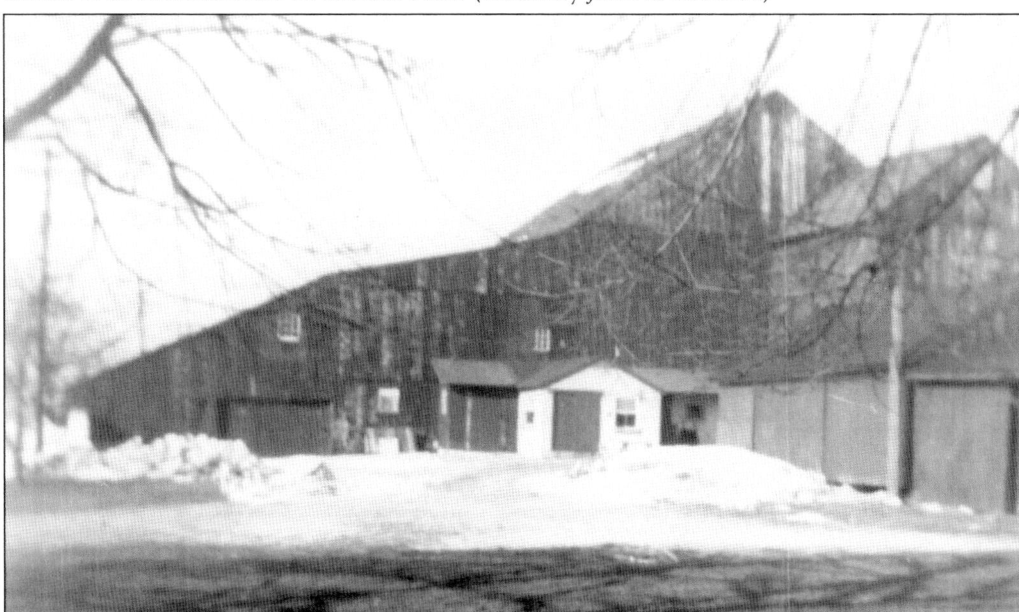

The red Quill barn has been described as the largest barn in Chester County. Built in the 1840s, it was unique for its enclosed barnyard. For the drover on the Gap-Newport Pike during the 18th and 19th centuries, this tavern was the only stand for 20 miles providing blacksmithing and livery services. The stable could accommodate 30 horses, while the transient visitor found a bed in the straw mow. (Courtesy Joan B. Procino.)

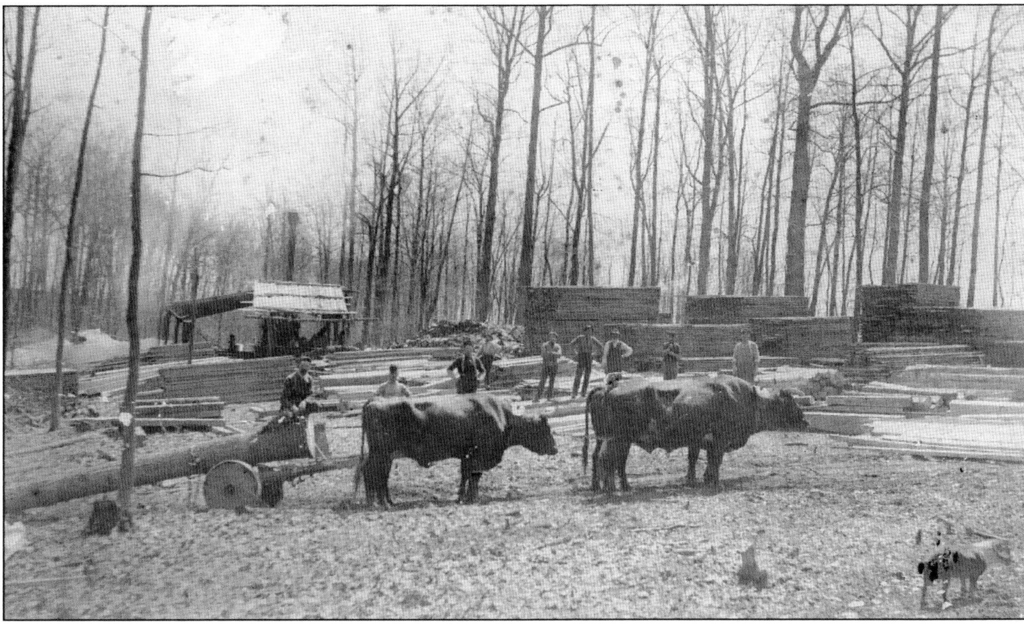

Established in 1915, Kennedy Crossan's mill operated for much of the 20th century. From New Garden's earliest days, sawmills powered by water supplied settlers with boards and timbers for buildings and fences. With the coming of steam power, sawmills could be located near roads or railroads or even be mobile, moving to a farmer's woodlot. (Courtesy Alma Rigler.)

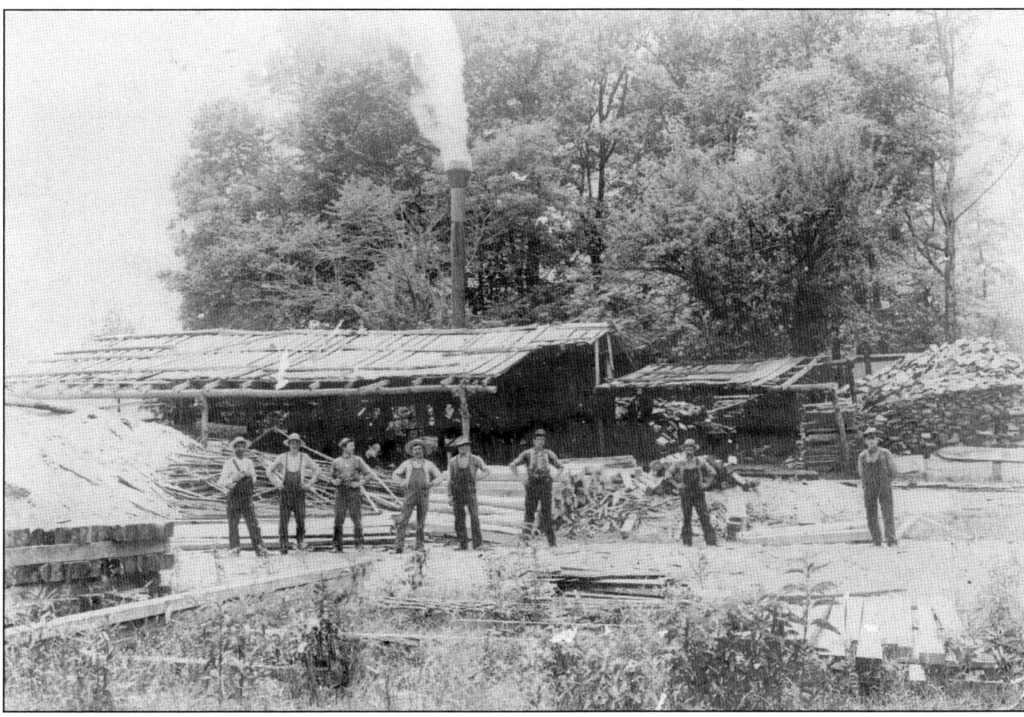

Some time in the 1920s, workers at Slater's sawmill, similar in operation to Kennedy Crossan's, lined up for a photograph. Much of the timber in buildings constructed in the southern part of the township during the 20th century was produced by Crossan's sawyers. (Courtesy Alma Rigler.)

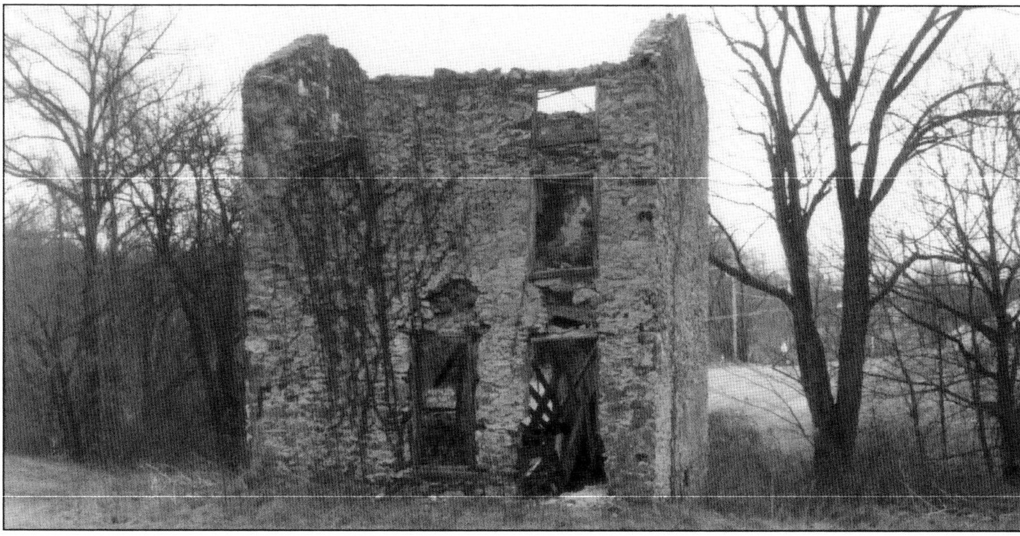

On Pemberton Road stands the ruin of a stone house once belonging to Nelson Wiggins and then to his son, Reuben. Nelson Wiggins, who owned his 24-acre farm from as early as 1851, was a farm laborer and lay preacher. Although there is no written record, it is possible that runaway slaves found shelter in his house; free black families were known to actively participate in the Underground Railroad. (Author's collection.)

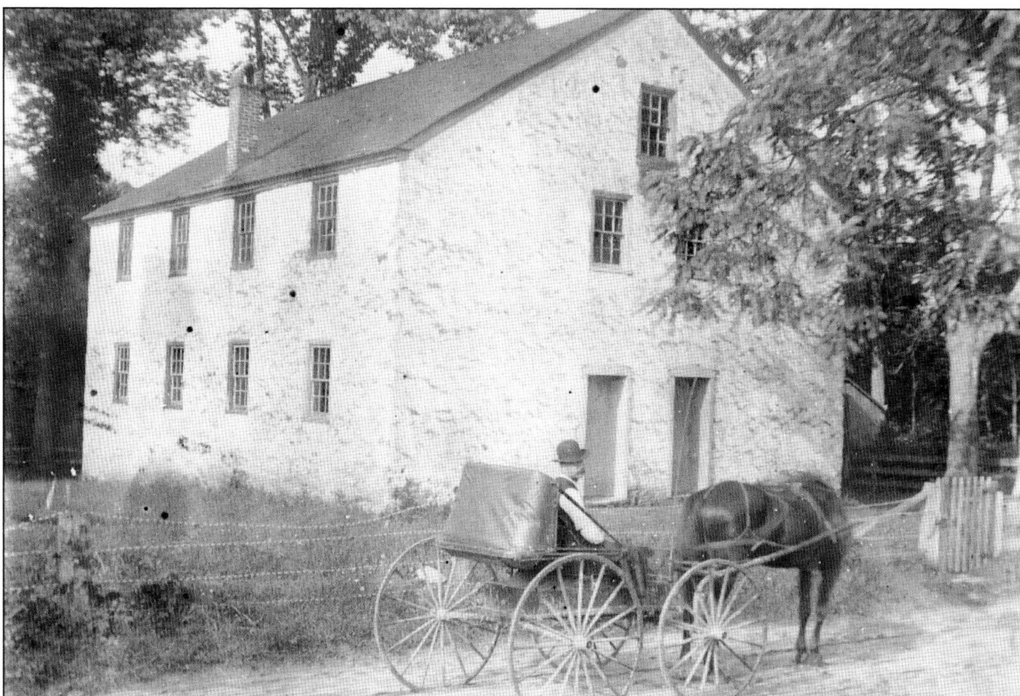

Undertaker Alexander Guthrie, who buried more than 112 persons in the Bucktoe Cemetery located just east of the New Garden line, is pictured in front of Bucktoe Church. The 1851 stone church, which replaced an 1824 log building, was home to the African Union Church of New Garden. Nelson Wiggins was the preacher for about 30 years until 1900, when dissension among the congregation caused the church to be abandoned. (Courtesy Kennett Township Historical Commission.)

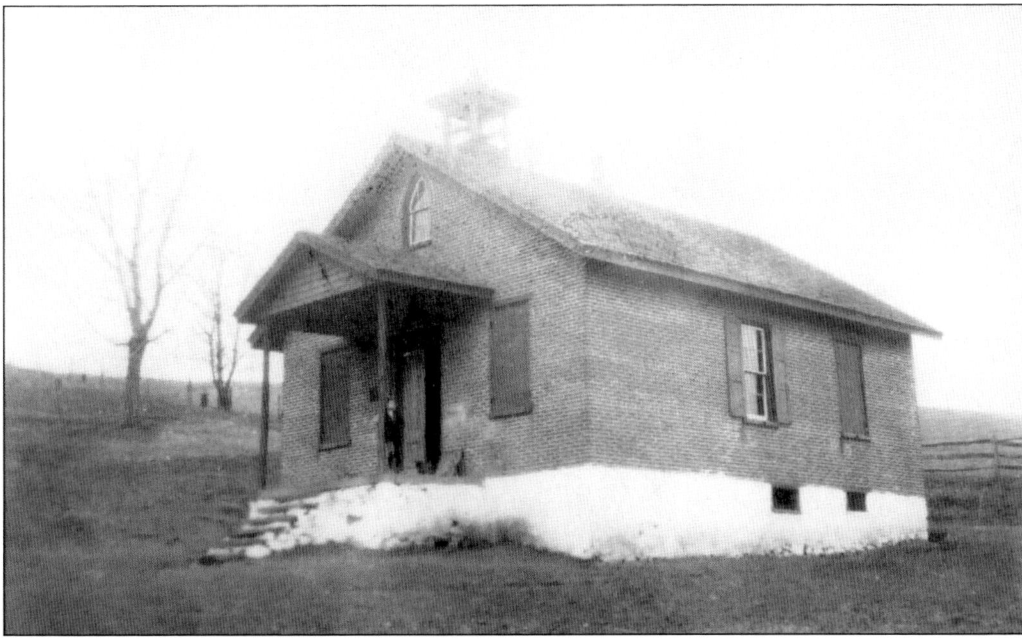

Walnut Run School was one of seven one-room schools closed when the Kennett Consolidated School opened in 1932. Other schools closed were Toughkenamon, Landenberg, Sunny Dell, Cedar Spring, Greenwood Dell, and Penn Green. (Courtesy NGTHC.)

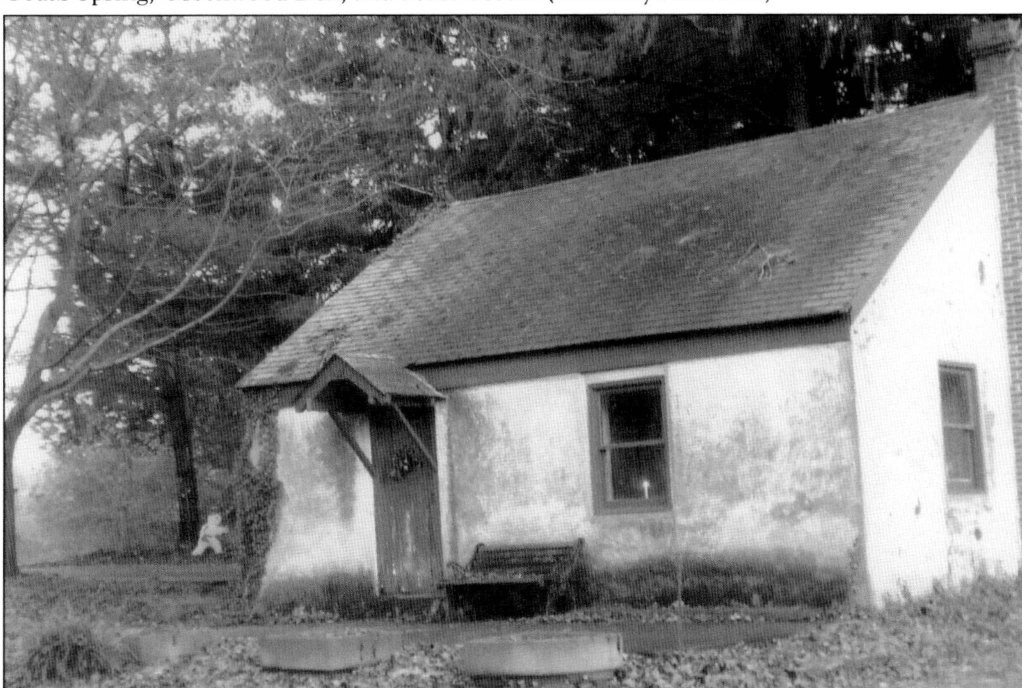

Chestnut Green School, located along Route 41 at Kaolin, was built sometime prior to 1822 for the education of poor children. Citizens contributed to the maintenance of the school and, because it was considered a "common school," it continued as a public school until the late 1860s. (Courtesy Andrea Tauson.)

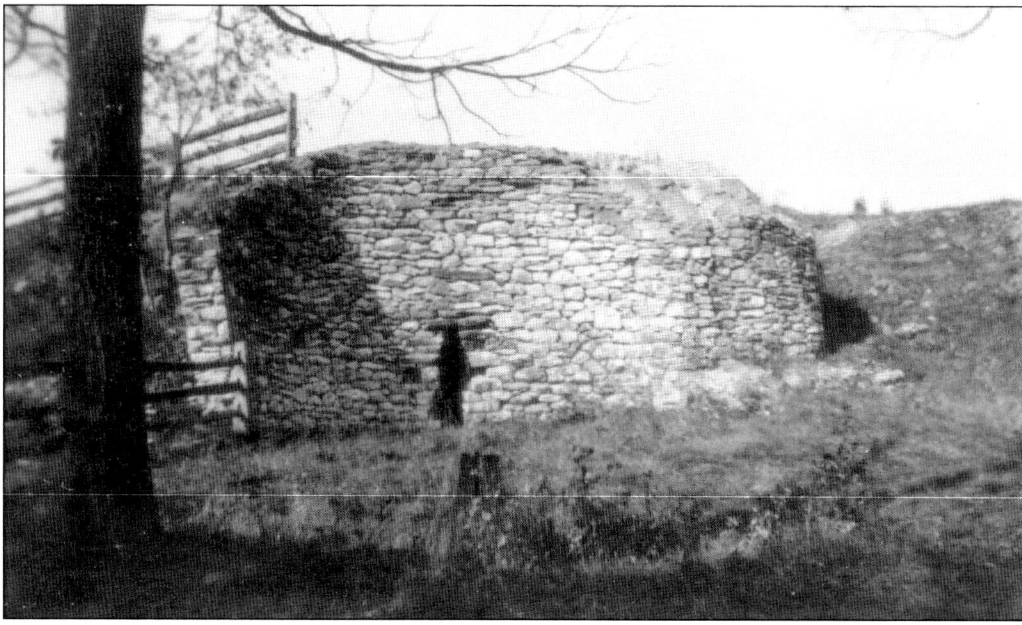

Some farmers in the 19th century built kilns where they burned limestone to make lime for fertilizer. A kiln was filled with alternating layers of wood scraps, coal, and chunks of limestone, then set afire. Burning from one to four weeks, the lime filtered down to the bottom of the kiln. After wetting down the mounds of lime, the slaked lime was shoveled into wagons and spread on fields. (Courtesy NGTHC.)

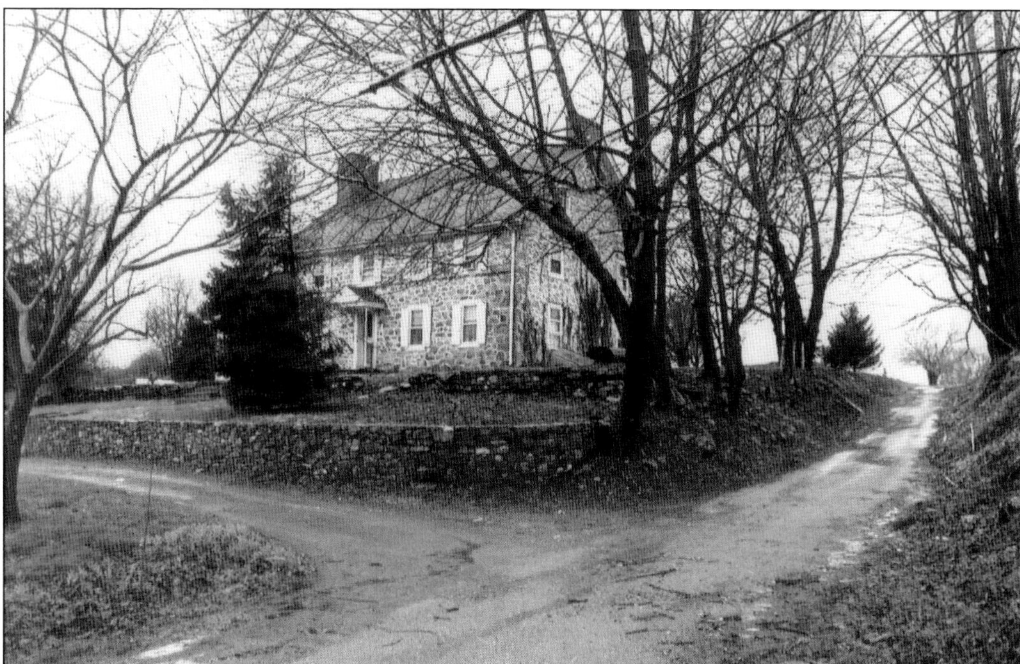

In 1814, James Walker, a tanner, built this stone house on Southwood Road, near the Delaware border. According to deed records from 1769 to 1874, there was an active tannery east of the house in the low area near the stream. (Courtesy Chris Robinson.)

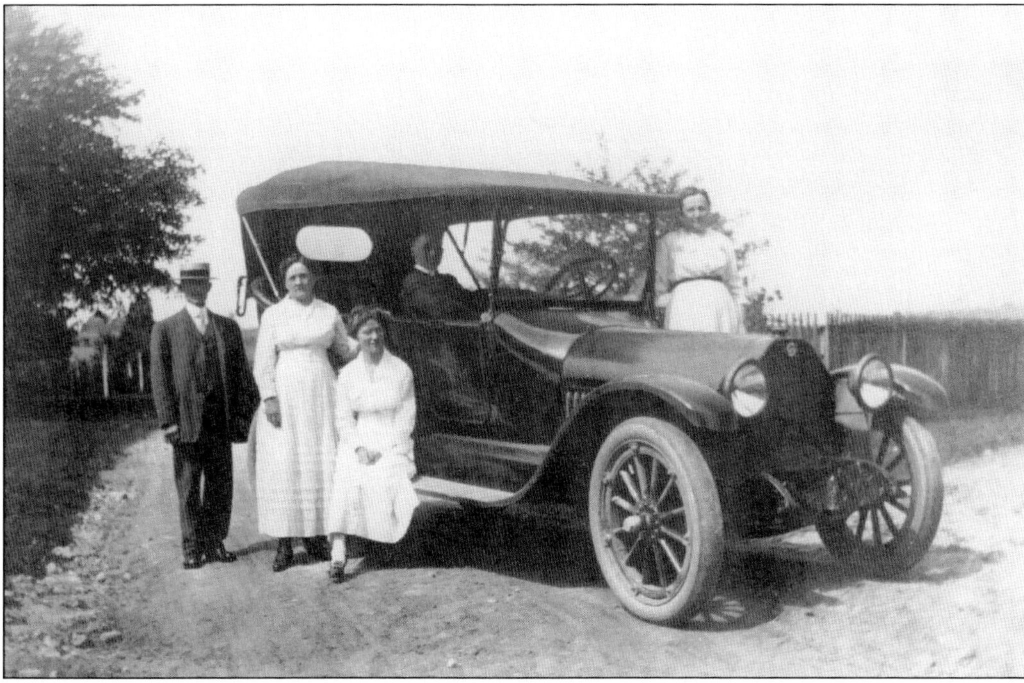

About 1920, Charles and Maluan Jones (standing at the rear of the car) and guests strike refined poses with their new Buick. Charles had moved his family to Crestfield Farm on New Garden Road in 1912. A proponent of education, he sat on the school board in 1932, when consolidation with Kennett took place. (Courtesy Margaret Jones.)

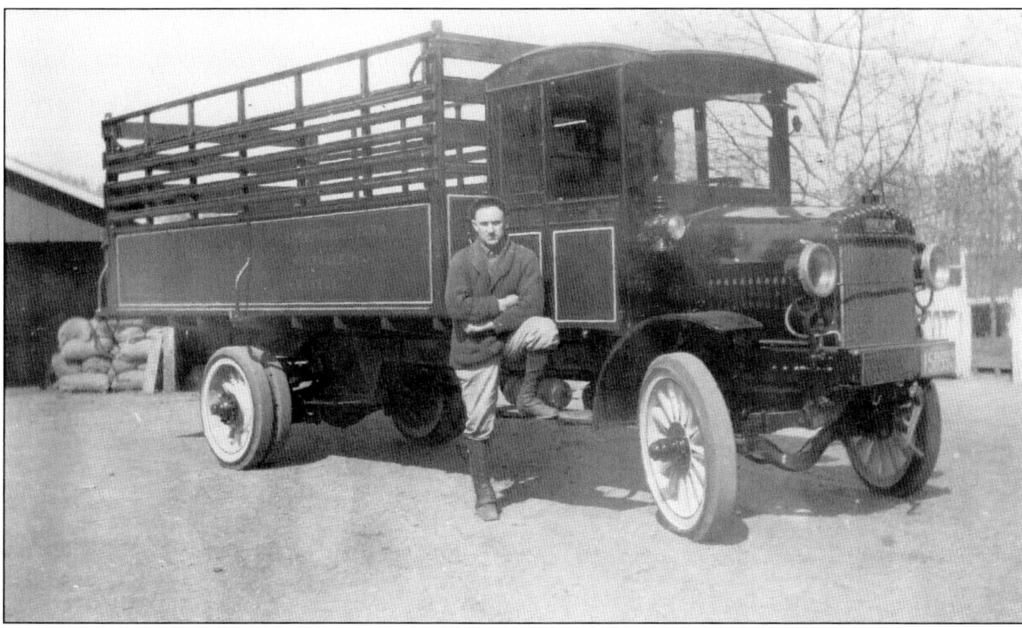

Jesse Hendrickson filled his truck daily with fruit and vegetables at the Wilmington or Baltimore wholesale market and then traveled the Landenberg neighborhood, selling his produce to housewives. The huckster was an important fixture in the days before fresh produce was readily available in a supermarket. (Courtesy Alma Rigler.)

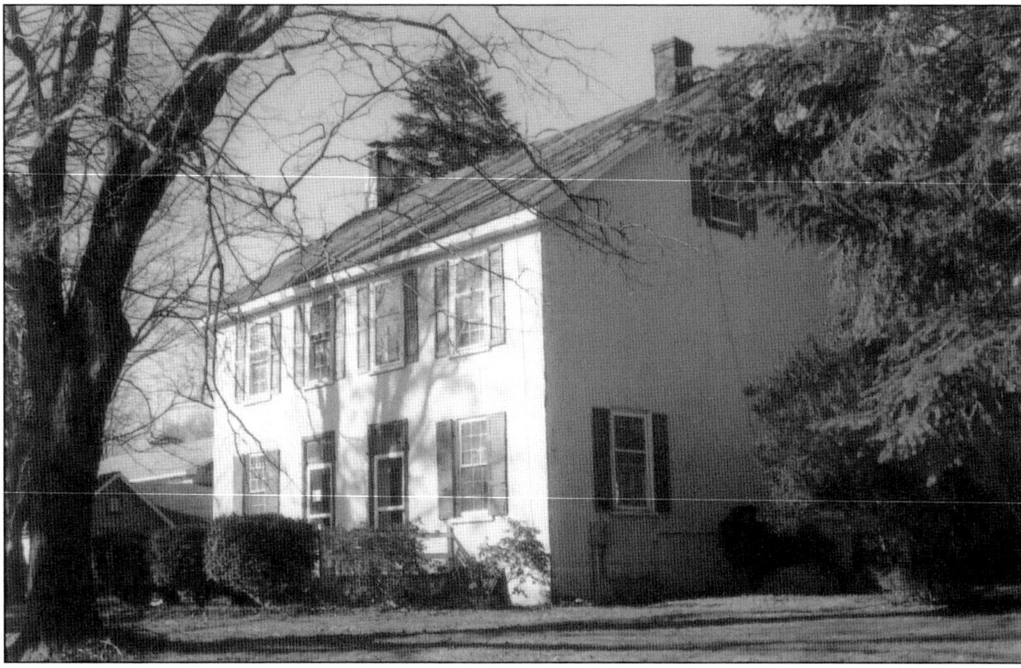

The only Federal-style house in the township was built by George Sharp sometime prior to 1782. Chester County judge Jesse Sharp made an addition to the early house with the refinement of finely detailed interior woodwork about 1818. During much of the 20th century, the home, located on Sharp Road, has been owned by members of the Robert Mendenhall family. (Author's collection.)

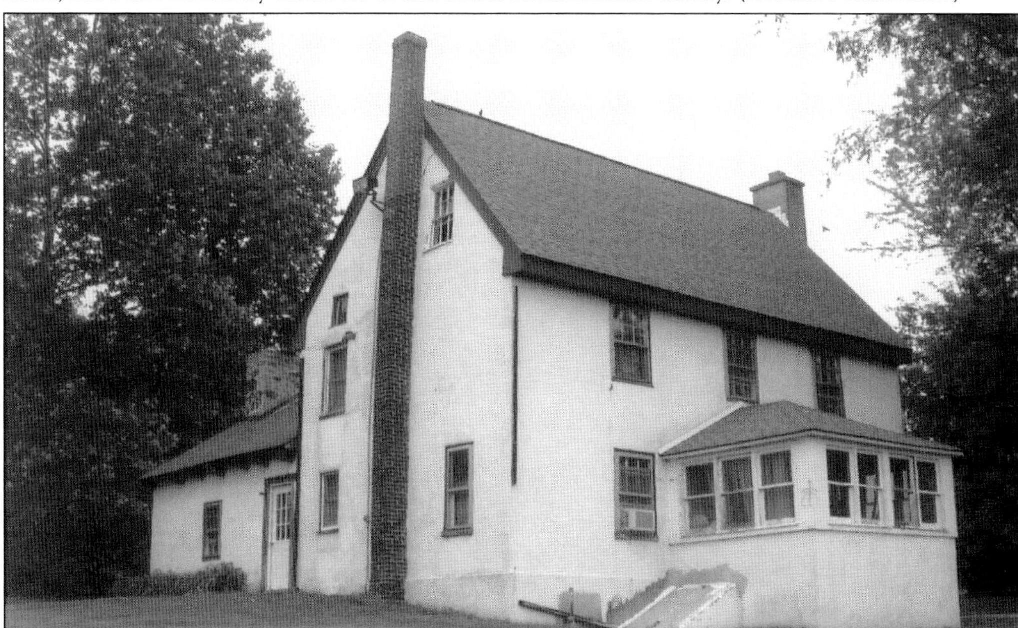

In 1817, Thomas Lamborn built his brick house with its steeply pitched roof in a style reminiscent of 100 years earlier. Until 1929, the house was home to Lamborn descendants who farmed the 115 acres. Despite a major fire and hard use by tenants, the house survived to eventually belong to New Garden Township, which acquired the property for a township park. (Courtesy Carla Lucas.)

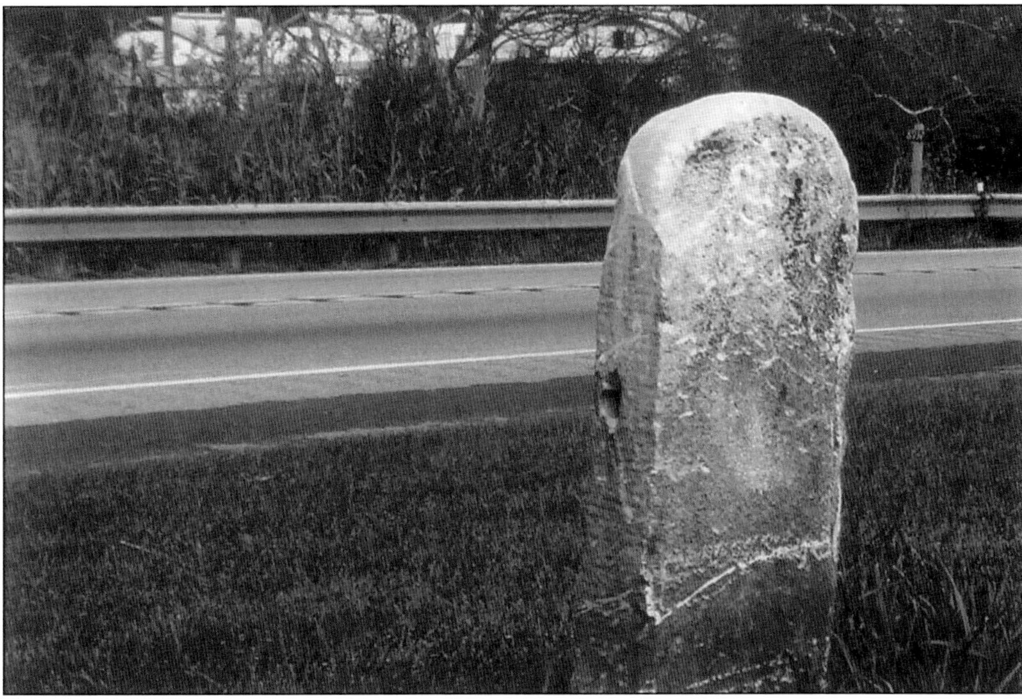

Stone posts to mark the miles were placed along the Gap-Newport Pike. "11 M to NP" (11 miles to Newport) was etched into this marker, still standing near the township garage. The turnpike, begun in 1808 and completed by 1818, was never financially solvent, going bankrupt by 1845. Nevertheless, it had been a navigable road, allowing Lancaster County farmers to readily transport livestock and produce to the port at Newport. (Courtesy Andrea Tauson.)

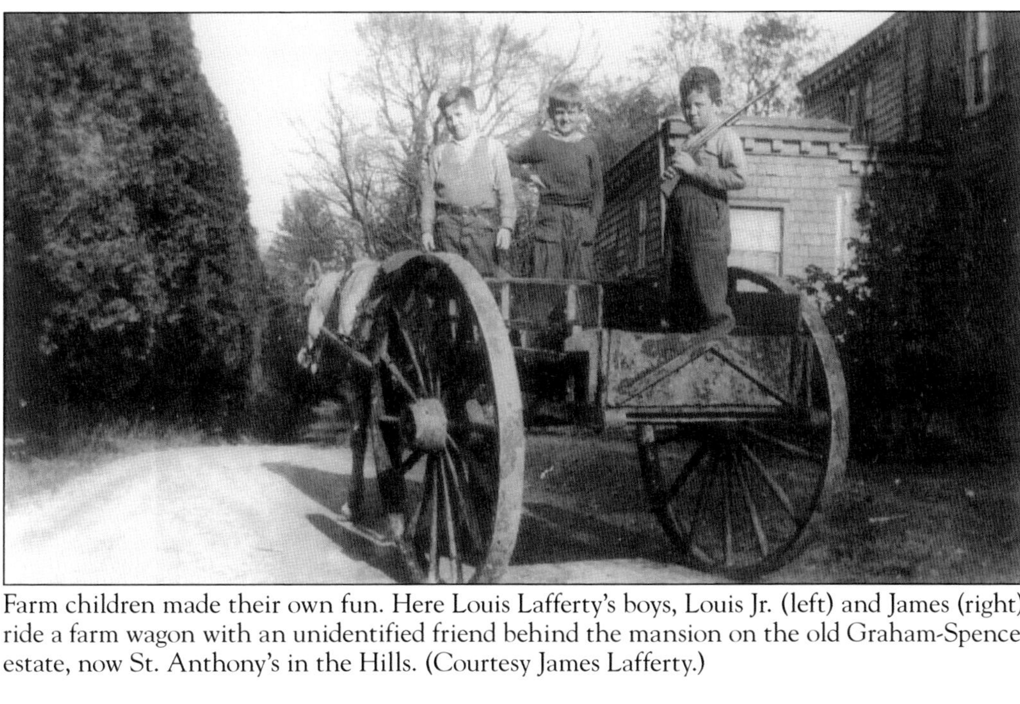

Farm children made their own fun. Here Louis Lafferty's boys, Louis Jr. (left) and James (right), ride a farm wagon with an unidentified friend behind the mansion on the old Graham-Spencer estate, now St. Anthony's in the Hills. (Courtesy James Lafferty.)

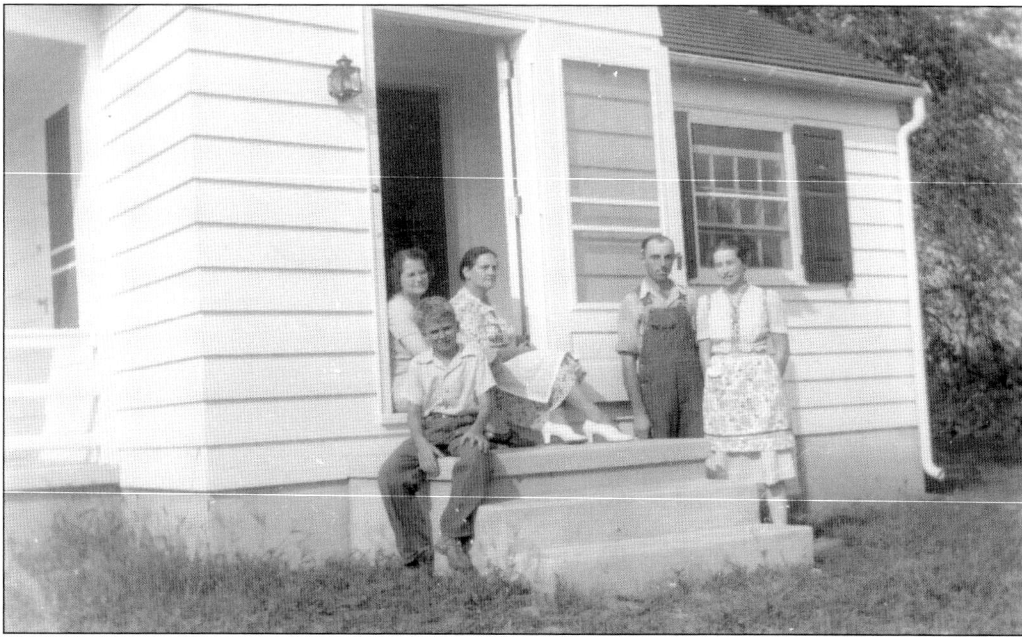

The traditional moving day for hired hands was April 1—early enough to help with springtime sowing at a new farm. In this picture, however, taken in the early 1940s, Calvin and Florence Hoopes move into their newly built, permanent house on the Walnut Run farm, owned for nearly a century by the family. (Courtesy Barclay Hoopes.)

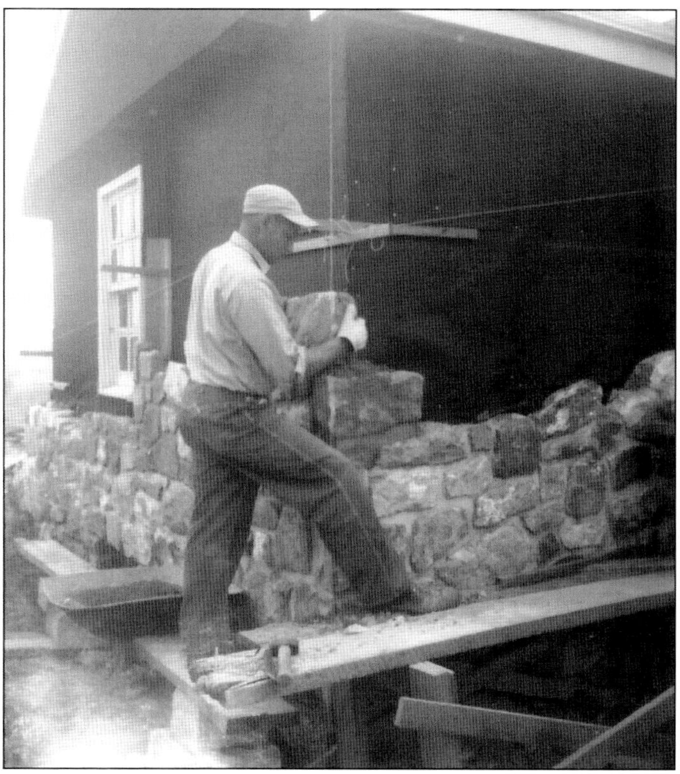

When Landenberg native Earl Rigler heard that the Brown house on Route 41 was to be demolished by Hewlett-Packard, he asked to raze it in exchange for the stone. It took Rigler nearly seven years to finish the stone house he always wanted on Sawmill Road. After its 1963 completion, Rigler imbedded the Brown house date stones in his retaining wall. The stones read "D & H B" (David and Hannah Brown). (Courtesy Alma Rigler.)

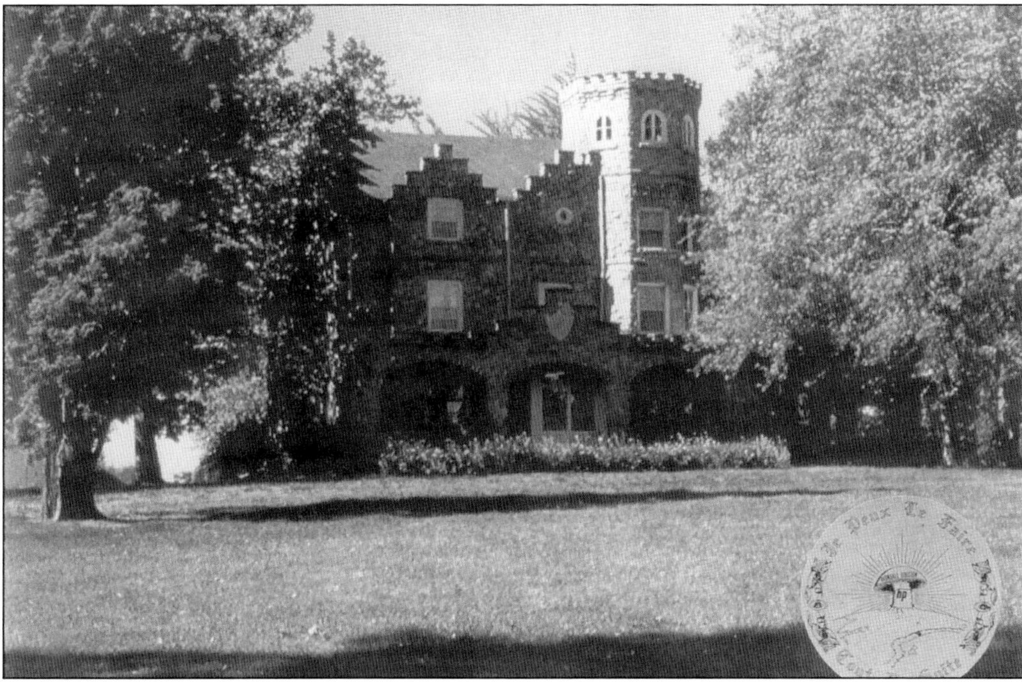

In 1911, Dr. Pusey de Foulke, a New York City surgeon and world traveler, purchased two farms on Sunny Dell Road and built a granite mansion he called Foulkleon. Dr. de Foulke was his own architect, creating a mansion with details that reminded him of castles he had seen in Europe. The house was demolished in the 1950s and replaced with a building that ultimately became a Hewlett-Packard plant. (Courtesy Margaret Jones.)

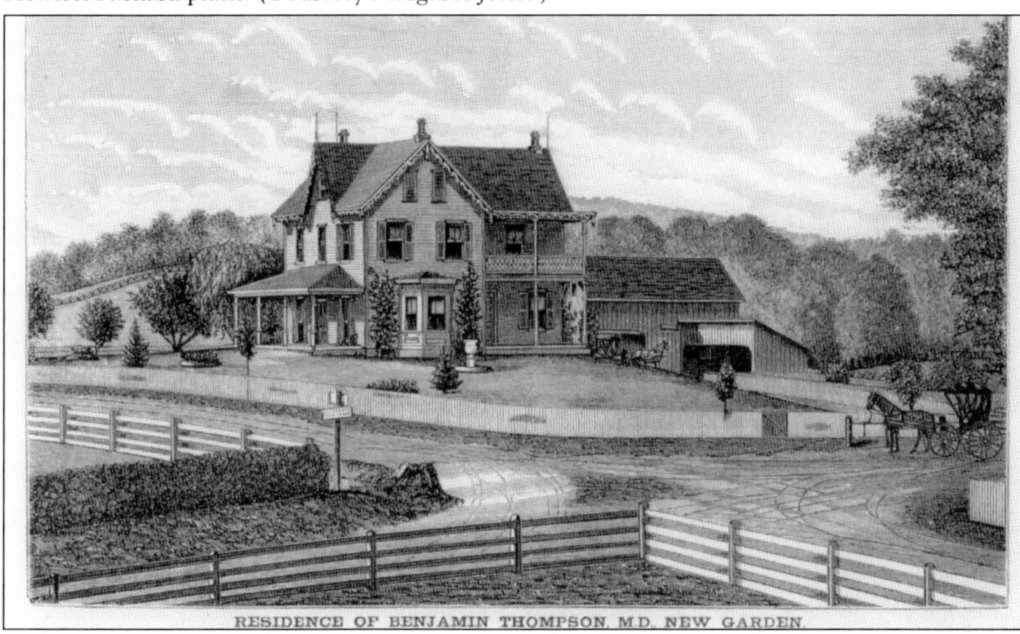

Dr. Benjamin Thompson's house stood at the intersection of Newark and Buttonwood Roads. Beginning in the 1880s, he was the country doctor in the southern part of New Garden Township. House calls were made by horse and buggy. (Courtesy *Futhey and Cope*.)

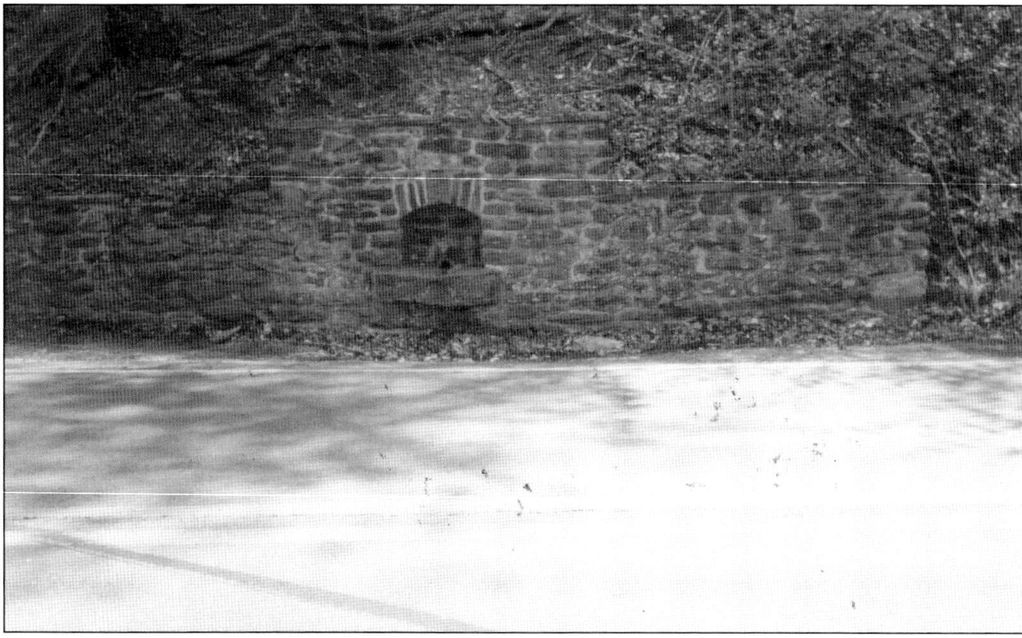

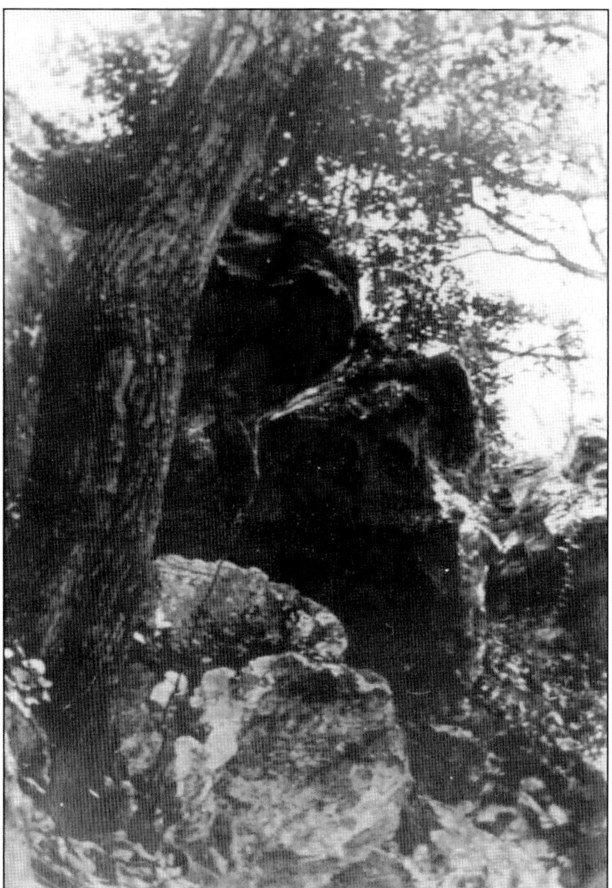

Generations of New Garden families brought their jugs and bottles to fill from the spring on Penn Green Road. Known for its sweet-tasting clear water, Laurel Spring became a landmark, giving its name to Laurel Spring Woods. (Courtesy Alma Rigler.)

Landenberg's old-timers say this is the site of Sandy Flash's cave. Located on the White Clay's west bank near the railroad cut, the cave was said to lead to a house high on the bank. James Fitzpatrick, known as Sandy Flash, was a Continental Army deserter who stole from tax collectors and gave to the poor. A reckless adventurer who became a folk hero, Sandy Flash was hanged in 1778. (Courtesy NGTHC.)

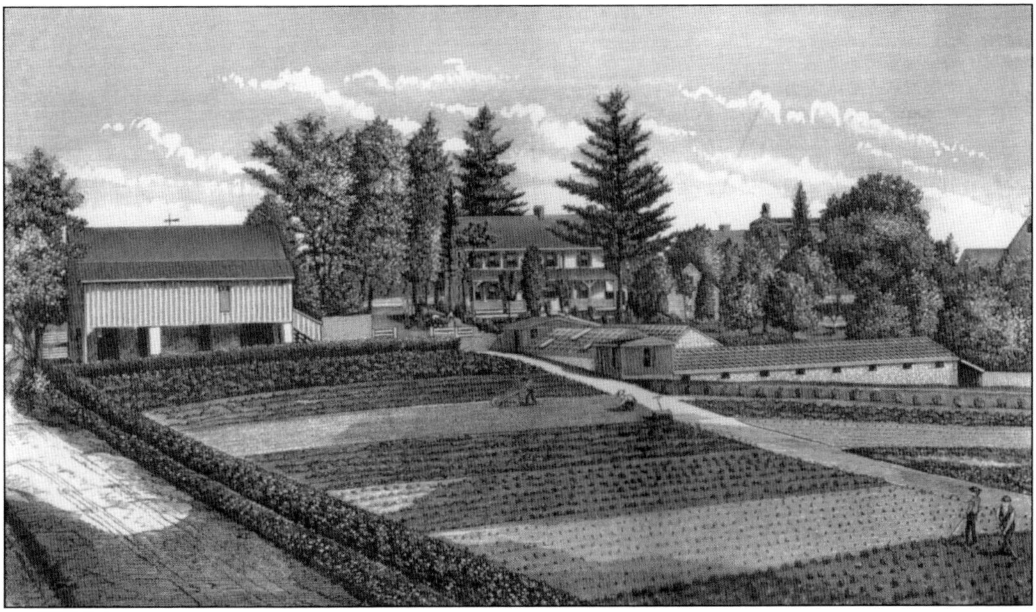

Charles Starr's nursery business, established in the early 1880s, was the first greenhouse operation in New Garden Township. He grew peonies, tuber roses, and carnations, which he shipped to city markets. Greenhouse culture expanded so much that by 1900, people were referring to New Garden Township as the "Township of Glass Houses." (Courtesy *Futhey and Cope*.)

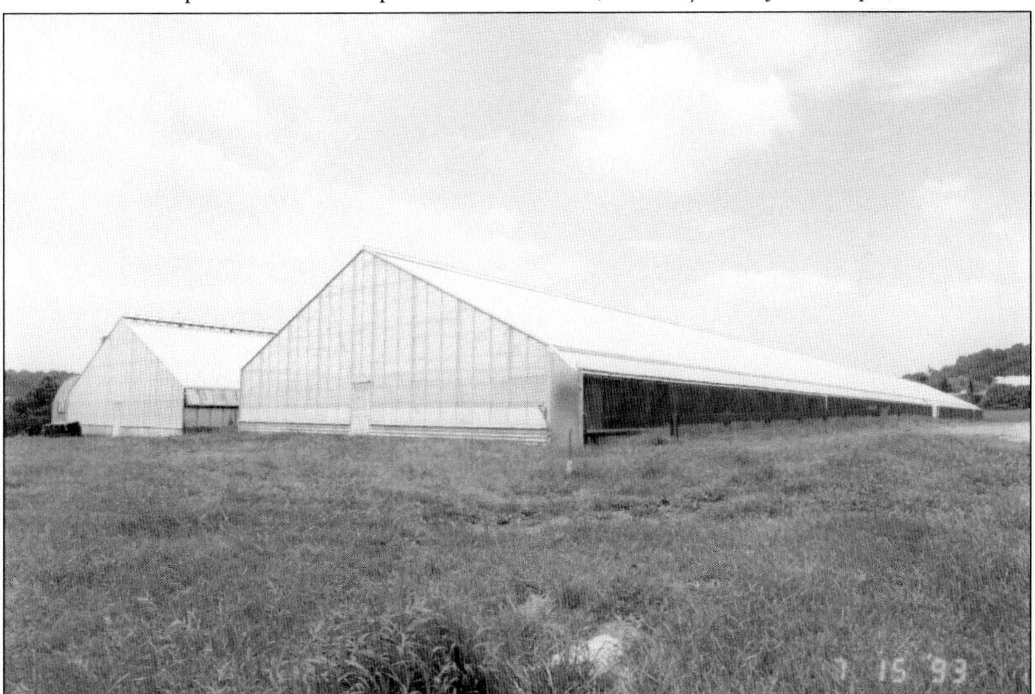

Another early greenhouse man was Samuel Thompson, whose original 1870s greenhouses began a family rose-growing business that extended until the end of the 20th century. (Courtesy Betsy Turner.)

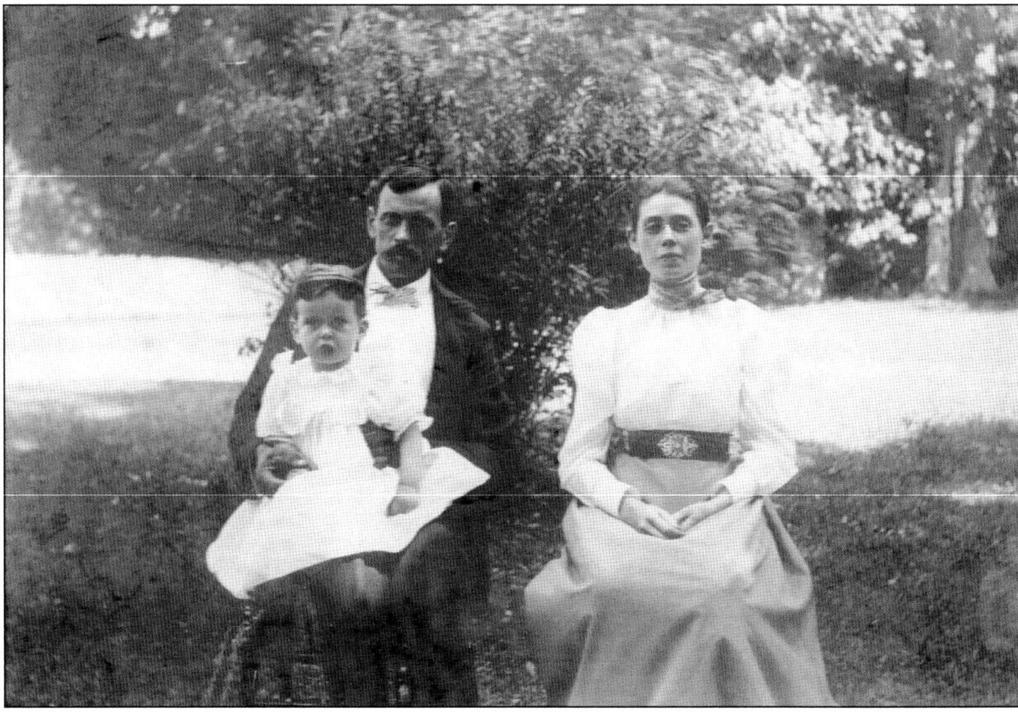

In a c. 1905 picture taken in the backyard of their 1810 farmhouse, Samuel Thompson's son, Joshua Howard Thompson, sits with his wife, Hannah Richards, and their son, Theodore Richards Thompson. Theodore, known as Ted, built the family greenhouse business into an enterprise that would prosper through two more generations. (Courtesy Betsy Turner.)

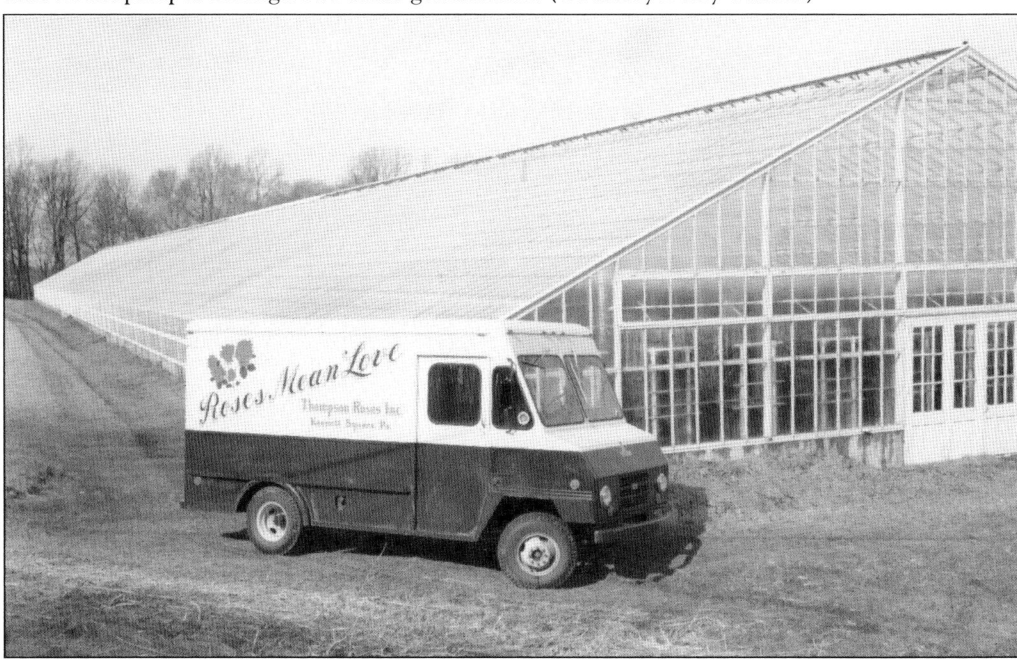

Deliveries of roses were made not only to city markets but also to local florists. The name Thompson became synonymous with roses. (Courtesy Betsy Turner.)

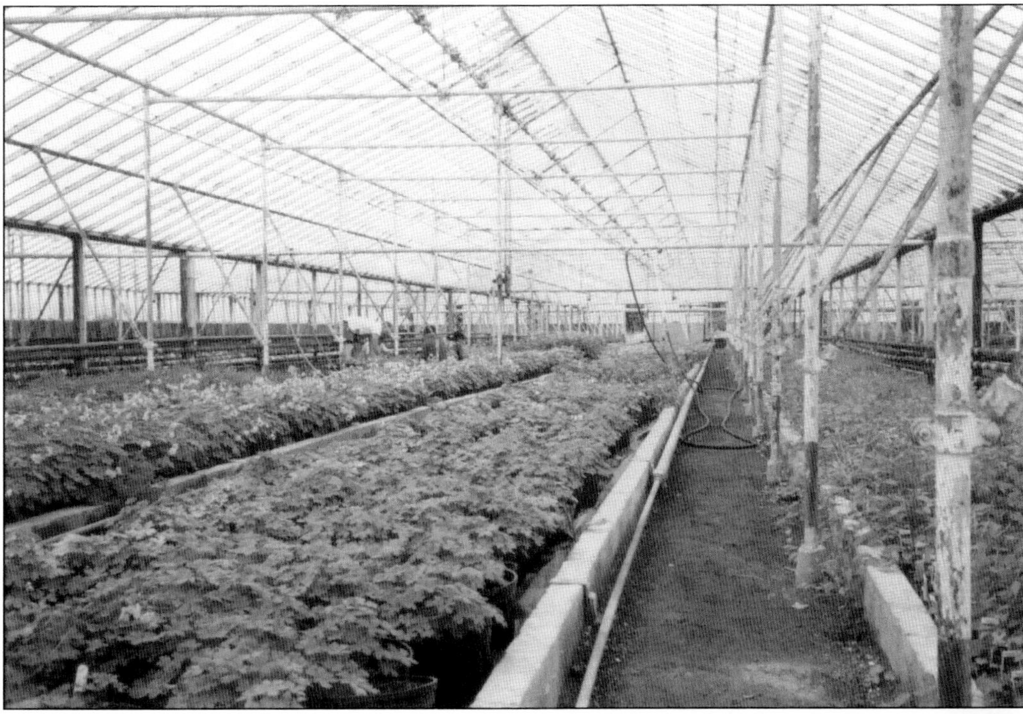

Literally acres of plants were under glass in the Thompson greenhouses. Other names from New Garden's greenhouse era included Starr, Marshall, Bancroft, Richards, Pratt, Pedicone, Mattascio, and Pratola. (Courtesy Betsy Turner.)

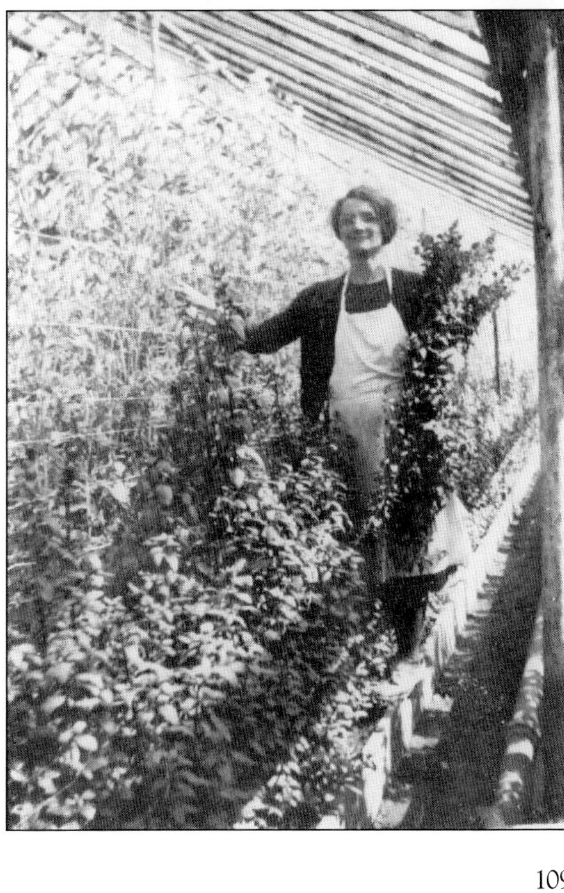

Producing flowers was often a family enterprise. In this picture, Grace Pratola holds an armload of snapdragons. When her husband, Michael Pratola, harvested peonies, it was a family affair; all the children helped to cut, sort, strip, and bundle the long-stemmed flowers. (Courtesy Annie Kelleher.)

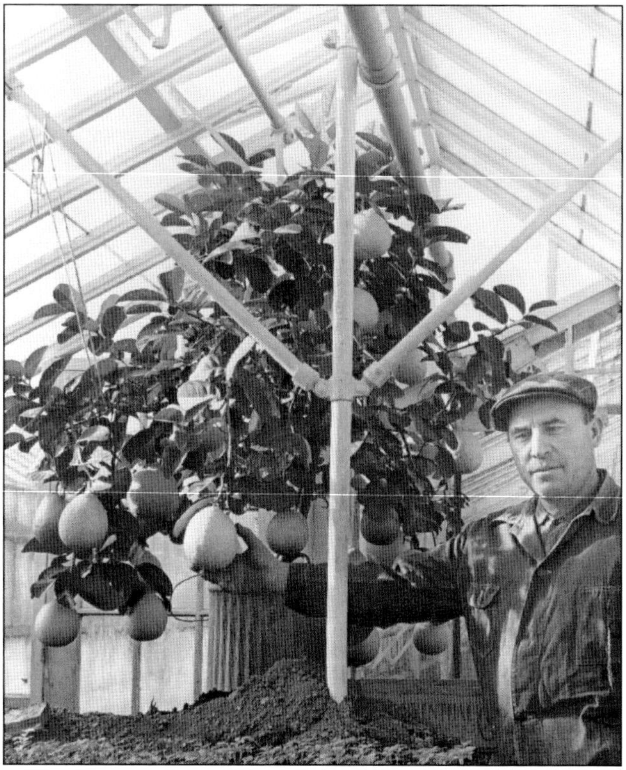

With its tall brick chimney and name written vertically, Camille Pedicone's greenhouse range on the western edge of Toughkenamon was a landmark. Pedicone, who learned the greenhouse business working for Thompson's, likewise grew roses. In this picture, he proudly shows oversized lemons cultivated in his greenhouse. (Courtesy NGTHC.)

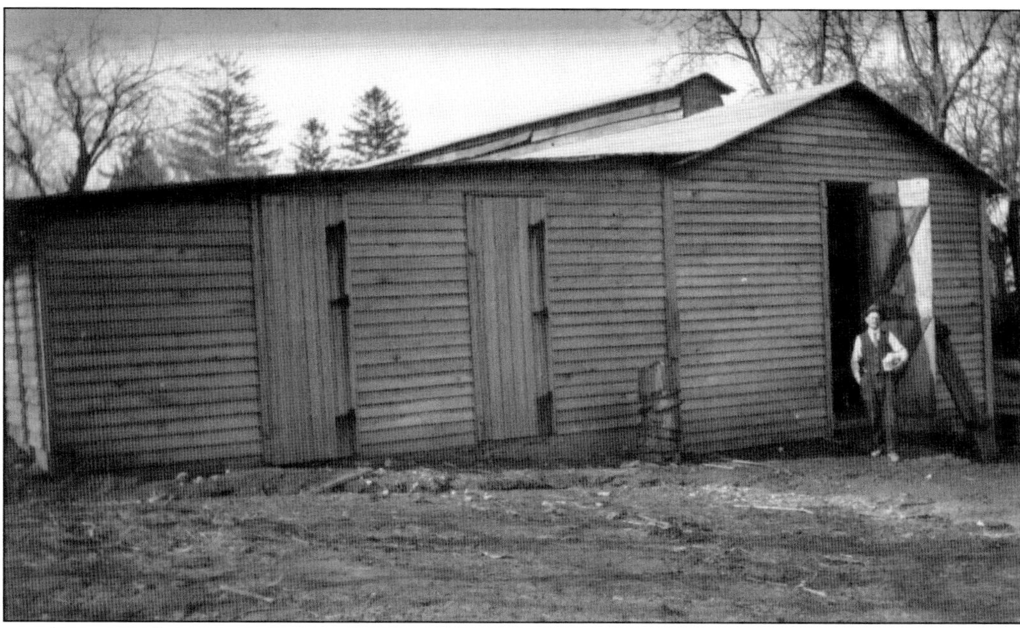

Mushroom culture in New Garden Township began when sons of greenhouse men began to experiment with the dark, damp space under greenhouse benches. Dairy farmers saw growing mushrooms as a way to supplement their income; in those days, mushrooms were only grown during the winter months. Farmers began to try mushroom culture in their barns, chicken houses, and basements and later built frame mushroom houses. (Courtesy Margaret Jones.)

As the 20th century dawned, industries like feldspar quarrying and railroad building yielded to the burgeoning mushroom farming as Italian immigrants embraced the mushroom as their bonanza. (Courtesy Jim Bertrando.)

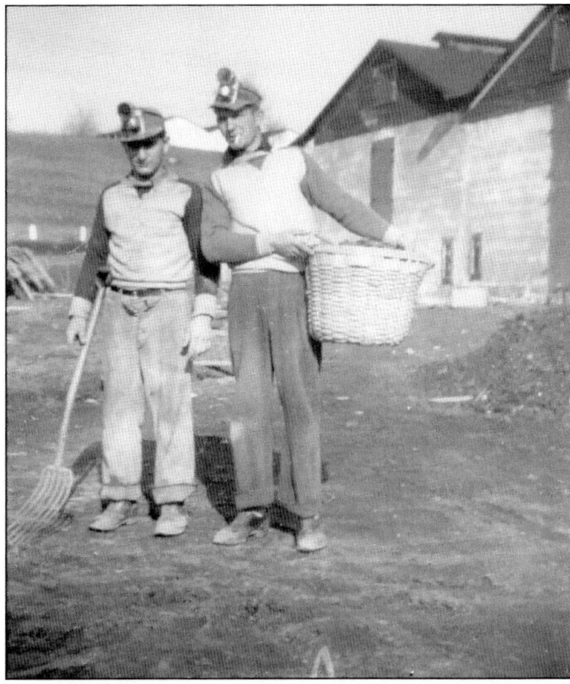

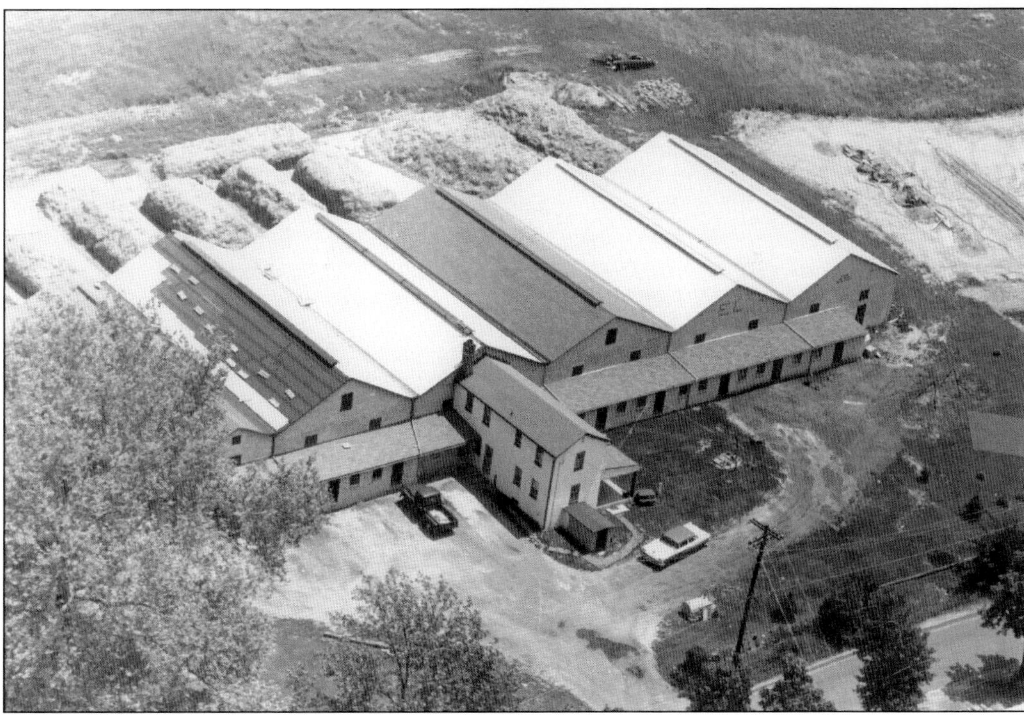

Because heat was generated by the pasteurizing of mushroom compost, there was always the danger of fire. Frame houses were replaced with cinderblock buildings. Double mushroom houses with two aisles and stacked beds, like these belonging to Ed Lafferty, were for many years the standard for the industry. A typical plant would have a row of connected mushroom houses, dirt shed, packing room, and boiler room. (Courtesy Ed Lafferty.)

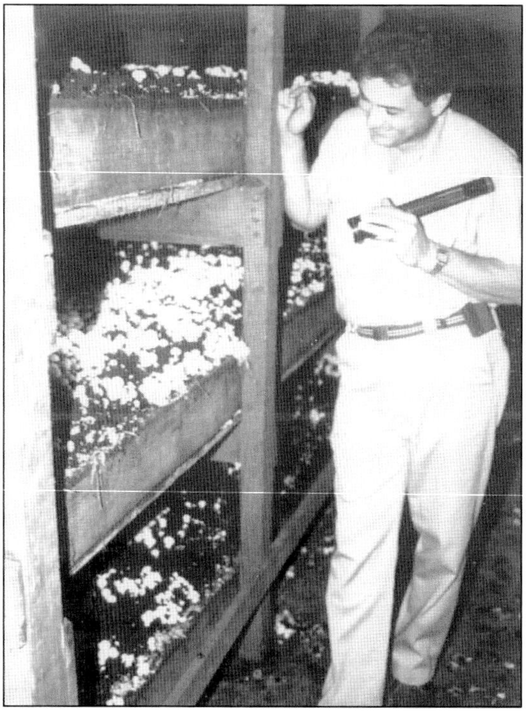

This first break of mushrooms was a sight every grower liked to see: a bed completely carpeted with smooth, rounded mushrooms. Growing mushrooms was risky: if a grower got a good crop, it was good luck; if he had a crop failure, it was bad luck. Not until the mid-20th century did the mushroom research labs at Penn State University begin to develop improved cultivating practices: compost formulae, spawn strains, and insect and disease control. New Garden's mushroom growers before the 1950s would not have believed how the industry would expand by the end of the century. They would have scarcely believed that 25 percent of the mushrooms grown in the United States would be grown in New Garden Township, or that by growing 4.5 crops a year, New Garden growers would be able to produce a total of 200 million pounds annually. (Left courtesy Rich Forte; bottom courtesy NGTHC.)

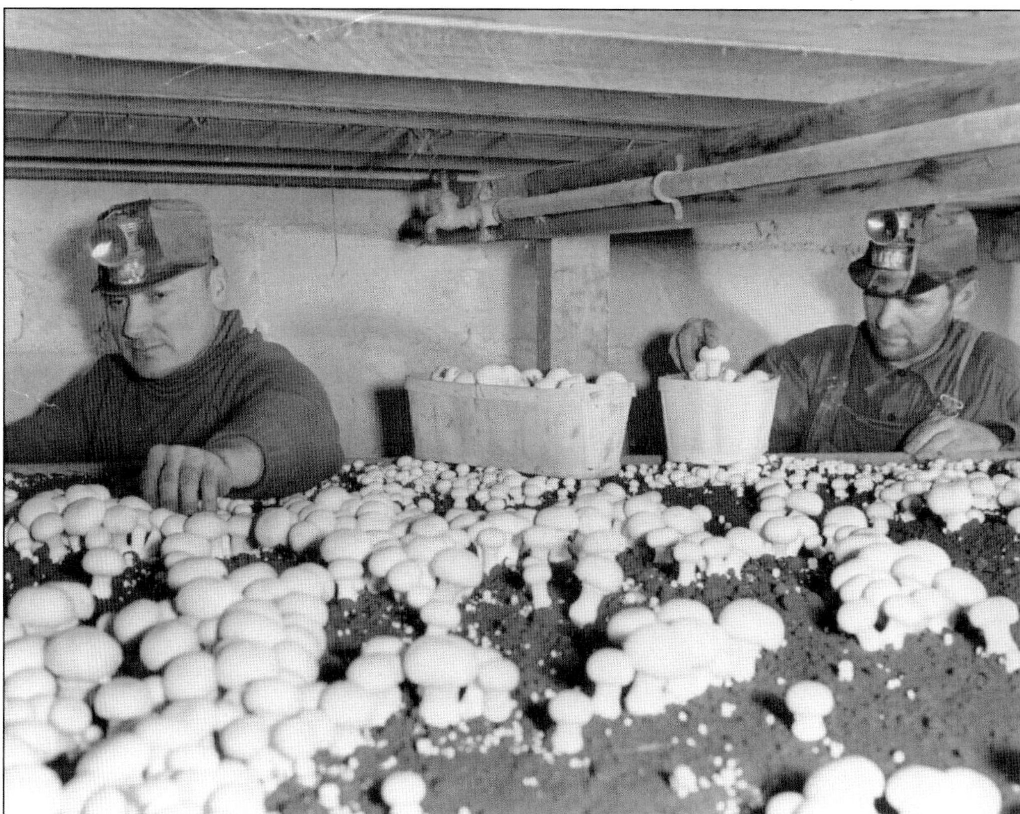

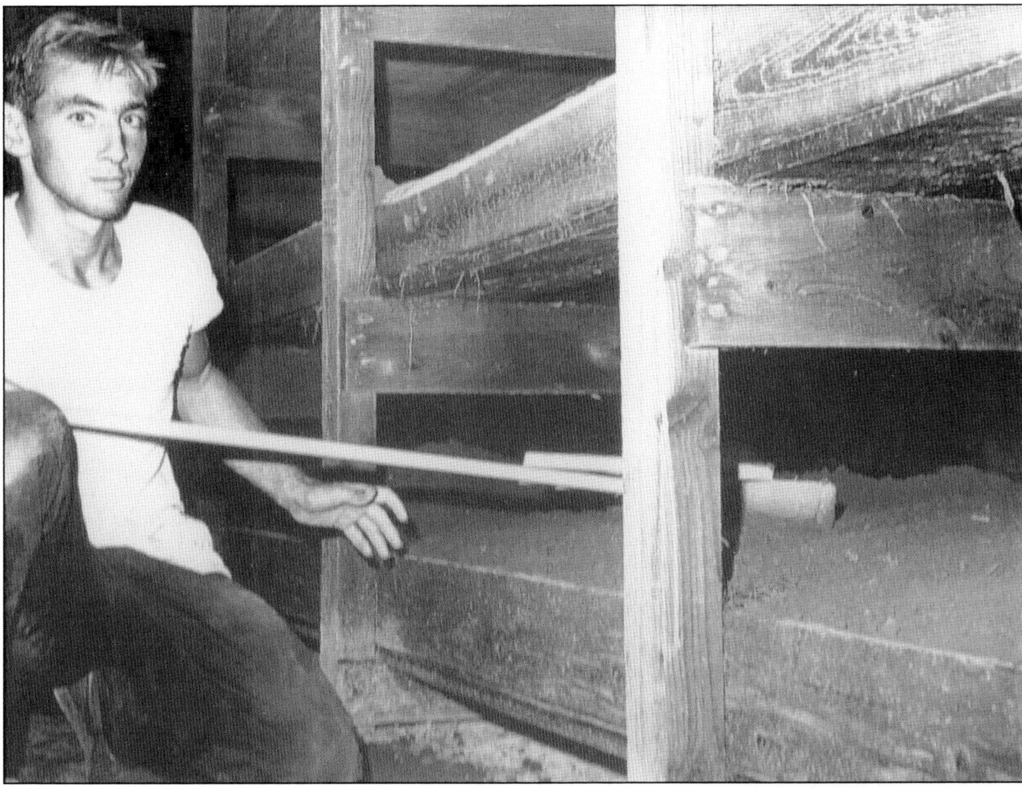

After a mushroom house was filled with pasteurized compost, beds were leveled and a layer of top soil spread on the surface. (Courtesy Rich Forte.)

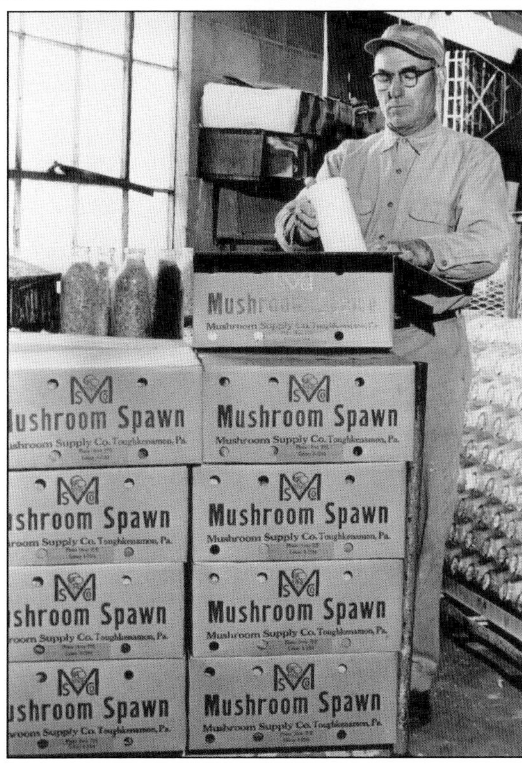

Spawn is spores or mushroom seed which is mixed with small grain. Originally imported from Europe in bricks, it was soon made in sterile facilities known as spawn plants. Mushroom Supply Company in Toughkenamon was one of these. Mushroom growers purchased the spawn in glass bottles and eventually in paper bags; they then poured it into open containers and broadcast the spawn over the beds of compost. (Courtesy NGTHC.)

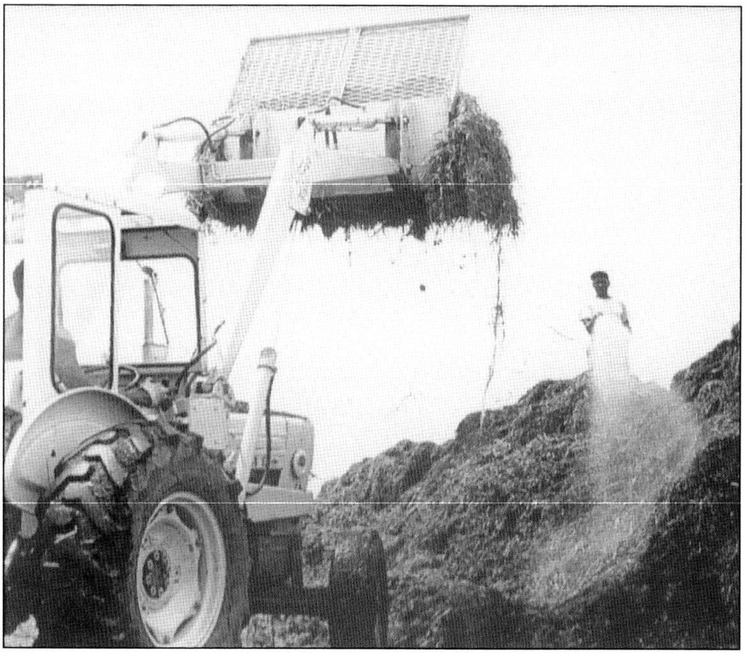

In the early days of preparing compost, horse manure was watered, mixed, and turned by men with forks. Eventually, front-end loaders and semi-automatic turners were used to wet and mix mulch hay, horse manure, and other supplements. (Courtesy Rich Forte.)

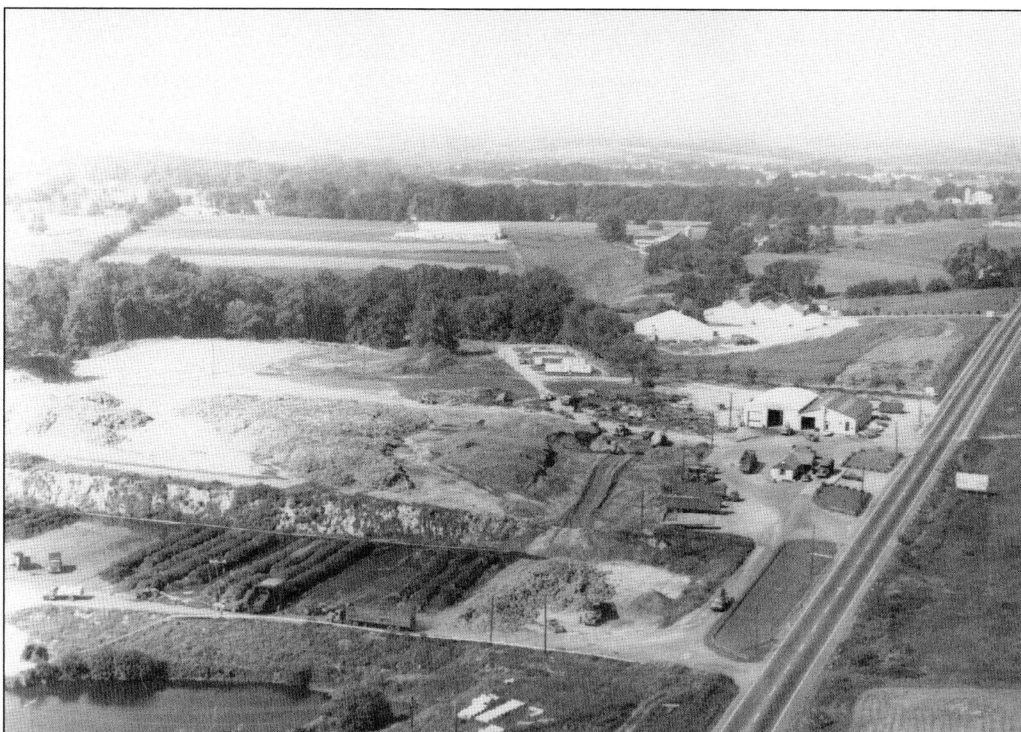

South of Route 41, an aerial view from the 1960s shows Lou Pia's mushroom composting wharf, with piles of hay, corncobs, and prepared compost. When horse manure, the traditional basis of mushroom compost, became scarce, Pia experimented with a formula created by Dr. James Sinden of Penn State. The experiment was successful; Pia's synthetic compost produced a tremendous increase in mushroom production. Soon he was selling it to other growers. (Courtesy Lou Pia.)

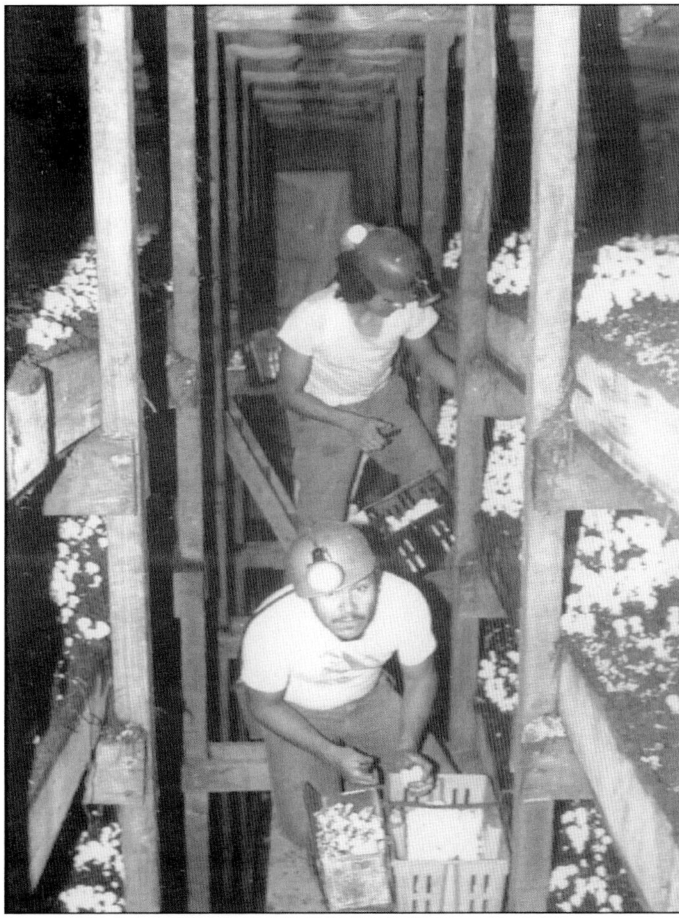

Harvesting mushrooms is labor intensive; each mushroom is pulled from the bed and the root cut off. Working in the dark (mushrooms are a fungus and do not require light), these workers, called pickers, wear individual lights. (Courtesy Rich Forte.)

Initially farmers packed their fresh mushrooms in three-pound baskets and shipped them by truck or rail to wholesale brokers in major cities. In Toughkenamon, there was a factory making mushroom baskets. (Courtesy Margaret Jones.)

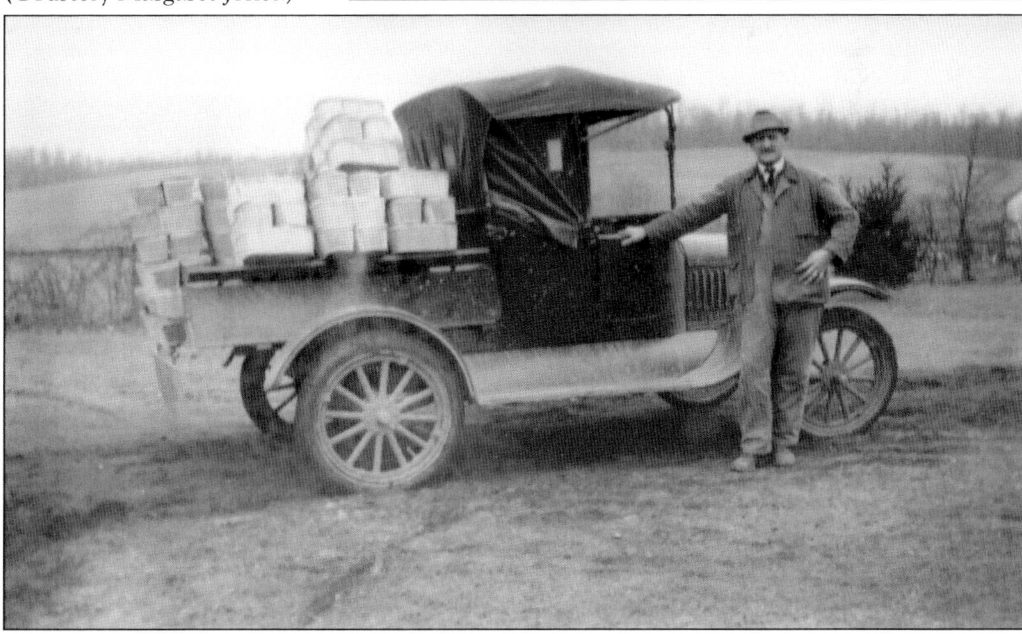

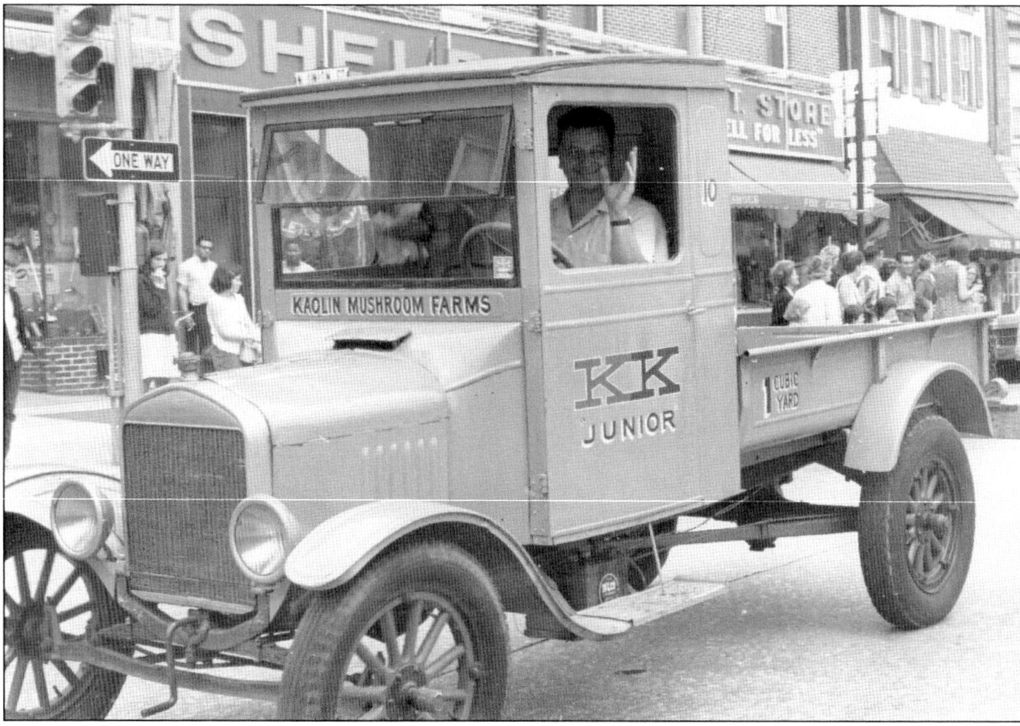

Lou Pia liked to collect classic cars, and this Model T truck was his first purchase. Painted to advertise his Kaolin Kompost, it was often parked along Route 41 to call attention to his business. This was his "play" truck, and Lou enjoyed driving it around Kennett and in parades. (Courtesy Lou Pia.)

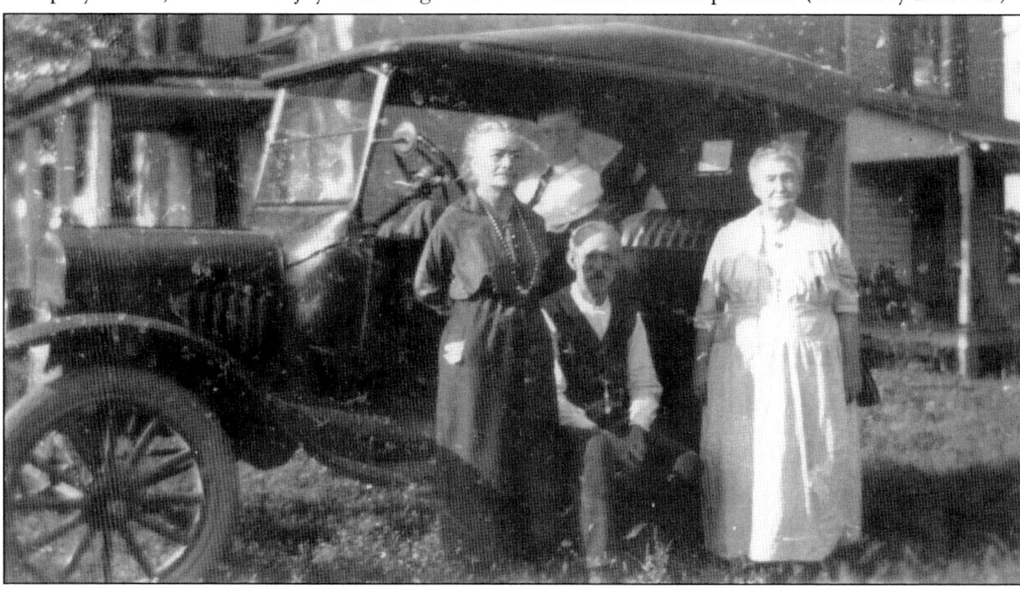

About 1916, Thomas and Ellen Cook pose with a friend in front of a car belonging to their son, Edwin Cook. The Cooks' house, in the background, was along Route 41 near the intersection with New Garden Road West. When road construction crews rebuilt Route 41, beginning in 1939, they raised the roadbed in such a way as to cause the Cooks' front walk to be below the surface of the highway. (Courtesy Vivian Miller.)

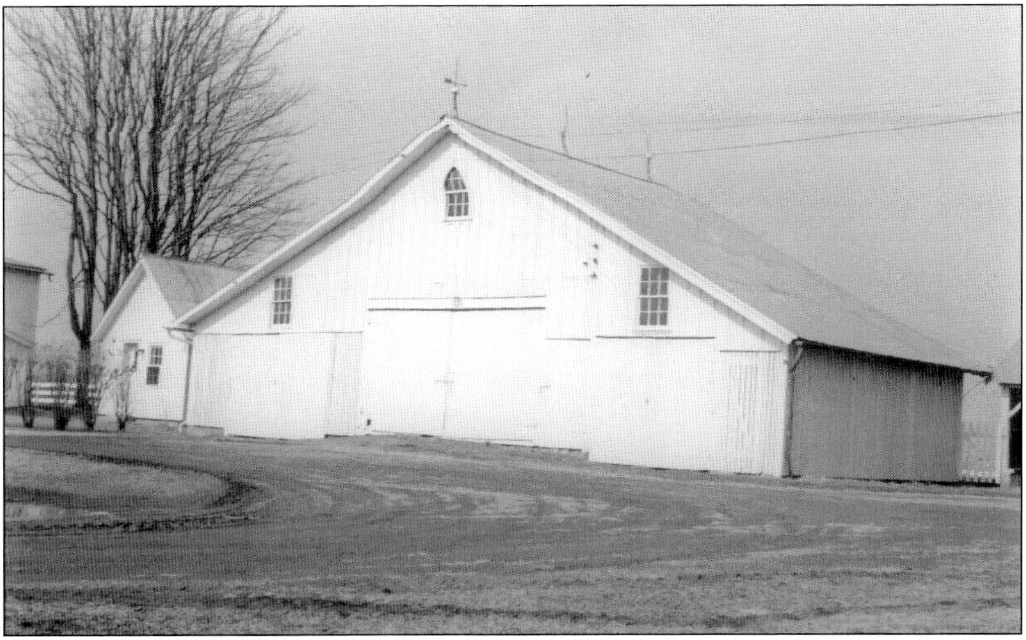

James Mendenhall built his granary in 1865. It had corncribs on either side, bins for grain on the second floor, and a potato cellar underneath the center section. The corncrib in the picture below was designed to allow ventilation and to prevent mold on his husked ear corn. In 1859, Mendenhall listed the crops he had grown on 18 acres under cultivation: 840 bushels corn, 190 bushels wheat, 200 bushels oats, 60 bushels potatoes, 26 bushels turnips, 120 bushels apples, and vegetables. He also had dairy cows, fat oxen, pigs, young cattle, horses, and 10 tons of hay. Mendenhall took his produce to the Wilmington market once or twice a week. (Both courtesy Margaret Jones.)

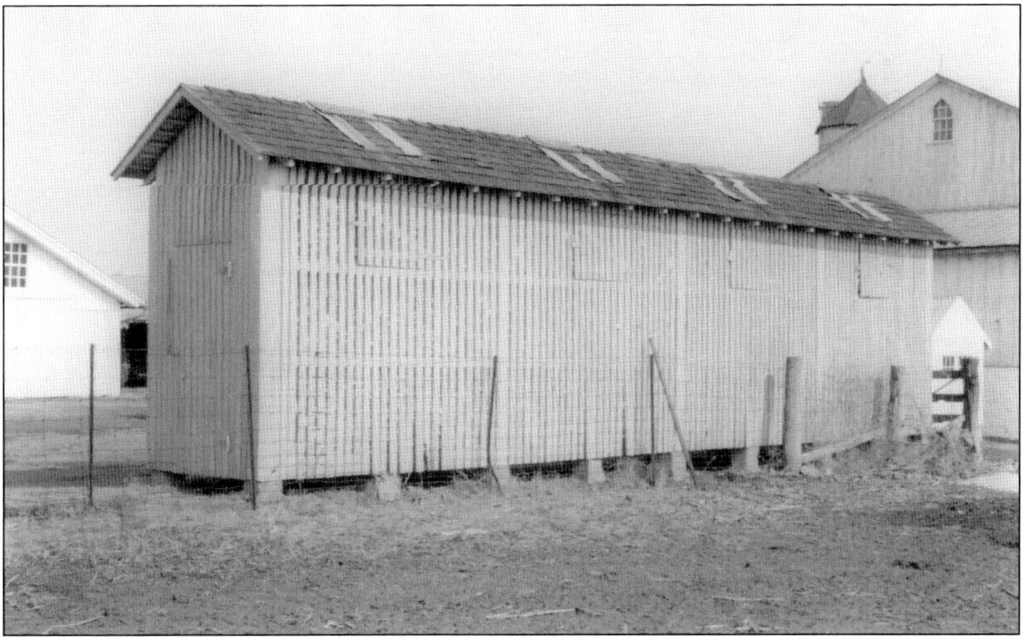

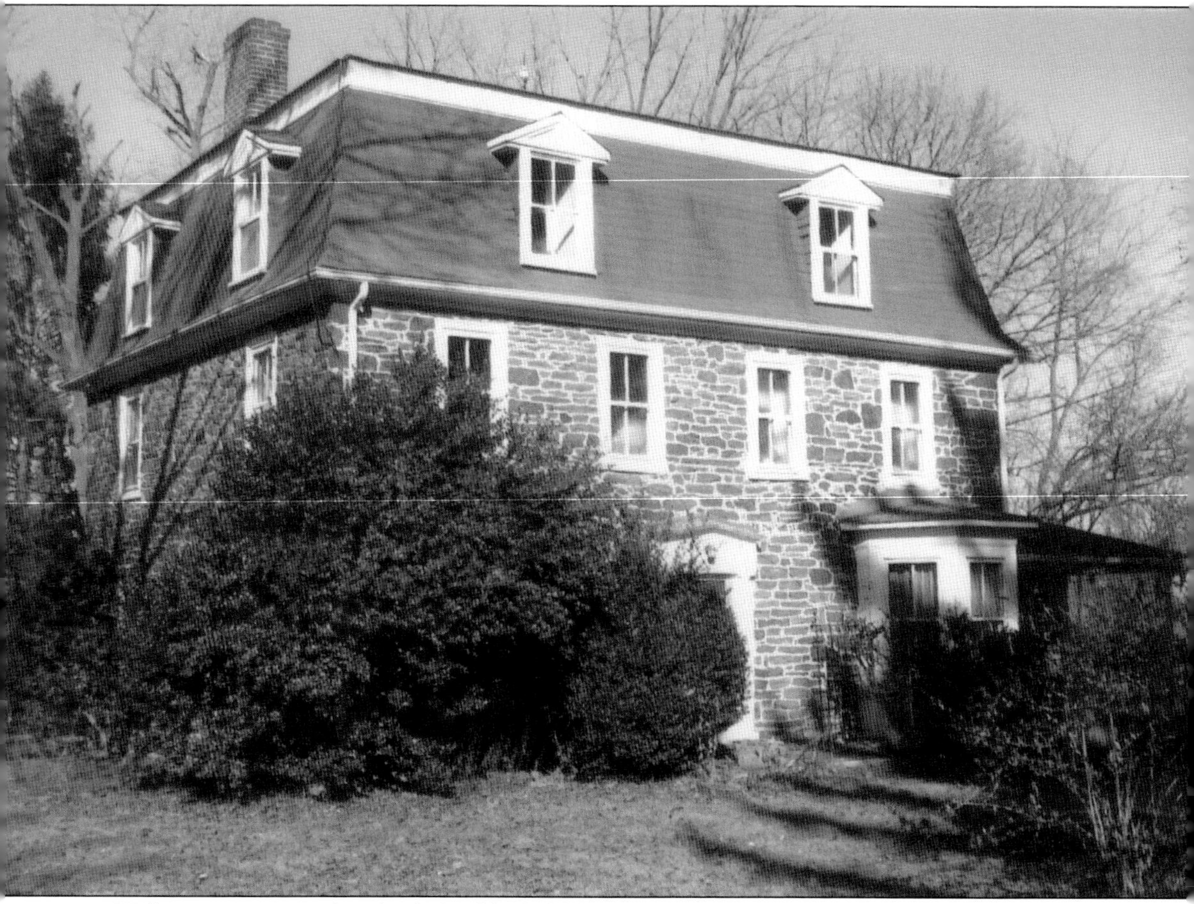

William McConaughey built his black feldspar granite house on Newark Road in 1817. The house was part of a rural industrial complex. McConaughey, a blacksmith, gained fame for developing a corn cultivator, a wooden harrow with an iron blade. Patenting his cultivator in 1824, McConaughey peddled this improved harrow throughout Chester County, traveling by horse and wagon. His manufacturing operation extended to both sides of Newark Road and included, in addition to his dwelling house, a stone smithy, a frame house for his mechanics, a barn for his horses, a charcoal house, and a grinding house. In the latter, horses walked in circles, their yokes attached to a wheel that operated a series of gears, which powered the grindstones used for sharpening cultivator blades. (Author's collection.)

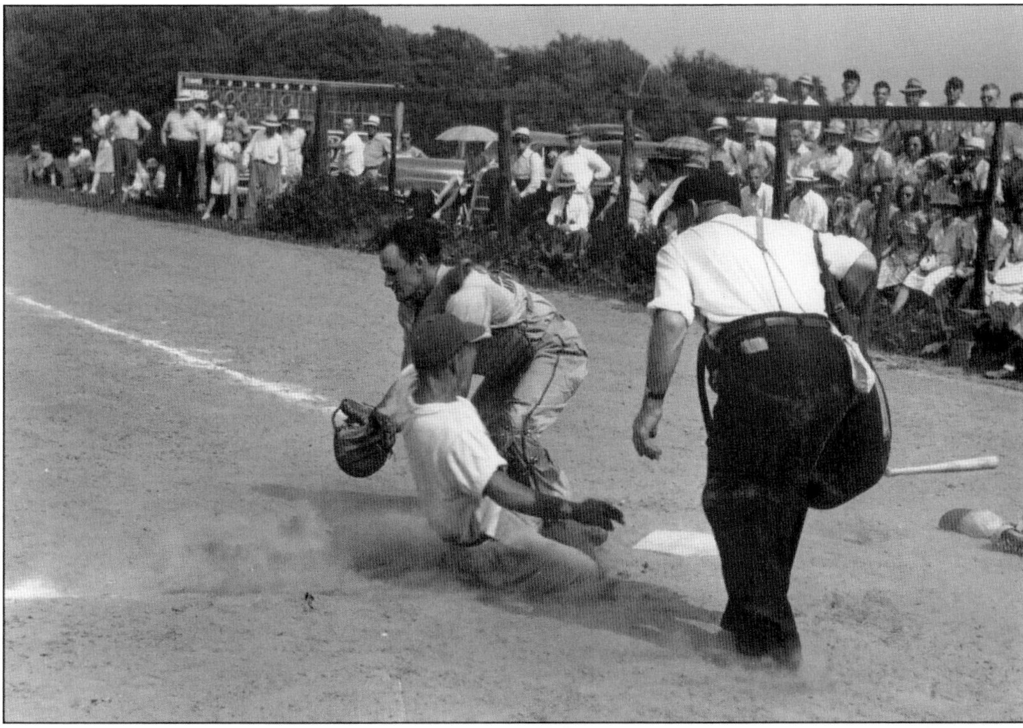

Earl Rigler, like his father before him, was a skilled baseball player even as a boy. Before and after he played for the U.S. Army in Germany during World War II, Earl starred for the Landenberg amateur team. In this picture from 1948, Earl applies a late tag to runner Dean Paisley as the umpire readies to make the call. Note the full bleachers. (Courtesy Alma Rigler.)

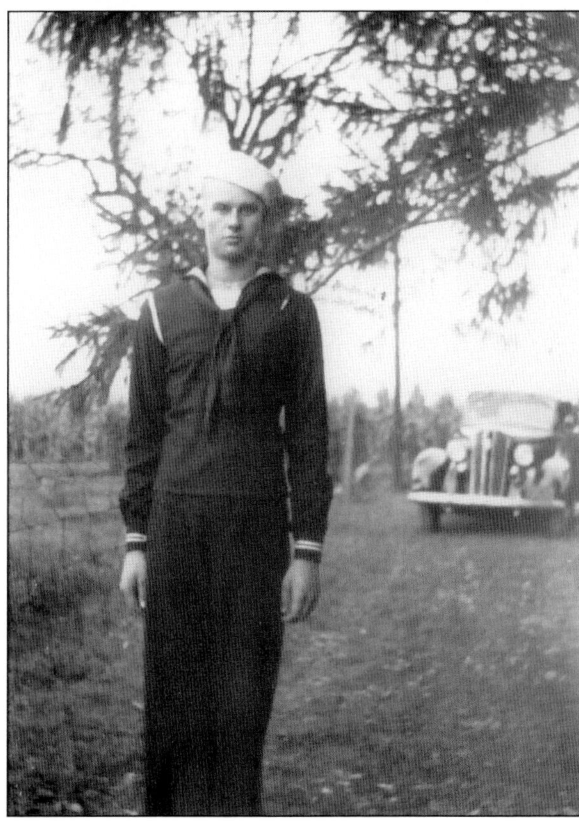

While home on leave during World War II, Ellery Robbins, son of George and Fanny Robbins, poses in the dress blues of the U.S. Navy. Ellery grew up on the Quill farm on Sharp Road. This photograph was taken outside the tenant house. Sharp Road lies behind the car. (Courtesy Joan B. Procino.)

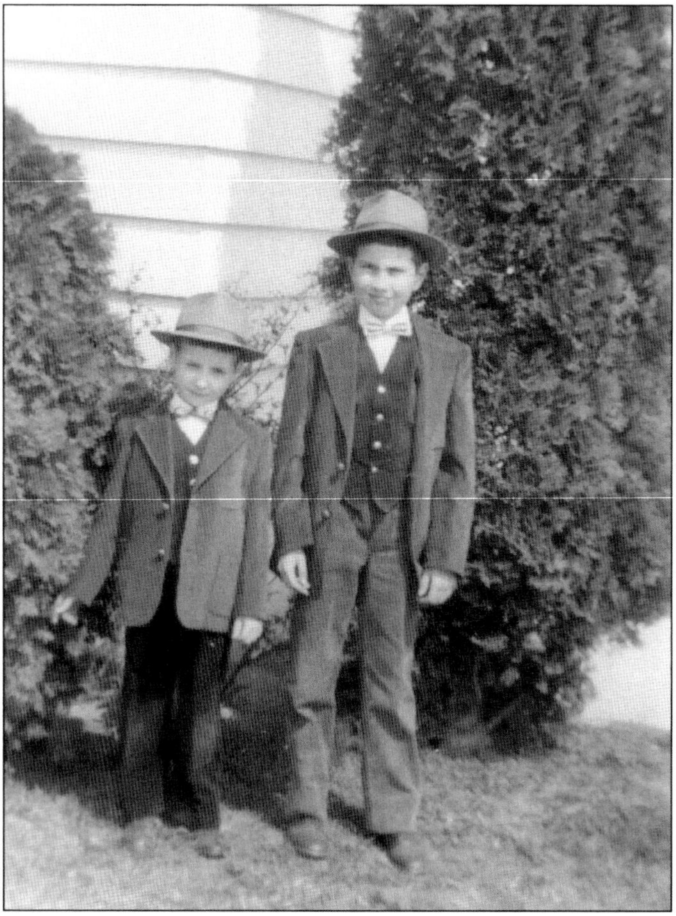

In the early 1940s, Harry (left) and Barclay, sons of Calvin and Florence Hoopes, dress for Quaker meeting on Easter morning. (Courtesy Barclay Hoopes.)

Farm children and dairy cows were usually on speaking terms. Here Eddie and Vivian Cook, children of Edwin and Marguerite Cook, take their red wagons to visit with their bovine neighbors. (Courtesy Vivian Miller.)

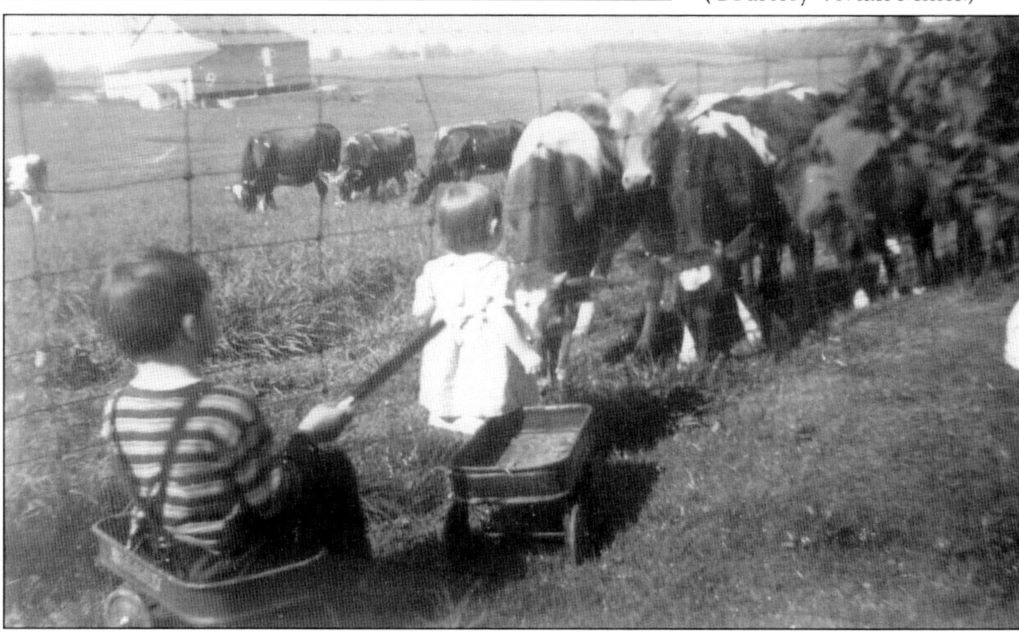

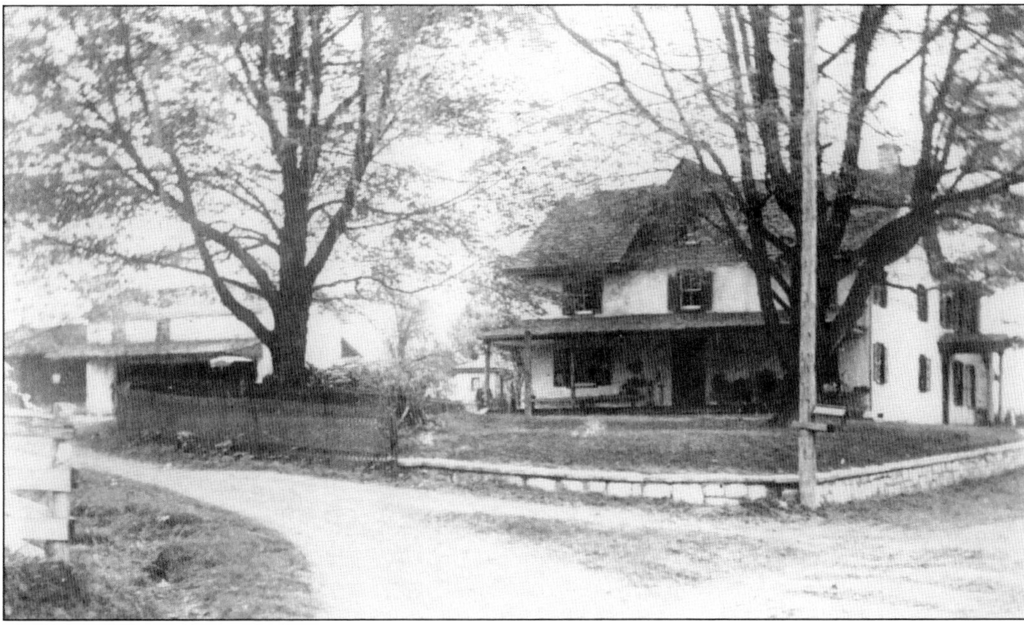

Isaac Frank Chandler's 80-acre farm on the west side of Newark Road stretched from Pine Street south to the top of the hill. Chandler was a prominent Quaker and member of New Garden Meeting who died in 1929. At that time, his children broke up his farm, selling the frontage along Newark Road and in this way extending the village of Toughkenamon south of the railroad. (Courtesy CCHS.)

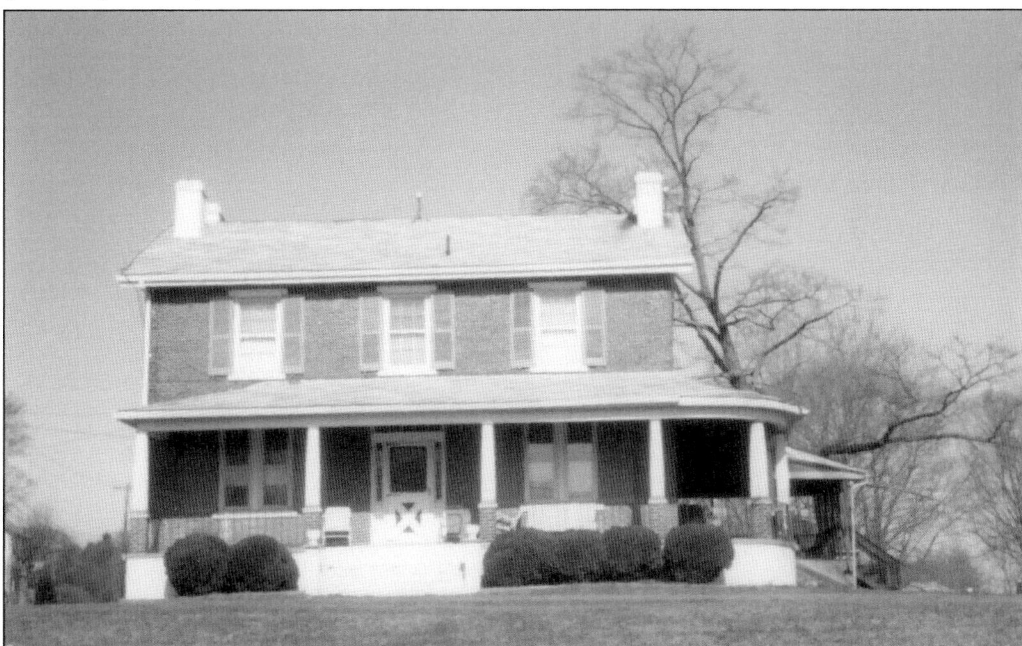

In 1871, John Brown replaced his log house with what the newspapers described as a brick "mansion house." This house was built on the northeast corner of New Garden Crossroads. (Author's collection.)

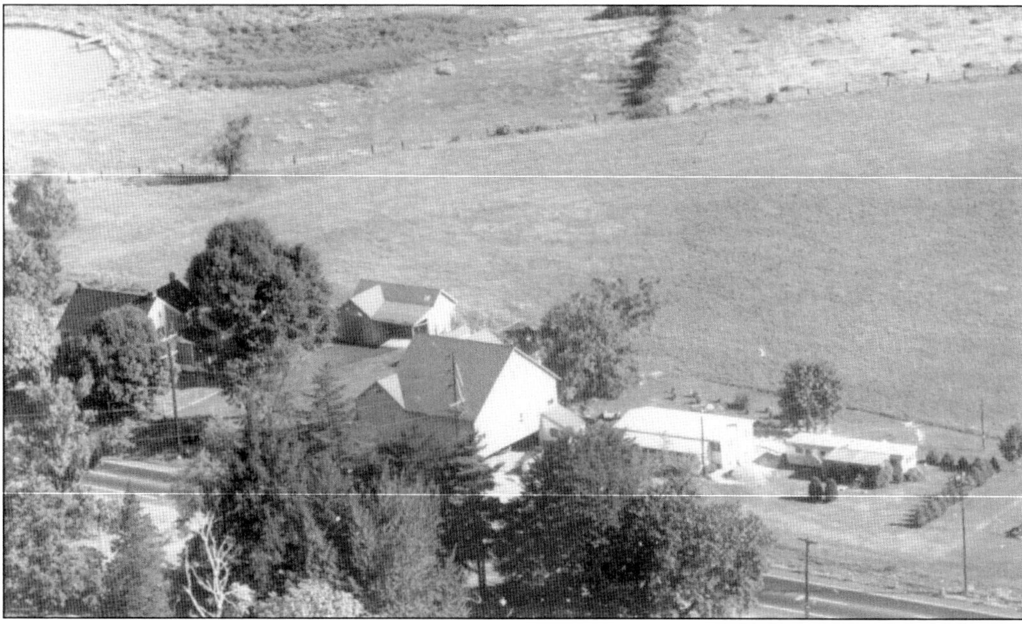

An aerial view of Route 41 shows the Percy Wollaston house and barn with adjoining house trailers. To the east of this picture was the ice cream/sandwich stand belonging to Austin "Bunny" Reynolds. As traffic increased on Route 41, his soft ice cream franchise flourished. Many children collected their coins saying, "Let's go to Bunny's." (Courtesy Skippy Reynolds.)

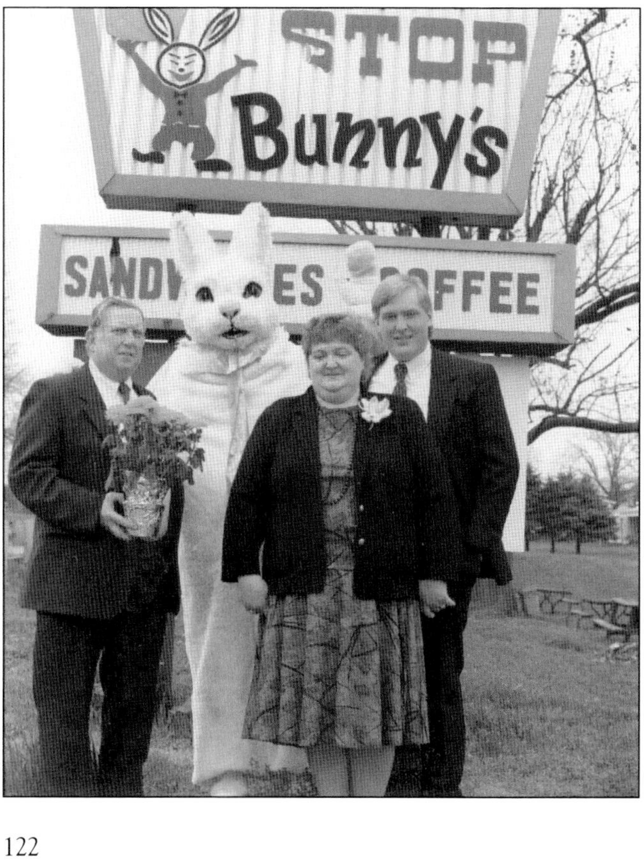

Bunny's became the local gathering place for workmen for lunch and for families seeking ice cream on summer evenings. Helena Reynolds's hamburger relish/sauce was a favorite with all the regulars. In this picture, the next generation, Maurice "Skippy," his wife Barbara, and son Mike, pose under the Bunny sign, which became a New Garden Township landmark. (Courtesy Skippy Reynolds.)

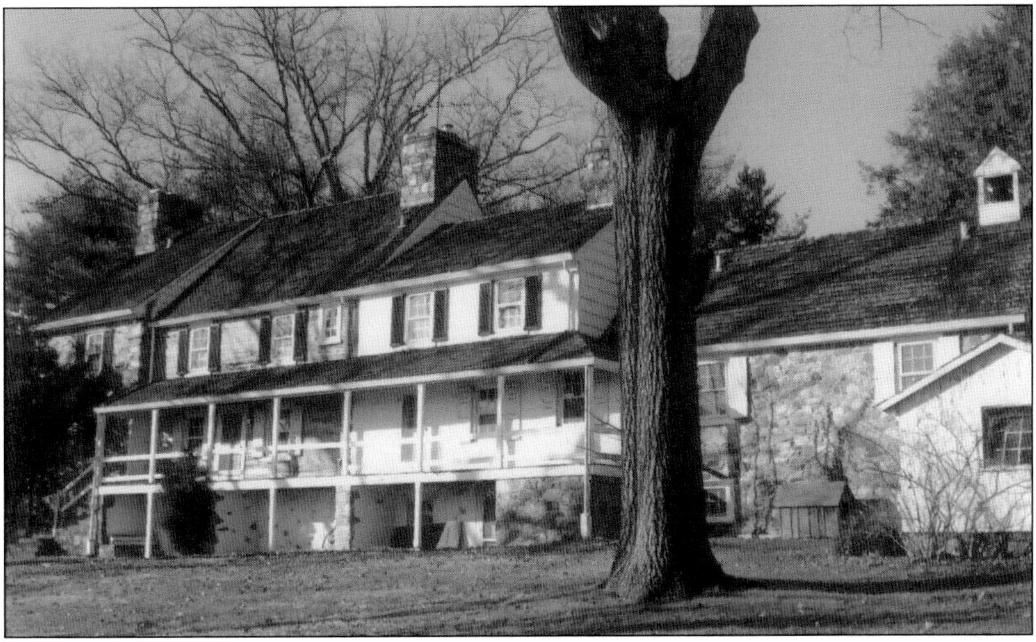

Merestone, so called because the name means boundary marker, straddles the Pennsylvania-Delaware line. The only house in New Garden Township that has been placed on the National Register of Historic Places, the log section dates from about 1730. Part of a 1,000-acre Penn grant to John Evans, the house remained in the Evans family until 1776. In this picture, the log and stone construction can be seen on the southern facade. (Author's collection.)

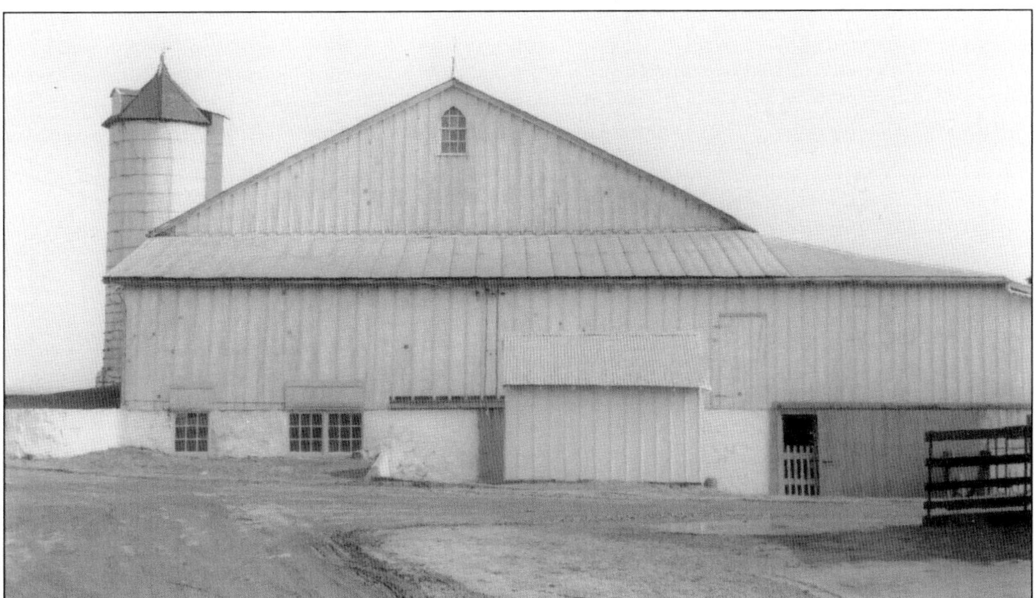

James Mendenhall's 95-acre farm on New Garden Road belonged at one time to Enoch Lewis and had a small barn. Mendenhall recycled many of the timbers of the early barn to build this large bank barn in 1873. The two-story structure faced south to provide maximum sunshine for the barnyard; on the north side was a sloping barn bridge to access the hay mow. (Courtesy Margaret Jones.)

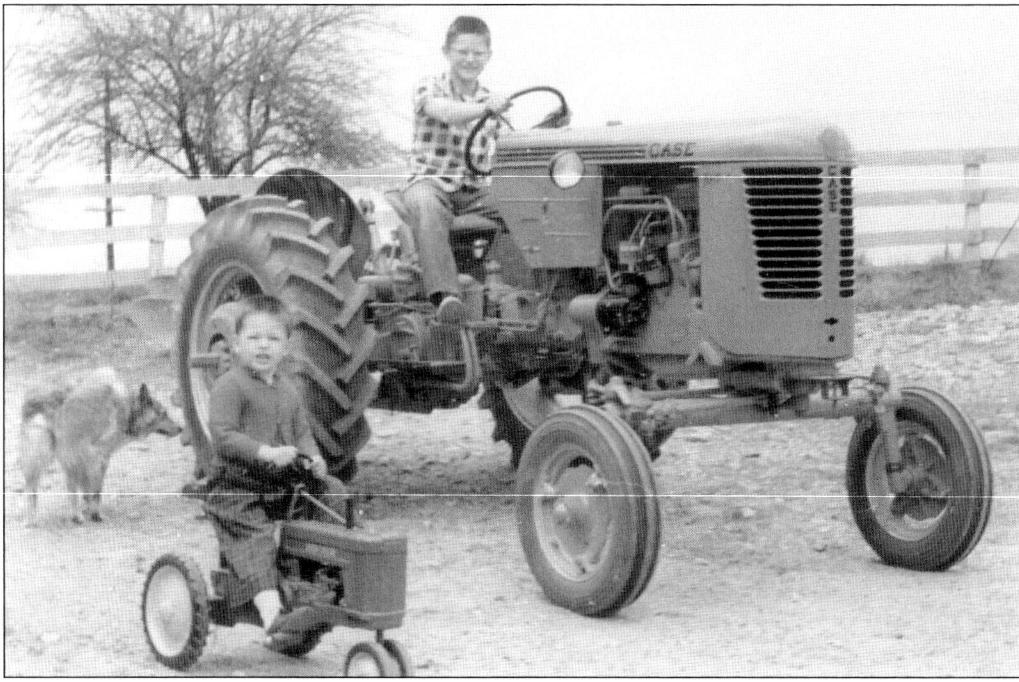

Farm boys all wanted to drive the tractor. In this picture, Rich Meinzer sits on Ed Slades's new Case tractor, and his younger brother, Ed, is on his new toy John Deere. Farm boys were an important source of farm labor, and most were eager to assume responsibility, especially when it came to operating tractors and machinery. (Courtesy Barclay Hoopes.)

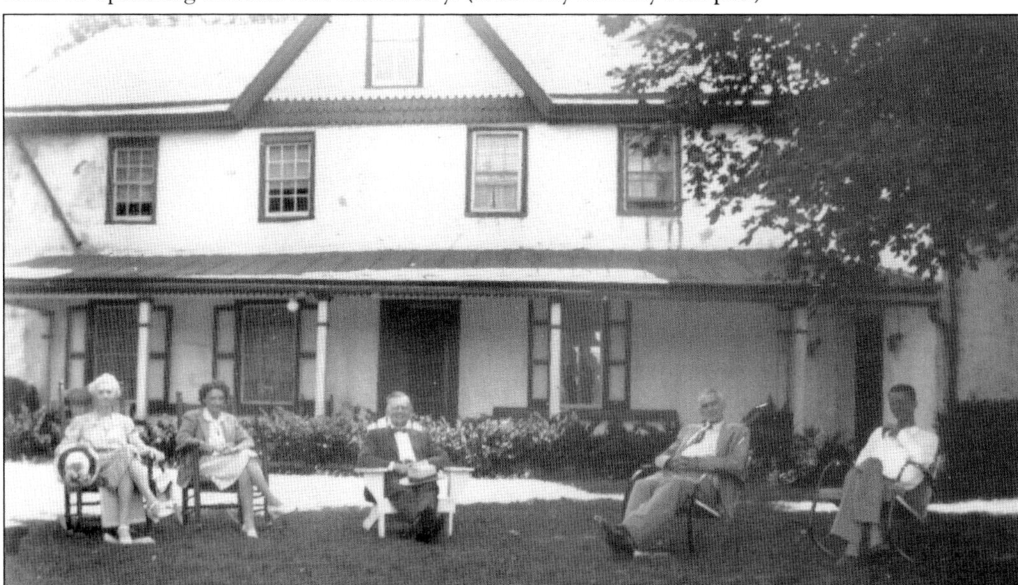

Evan (second from right) and Carsye (second from left) Reynolds with their son Ben (far right), entertain guests on the lawn of their Green Valley Farm in this picture from about 1940. This was ancestral Reynolds land; Evan Reynolds's forbear, John Miller, had acquired a Penn patent in 1714. The core of the stone farmhouse was built about 1770; subsequent additions created the large farmhouse. (Courtesy Warren Reynolds.)

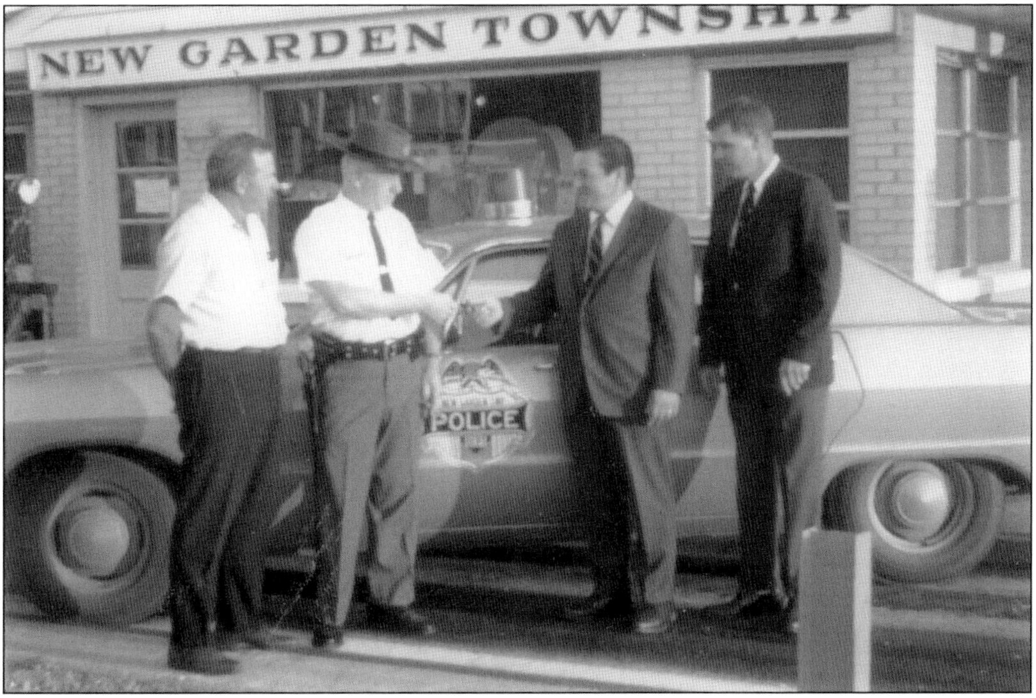

As traffic on Route 41 increased, the township supervisors saw the need for a township policeman. From left to right, Bob Taylor, Ofc. McKinley Hall, Dino Ruggeri, and Chip Smedley posed with their new police car around 1969 outside the township building and public scales. (Courtesy NGTHC.)

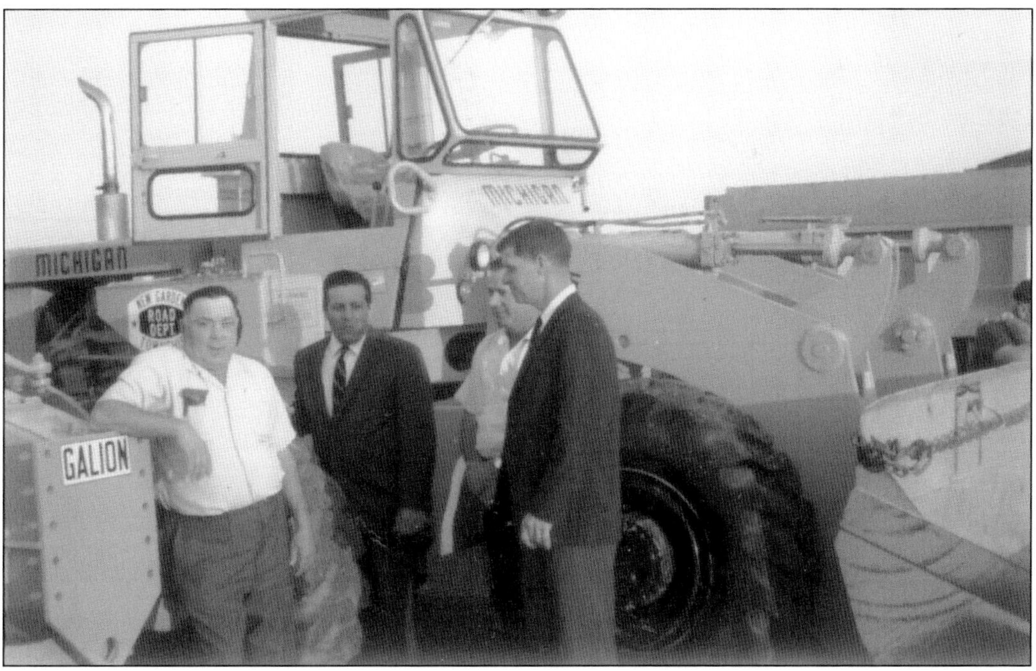

New equipment was always an opportunity for a picture. Here Augie Testa (left), township road master, stands in front of a new road grader with township supervisors (second from left to right) Dino Ruggeri, Bob Taylor, and Chip Smedley. (Courtesy NGTHC.)

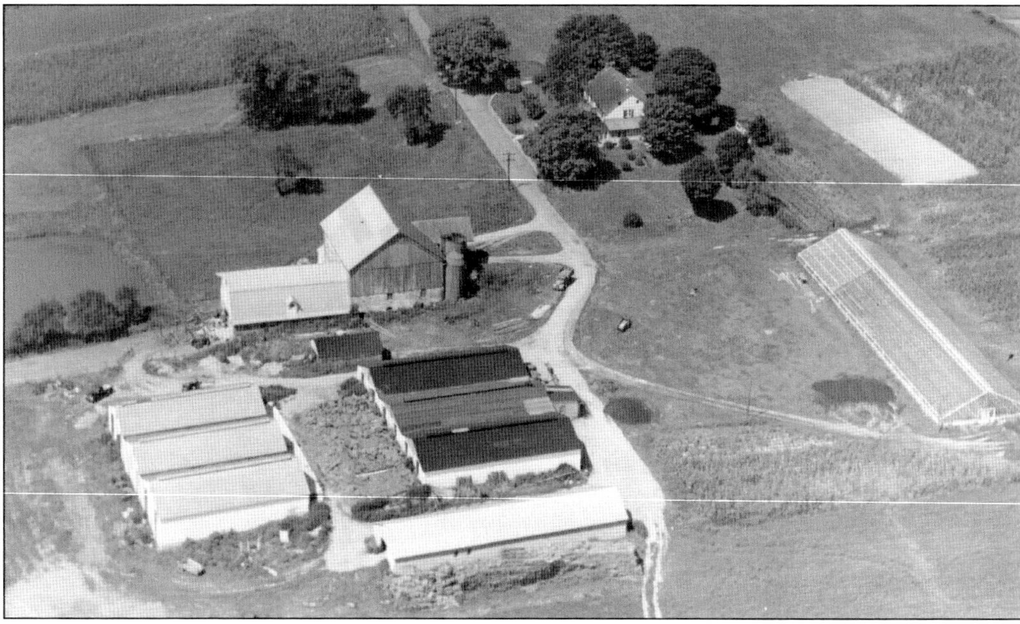

This picture of the Howard Pratt farm taken in the 1940s shows not only a house and dairy barn but also mushroom houses and a greenhouse range. Diversification among farmers was common; to allow for adverse weather conditions or insect infestation, farmers grew a variety of crops. For a crop to raise in the winter, many turned either to growing mushrooms or to building greenhouses. Howard Pratt was unique; he did both. (Courtesy NGTHC.)

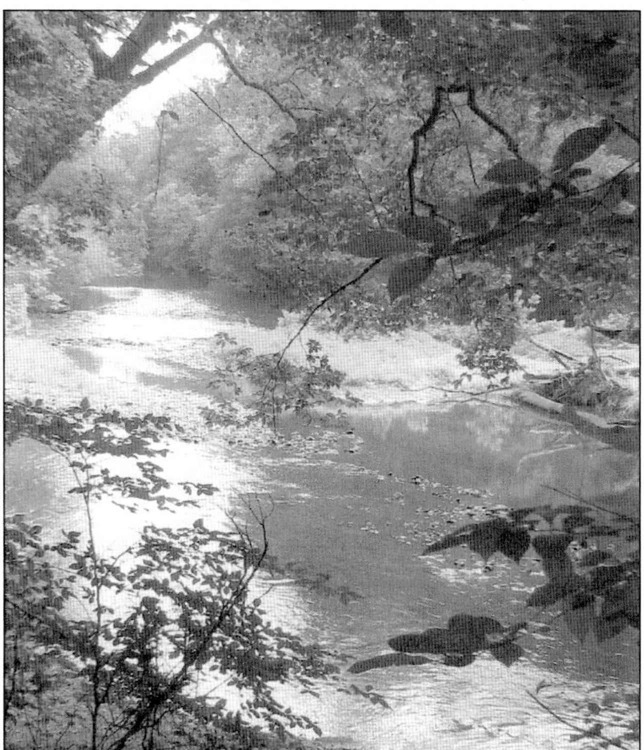

The White Clay Creek still meanders past the crop and mushroom farms of New Garden Township. Although the mills and railroads have fallen silent, the natural beauty affords more recreational splendor today than the economic profit sought by yesterday's industrial barons. (Courtesy Carla Lucas.)

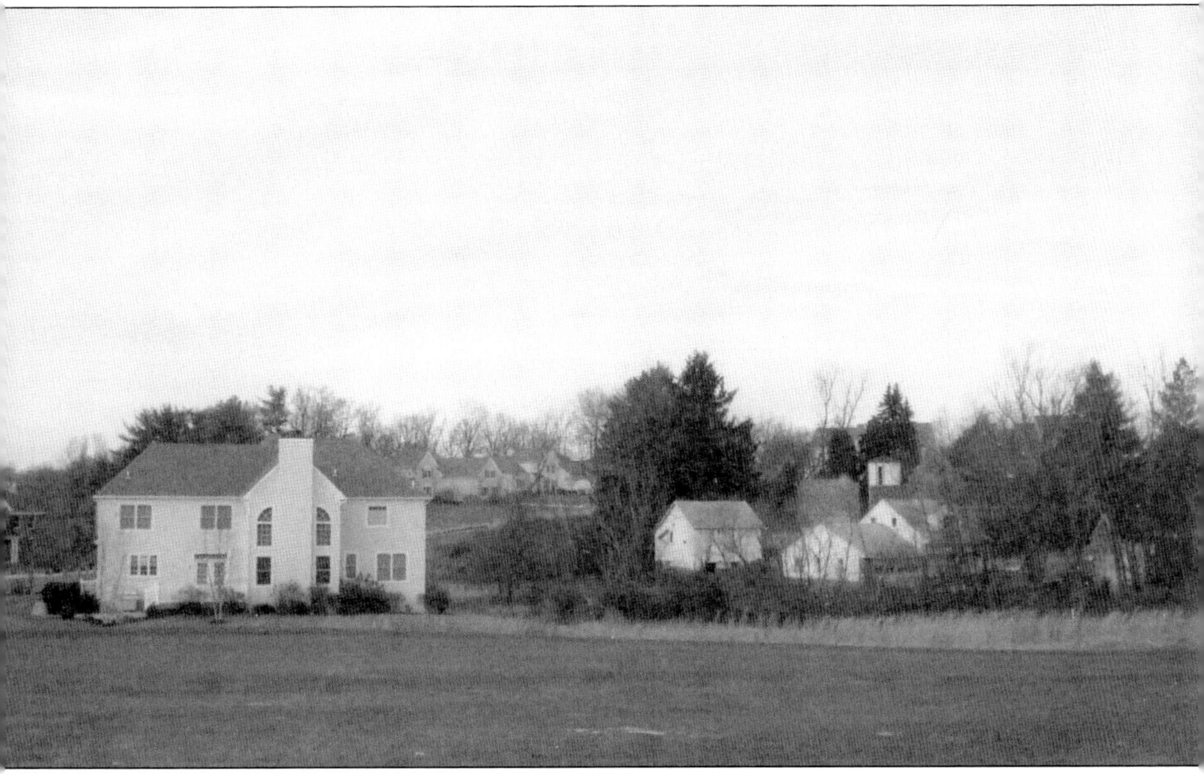

The rolling hills—from which Lenni Lenapes defended their territory, streams plunged to provide industrial power, minerals were mined, cattle grazed, and corn and crops sprouted—remain. However, the land's purpose has shifted. As development encroaches, the past fades. Today developers are required to preserve vestiges of the township's agricultural legacy—like the 19th-century homestead, dilapidated barn, and outbuildings of the 1850s Hoopes/Herdube Farm above—amid modern, palatial homes and fairways. (Author's collection.)

www.arcadiapublishing.com

Discover books about the town where you grew up, the cities where your friends and families live, the town where your parents met, or even that retirement spot you've been dreaming about. Our Web site provides history lovers with exclusive deals, advanced notification about new titles, e-mail alerts of author events, and much more.

MADE IN THE USA

Arcadia Publishing, the leading local history publisher in the United States, is committed to making history accessible and meaningful through publishing books that celebrate and preserve the heritage of America's people and places. Consistent with our mission to preserve history on a local level, this book was printed in South Carolina on American-made paper and manufactured entirely in the United States.

This book carries the accredited Forest Stewardship Council (FSC) label and is printed on 100 percent FSC-certified paper. Products carrying the FSC label are independently certified to assure consumers that they come from forests that are managed to meet the social, economic, and ecological needs of present and future generations.

FSC
Mixed Sources
Product group from well-managed forests and other controlled sources

Cert no. SW-COC-001530
www.fsc.org